M000107512

The Making of the 1963
Baptist Faith and Message

The Making of the 1963 Baptist Faith and Message

A. J. Smith

WIPF & STOCK · Eugene, Oregon

THE MAKING OF THE 1963 BAPTIST FAITH AND MESSAGE

Copyright © 2008 A. J. Smith. All rights reserved. Except for brief quotations in critical publications or reviews, no part of this book may be reproduced in any manner without prior written permission from the publisher. Write: Permissions, Wipf and Stock Publishers, 199 W. 8th Ave., Suite 3, Eugene, OR 97401.

Wipf & Stock
A Division of Wipf and Stock Publishers
199 W. 8th Ave., Suite 3
Eugene, OR 97401

www.wipfandstock.com

ISBN 13: 978-1-55635-426-7

All rights reserved. The Southern Baptist Theological Seminary has permission to reproduce and disseminate this document in any form by any means for purposes chosen by the Seminary, including, without limitation, preservation or instruction.

Manufactured in the U.S.A.

To my wife Michelle,
and our children, Kayla, James, and Victoria,
whose love, support, prayers, and patience
made this project possible.

And to the late Rev. Almer Douglas Smith, my father,
who instilled in me a love for
God, the Bible, and Baptist History.

Contents

Preface

INTEREST IN THIS TOPIC began during my master's studies. Over a period of several years it became apparent that no one had sat down and looked through the records of the Committee on Baptist Faith and Message, examining what it did, how it did it, and what changes it made in the Baptist Faith and Message approved at the Southern Baptist Convention in Kansas City, in 1963. This research has provided, one hopes, a valuable window into life in the Southern Baptist Convention in the early 1960s and into the process of writing a confession of faith for a denominational body.

I would be remiss if I did not take this opportunity to express gratitude to all those who have made this project possible. First, my wife, Michelle, and our children, for their loving patience, prayers and support during these years of study. Secondly, my in-laws, James McDonald and Kaye Curran McDonald, who have been both generous and encouraging during the financially lean years of my seminary education. I would also like to thank my mother, Inez Smith, whose prayers I know have been a great help to me through the years.

I have received a great deal of assistance from my peers and mentors in the faith. First, I would like to thank my original doctoral committee— Tom Nettles, Bruce Ware, and Craig Blaising, for allowing me into the doctoral program and mentoring me through to the completion of my prospectus. Secondly, I would like to thank my defense committee—Tom Nettles, Gregg Allison, and Greg Wills, for seeing this process through to completion with me. Special thanks are due to Wayne Ward, who graciously shared his personal files with me from the period under consideration, James Leo Garrett, who also shared valuable information from his personal files, and Marvin Tate, who graciously shared personal recollections of life at Southern Seminary in the early 1960s and his own thoughts then and now on the 1963 Baptist Faith and Message.

I would also like to thank Bill Sumner and his fine staff at the Southern Baptist Historical Library and Archives, in Nashville, Tennessee. Never have I seen a more pleasant place to do research, or found a more knowledgeable, cooperative, and capable staff. I would also like to thank my peers in the doctoral program. They have offered encouragement during times of despair and thoughtful insight when confronted with difficult problems in research or writing. I am also grateful for the great Christian fellowship we have enjoyed together. A special word of gratitude goes to Monty Self and Dr. Charles Burton, both who graciously agreed to proofread the manuscript. Any errors are mine, not theirs.

I would also like to thank the members of the Southern Baptist churches throughout the Convention whose generous gifts through the Cooperative Program made this learning experience financially possible. May the Lord bless and use the people called Southern Baptists for the spread of his gospel to the end of the age.

Finally, there is one typographical matter that must be pointed out. In chapter 4 I have replaced the archaic "y" = "th" in a quote to improve readability.

—Almer J. Smith
Louisville, Kentucky
December 2004

Abbreviations

AkB	Arkansas Baptist
AlB	Alabama Baptist
B&R	Baptist & Reflector
BCL	James P. Boyce Centennial Library, the Southern Baptist Theological Seminary
BD	Baptist Digest
BFM	Baptist Faith and Message
BHH	Baptist History and Heritage
BM	Baptist Message
BNM	Baptist New Mexican
BP	Baptist Press
BS	Baptist Standard
BT	Baptists Today
CI	The Christian Index
F&T	Facts & Trends
GBTS	Golden Gate Baptist Theological Seminary
MBF	Millard Berquist Files, Midwestern Baptist Theological Seminary Library
MBTS	Midwestern Baptist Theological Seminary
NOBTS	New Orleans Baptist Theological Seminary
R&E	Review & Expositor
RH	Religious Herald
SBC	Southern Baptist Convention
SBHLA	The Southern Baptist Historical Library and Archives, Nashville, Tennessee
SBJT	Southern Baptist Journal of Theology
SBT	Southern Baptist Texan
SBTS	Southern Baptist Theological Seminary
SEBTS	Southeastern Baptist Theological Seminary
SWBTS	Southwestern Baptist Theological Seminary
TB	Texas Baptist
WR	Western Recorder
WWC	Wayne Ward Private Collection

1

Introduction

HERSCHEL H. HOBBS STANDS out as one of the most prolific writers in Southern Baptist history. He wrote a vast amount of Sunday
School literature and many commentaries for the laity. He also wrote
several works on Baptist doctrine, including a commentary on the BFM
1963. During Hobbs's presidency of the Southern Baptist Convention,
the publication of Ralph Elliott's *The Message of Genesis* and questions
about Dale Moody's teaching on apostasy rocked the SBC. These inci-
dents caused many in the churches to question the doctrinal soundness of
the seminaries of the Convention. Other concerns also in play within the
Convention included the civil rights movement, socialism, materialism,
and Catholicism. Some feared that the Convention would either be taken
over by theological liberals or fragment along doctrinal lines. In this context the Convention called for a committee to revisit the Statement on
Baptist Faith and Message the Convention adopted in 1925. As President of
the Convention, Hobbs chaired this historic Committee. Mark Coppenger
wrote of Hobbs's role in framing the revised document:

> In some sections Hobbs introduced concepts and phrases. In oth-
> ers he coordinated the thinking of the committee. Throughout,
> he was the writer, presenting successive drafts for committee ap-
> proval. His enthusiasm for the document in whole and in part is
> obvious in his explanation and defense of the text in a widely used
> study course book.[1]

1. Coppenger, "Herschel Hobbs," in *Baptist Theologians*, 438.

According to David Dockery, Hobbs considered his work on the 1963 BFM his most enduring achievement for the cause of the kingdom.[2] Dockery also noted that

> he nevertheless was hesitant to acknowledge the place of doctrinal confessions as normative for the Christian community. His emphasis on individualism and the competency of the soul in each believer moved him to a false dichotomy between a "living faith" and a "confessional or creedal faith."[3]

What emerges from Coppenger's and Dockery's articles on Hobbs is the impression that he was, in many respects, the determining factor in the revised form of the document.

THESIS

This work will argue that Herschel Hobbs through his work on the BFM sought to avert an immediate denominational split through the reformulation of key historic Baptist doctrines, wording some broadly to allow for widely divergent interpretations without sacrificing the Convention's conservative base.[4] Hobbs did this by a consistent application of the accepted views of soul competency and the role of Baptist confessions as a "consensus of opinion" outlined in the Preamble to the 1925 BFM.[5] In pursuit of this goal this dissertation will demonstrate what influences shaped the final form of the document, examine key theological shifts, explore the Baptist confessional heritage, and the principles of soul liberty and soul competency as these issues related to the Committee's work.

In order to accomplish this it will be necessary to explore the wealth of available primary source documents, mostly in the form of letters,

---

2. Dockery, "Herschel H. Hobbs," in *Theologians of the Baptist Tradition*, 219.

3. Ibid., 221.

4. An example of how outside influences battled to determine the final outcome of the statement in key areas can be seen in a letter from Moody to McCall. Ward had proposed to Hobbs that the statement affirm that "the criterion by which the Bible is to be interpreted is the person, work and teaching of Jesus Christ." Moody argued that the sentence should be amended to exclude "the teaching of Jesus Christ," because "it is already being used by fundamentalists to prove that Moses wrote all five books of the Pentateuch . . . the unity of the book of Isaiah . . . and the Exile date for Daniel." Moody to McCall, 7 January 1963, Dale Moody Collection, BCL. The final draft which the Convention approved followed the wording suggested by Moody.

5. Mullins, et. al., "Report of the Committee on Baptist Faith and Message," 71.

pertaining to the Committee on Statement of Faith and Message that was organized in 1962 and charged with the task of reviewing the 1925 Statement with a possible view to revising or replacing it. The Millard Berquist Files, housed at the library at Midwestern Baptist Theological Seminary, Kansas City, Missouri, contain valuable materials related specifically to the Genesis Controversy and Ralph Elliott and will be examined in regard to this controversy.

What will come to the fore is the fact that the Committee went about its work very conscious that it was acting on behalf of the entire Convention. A select subcommittee prepared a preliminary draft, solicited comments, and the whole Committee made further revisions, all the while soliciting more comments from Southern Baptists until the final draft was prepared for release to BP in February 1963.

This research project is intended to foster an advance in knowledge with regard to the functional role of confessions within the Baptist tradition, how theological trends shaped the confessional expression of the Southern Baptist Convention, and how the 1963 Committee on Baptist Faith and Message carried on its work under the leadership of Herschel H. Hobbs.

BACKGROUND

Recent events, culminating in the third edition of the BFM, as well as the need for a historical analysis of how the second edition was prepared, prompted this study.

Development of the Confession

An exploration of electronic databases cataloging journal articles and dissertations has shown that some academic work has been done on the content and influence of the BFM1963 (three dissertations have been written on various aspects of the statement);[6] however, to date there has been no extensive research done on the Committee's work or the formative influences that helped determine the final shape of the document.

---

6. Downs, "The Use of the 'Baptist Faith and Message,' 1963–1983." Durden, "A Selected Issue in Southern Baptist Ecclesiology." Gaines, "An Analysis of the Correlation Between Representative Baptist Hour Sermons by Herschel H. Hobbs."

David Downs, in his fourth chapter, viewed the use made of the 1963 BFM as a further move toward creedalism in the Convention.[7] In his second chapter he traced the nature and uses of confessions in Baptist life. He noted that confessions functioned as voluntary statements that reflect historic Baptist beliefs.[8] Further, he observed that, pragmatically, confessions have been used to settle doctrinal disputes, but that they derive their authority from the voluntary consent of those who embrace them. Baptist confessions always point back to the Scriptures as the final authority in religious disputes.[9]

Steve Gaines, in his dissertation, first examined the impact that Hobbs had on Baptist preaching and theology.[10] In chapters 2 through 4 Gaines traced out Hobbs's *Baptist Hour* preaching on the doctrines of Christ, man and the fall, and salvation.

Thorough research requires an investigation of the Committee's records and related documents. These records are housed in the Southern Baptist Historical Library and Archives, in Nashville, Tennessee. Other records are privately owned or are archived in the James P. Boyce Centennial Library at the Southern Baptist Theological Seminary.[11] The needed journal materials and state papers are accessible, as is one dissertation written at Southern Seminary in the 1980s. Other dissertations are available via inter-library loan.

That there were outside influences that shaped the final form of the document can be illustrated by a letter from Wayne Ward to Dick Hall

---

7. Downs, "Use of 'The Baptist Faith and Message,'" 103–48. Downs also wrote a Th.M. thesis at Southern dealing with the McDaniel Statement adopted by the 1926 Southern Baptist Convention, Houston, Texas, which he sees as an early movement toward creedalism in the Convention. Downs, "The McDaniel Statement: An Investigation of Creedalism in the Southern Baptist Convention," 36–38.

8. Downs, "Use of 'The Baptist Faith and Message,'" 19, 25.

9. Ibid., 23, 26.

10. Gaines, "An Analysis of Sermons by Herschel Hobbs," 16–33.

11. Letters written to the other five seminaries requesting any archived materials regarding faculty interaction with the committee have turned up no available records. The Boyce Library has the Dale Moody records in its archives, but the records of faculty involvement with the Committee are in the Office of the President and have been deemed too sensitive for release at this time. Wayne Ward, retired professor of theology at Southern, has very graciously shared his personal files for the purpose of researching and writing this dissertation. James Leo Garrett kindly shared from his files, and Marvin Tate shared from his recollections of the events concerning Southern Seminary's involvement with the Committee.

Jr., Committee secretary, dated 20 October 1962.[12] In this letter Ward commended the subcommittee for certain aspects of its work, but he also pointed out significant weaknesses in the first draft, suggesting several areas that needed further clarification, even suggesting a complete re-write of the article on Christ. Later drafts indicate that the Committee heeded his advice. In an interview Ward said that Hobbs made a deliberate choice to solicit input from a broad cross-section of the Convention. Letters to and from the Committee support this contention.[13]

Hobbs organized a select subcommittee to make an initial draft document. After they completed their work (sometime before 3 December 1962),[14] subcommittees of two members each were appointed to meet with representatives of each of the seminaries to gather input from their faculties.[15] The subcommittees to the seminaries were assigned as follows: Golden Gate—Doug Hudgins and Jimmy Landes; Midwestern—C. Z. Holland and Robert Woodward; New Orleans—Howard Reaves and David G. Anderson; Southwestern—Warren Rust and Paul Weber Jr.; Southern—Verlin Kruschwitz and R. P. Downey; Southeastern—Dick Hall Jr. and Nane Starnes.[16] The Committee produced the final draft of the document and distributed it to state papers for publication in February, 1963.

Soul Competency and Confessionalism

Both the 1925 and 1963 Committees had to grapple with how a confession adopted on behalf of and in the name of the Convention should be used in relation to the principle of soul competency. In the debate over the 1925 confession W. O. Carver accused E. Y. Mullins of "presbyterianizing" the Convention, and others in state papers raised a loud cry against "creeds" in the name of soul liberty and soul competency.[17] Indeed, even before

12. Ward to Hall., 20 October 1962, BFM file, folder 4, SBHLA.

13. Interview with Dr. Wayne E. Ward, April 17, 2002. See also the following letters: Starnes to Hobbs, 27 June 1962, BFM file, folder, File 1; Hobbs to Koons, 17 July 1962, BFM file, folder 2; Hobbs to Nelson., 26 July 1962, BFM file, folder 2; Hobbs to Hall, 22 October 1962, BFM file, folder 4; there is also a draft of the document with notations from the Department of Christianity, Mercer University, BFM file, folder 4, SBHLA.

14. Hall to Hobbs, 3 December 1962, BFM file, folder 5, SBHLA.

15. Ibid.

16. Hobbs to members of the seminary subcommittees, 10 January 1963, BFM file, folders 5 and 7, SBHLA.

17. For examples see Carver, "The Baptist, His Creed, and His Fellowship," *RH*, 7 May

the 1925 Convention the question of Baptist confessionalism had become a growing concern. W. B. Johnson, first president of the Convention, was decidedly anti-confessional and wrote of Baptists, "The Bible is their only standard of doctrine and unity."[18] Meanwhile, Joseph Baker assumed that Baptist churches had and used doctrinal statements as a basis for church and associational unity.[19] In a strongly worded statement on the necessity of confessions, J. L. Reynolds noted that Socinians decried confessions as impositions on the conscience and freedom of the believer. They were "an encroachment upon the prerogative of the Supreme Teacher." Reynolds noted that Baptists, along with all Protestants, strongly resisted this anti-confessional sentiment and argued for the use of confessions in promoting the advance of the Kingdom.[20]

The 1963 Committee faced the same challenge. The issue has continued in Southern Baptist life even to the present. The entire winter 1979 issue of *R&E* was devoted to the question of creedalism and Baptist confessions.[21] Numerous articles have also appeared on the subject in *BHH*.[22] Moderate Southern Baptists have addressed the issue in *Sacred Mandates of Conscience*.[23] In *The Southern Baptist Convention and the Judgement of History*, E. Luther Copeland commented that for decades "the waters of creedalism had been creeping upward," and when the conservatives came to power in the Convention in 1979 these waters "reached flood stage."[24]

1925, 11. White, "An Old and Strong Statement of the Baptist Position on Creeds," *RH*, 2 April 1925, 3. Jackson, "That Creedal Business," *RH*, 16 April 1925, 3, 7.

18. Johnson, *The Gospel Developed through the Government and Order of the Churches*; reprinted in *Polity*, ed. Mark Dever, 187.

19. Baker, *Queries Considered*; reprinted in *Polity*, ed. Mark Dever, 288.

20. Reynolds, *Church Polity*; reprinted in *Polity*, ed. Mark Dever, 334–35.

21. Articles include Hinson, "Creeds and Confessions in the Christian Tradition," *R&E* 76 (Winter 1979): 5–26. Hobbs, "Southern Baptists and Confessionalism," *R&E* 76 (Winter 1979): 55–68. Hurt, "Should Southern Baptists Have a Creed/Confession?— No!" *R&E* 76 (Winter 1979): 85–88. Odle, "Should Southern Baptists Have a Creed/Confession?—Yes!" *R&E* 76 (Winter 1979): 89–94.

22. Examples include Carter, "Southern Baptists' First Confession of Faith," *BHH* 5 (January 1970): 24–28, 38. Garret, "Sources of Authority in Baptist Thought," *BHH* 13 (July 1978): 41–49. Hobbs, "The Baptist Faith and Message—Anchored but Free," *BHH* 13 (July 1978): 33–40.

23. Pool, "Chief Article of Faith," in *Sacred Mandates of Conscience*.

24. Copeland, *The Southern Baptist Convention and the Judgement of History*, 117.

He devoted all of chapter 7 of the work to detailing conservative efforts at maintaining doctrinal uniformity (i.e., creedalism).

During the debate over the adoption of the 2000 BFM several moderates raised some objections in an attempt to reclaim the original wording of the 1963 Preamble.[25] Against these accusations Adrian Rogers, Richard Land, and R. Albert Mohler Jr. stressed that no church was required to adopt the new confession and that the Convention had a long standing policy of requiring denominational agencies to subscribe to the BFM in its most current form.[26] Conservatives have spoken on the issue, endorsing the use of confessions recently in two Baptist Press articles, both dated 16 April 2002. One was published in Texas headlined "Creeds, Confessions, Beliefs & Integrity," and the other, addressing recent actions taken by the new Baptist General Convention of Missouri, bore the headline "New Mo. convention requires voters to sign 'agreement' form." The 18 May 2002, issue of the *SBT* contained an article by Michael Foust reporting on comments by Mohler on the role of confessions in Baptist life.[27] In the aftermath of the approval of the latest revision of the BFM the question of how doctrinal statements should function continues to be a source of debate.

METHODOLOGY

This project focuses on three major factors: (1) the influences upon the Committee that prompted it to make the changes it did; (2) the relation

25. Miller, "Southern Baptists overwhelmingly adopt revised Baptist Faith and Message," Baptist Press, June 14, 2000 [online]; accessed 15 June 2000; available from http://www.sbcannualmeeting.org/sbc00/news.asp?ID=1927611432&page=2&num=5; Internet.

26. Hinson, "Baptist Faith and Message Committee members say report embraces biblical authority," Baptist Press, June 14, 2000 [online]; accessed 15 June 2000; available from http://www.sbcannualmeeting.org/\sbc00/news.asp?ID=1927611428&page=3&num=5; Internet.

27. Foust, "Baptist forefathers never questioned confessions," *SBT*, 18 May 2002, 16. For a fuller list of articles on the issue of Baptist confessions, see the bibliography. Also note the difference in how Wills interprets the use of confessions in Southern Baptist life in *Democratic Religion*, 87–88; 98–101, with how Lumpkin sees their use in *Baptist Confessions of Faith*, 15–16. Lumpkin argues that "The Baptist Movement has traditionally been non-creedal in the sense that it has not erected confessions of faith as official bases of organization and tests of orthodoxy" (16). Wills argues that Baptist churches and associations routinely used confessions of faith as a benchmark for testing the doctrinal orthodoxy of ministers and churches (see chap. 4 of this work).

of confessions to Baptist life; and (3) the theological significance of key changes made in the 1963 document.

The Committee did not work in a vacuum. Competing perspectives within the Convention provided a dynamic that called for a delicate balance between conviction and a desire for denominational coherence. Correspondences received from concerned Southern Baptists influenced the various members of the Committee as well.

The question of the role of confessions in relation to the priesthood of believers, soul liberty and soul competency resurfaces every time there is a need to revisit a doctrinal formulation. The Committee had to face this question, and so it is appropriate to investigate the historical data and attempt to discern the Committee's views on this historically informed issue.

Changes in wording may reflect attempts to clarify a theological point or changes in theological understanding among Southern Baptists of the time. It is appropriate to examine those changes to see how the Committee sought to clarify doctrines, and in what direction Southern Baptist thinking had moved and where changes exhibited substantive doctrinal shifts.

In order to determine how much outside influences helped shape the final form of the document, various drafts have been compared to the letters, resolutions, and articles of faith which the Committee received, noting changes in the various drafts that reflect the influence of these documented sources. Doing so made it possible to distinguish those changes that were advanced from within the Committee from those that were the product of outside influences. Four appendices contain drafts prepared by the Committee, notes from various sources, and one independent document received from James Leo Garrett. These appendices serve as reference points throughout much of the dissertation to demonstrate progressive changes in the document and show also the sources for those changes.

LIMITATIONS AND OTHER AVENUES OF RESEARCH

Investigation of the controversies which prompted the formation of the Committee, Hobbs's leadership, and the prevailing concept of the role of Baptist confessions at the time raise a number of issues and other avenues for research. It would be impractical to pursue all of these, and so certain limitations must be placed on the scope of the research. Also, it will be helpful to note areas that deserve significant research in the future.

Scope and Limitations of the Research

This research project will focus on the work of the Committee, the controversies which prompted the formation of the Committee, and a brief examination of soul competency and the role of confessions in Baptist life, both as they functioned historically and as they were perceived by denominational leaders to have functioned at the time.

A full exploration of the concept of soul competency would take the dissertation too far afield from the primary focus of the research to delve into the subject fully. More serious research needs to be done on this important Baptist concept.

Likewise, the full exploration of the role of Baptist confessions as instruments of identity and accountability deserves more attention, but for the purposes of this dissertation only Baptist instruments of accountability will be surveyed relative to British Baptist life to approximately1800, and American Baptist life (especially in the South) to 1963. Sources of doctrinal expression and accountability in Baptist life subservient to Scripture include confessions, covenants, and especially after 1900, individual experience.[28] This work will only survey and summarize how each of these functioned in Baptist life at the level of the local church and the association. In this way a snapshot will be presented that demonstrates, historically, how Baptists of the past used confessions and covenants in churches and associations.

Other Avenues of Research

Several issues demand further attention. First among them would be an exploration of the pastoral methodology of Herschel H. Hobbs. His careful attention to the concerns of everyday Southern Baptists dur-

---

28. Norman identifies two approaches to Baptist identity. The first is rooted in the Reformation understanding of Scripture and a normative role for confessions. The second approach is rooted in the Enlightenment and focuses on the competency of the individual before God. While Norman's chapters on soul competency and religious liberty are, perhaps, his weakest chapters, he does highlight the need for further research in these areas of study. Norman, *More than a Name*, 41. Nettles has recently opened a new window on this subject with his three volume work, *The Baptists*.

ing this tumultuous period suggests a model of pastoral care worthy of investigation.

Stan Norman's work on Baptist identity raises the question of how soul competency and religious liberty should be understood. There is need for a thorough investigation of these two concepts from within both the Reformational and Enlightenment approaches, beginning with early Baptist struggles for religious liberty. Such an investigation should cover the subject exegetically, historically, and systematically. Further research into the developing understanding of soul competency in the aftermath of 1963, and especially after Hobbs's commentary on the BFM in 1971 would reveal how Southern Baptists perceived the Committee's understanding of this principle of Baptist life.

A third area in need of research is the nature of theological education in SBC seminaries during the 1950s and 1960s. How much latitude did faculty enjoy in regard to core doctrinal issues in these schools at the time? How often was "doublespeak"[29] employed by members of the faculty to cover the true intent of their teaching?

PREVIEW OF THE WORK

Chapter 2: Historical Crises Leading to the Formation of the Committee on Baptist Faith and Message

In this chapter the historical context for the formation of the Committee on Baptist Faith and Message will be examined. The tendency toward conservatism in the South and the rise of progressive thought set the stage for the examination of the Apostasy Controversy involving Dale Moody at SBTS and the Genesis Controversy at MBTS. The Controversy surrounding Moody remained somewhat isolated to the Southern Seminary community because he had not yet published a major work voicing his views on falling from grace. Nevertheless, there were expressions of concern

---

29. Elliott, *The "Genesis Controversy" and the Continuity in Southern Baptist Chaos*, Elliott notes on 10 that "in those days theological education at Southern Seminary was far more liberal and open than it was at Central [Baptist Theological Seminary]." Elliott cites Hinson as saying that "doublespeak" was part and parcel of life at Southern Seminary from the very beginning. "Professors and students learn to couch their beliefs in acceptable terminology and in holy jargon so that although thinking one thing, the speaker calculated so as to cause the hearer to affirm something else" (33–34).

about Moody's teaching from outside the seminary community.[30] Because Elliott published *The Message of Genesis* his controversy took center stage in the life of the SBC.

Chapter 3: Concerns Faced by the Committee

Societal concerns faced by the Committee included: (1) racism and the Civil Rights Movement; (2) global Communism; (3) materialism; and (4) Catholicism. Allegations surfaced of socialist tendencies in some literature published by the SSB, and racism within the churches of the SBC concerned the Committee as well.[31] Both the Genesis Controversy and the Apostasy Controversy raised concerns over the general doctrinal health of SBC institutions. Doctrinal concerns included the understanding of the nature and authority of Scripture, the doctrine of the church,[32] and salvation, especially the security of the believer. They also raised the issue of confessional authority for employees of Baptist institutions.[33] Chapter 3 explores these concerns.

Chapter 4: Confessionalism and Soul Liberty

Because the Committee had to address the relationship between confessional accountability and employees of Baptist institutions, this chapter will focus on the uses of Baptist confessions since the beginning of modern

30. Note for example the letter of Breining to Hobbs, 23 May 196[2], BFM file, folder 1, SBHLA, which she also claims to have sent to both Elliott and Moody. Also note the Resolution adopted by the Highland Avenue Baptist Church of Montgomery, Alabama, 25 July 1962, BFM file, folder 2, SBHLA, where Dale Moody is cited specifically as a source of concern.

31. Breinging to Hobbs. Highland Avenue Resolution. Breining mentions socialism and the Highland Resolution refers to Martin Luther King Jr. having been invited to preach in Alumni Chapel in 1961.

32. Moody suggested adopting the language of the Abstract of Principles. Moody to McCall, 7 January 1963, Dale Moody Collection, BCL. Barr sent the Committee an unpublished essay entitled "Universal Churchhood," in which he advocated a solution as to how to relate the concepts of local and universal church to one another based on the teachings of W. O. Carver, BFM file, folder 5, SBHLA.

33. Stealey to Hobbs, 1 December [1962], BFM file, folder 5, SBHLA. Stealey wants to be very clear that Southeastern neither affirms nor condemns the statement of faith prepared by the committee. Compare this to Ward's comment to Hall, "It is certainly within the realm of possibility that all our teaching faculties, college or seminary, might one day be called upon to accept [the *Baptist Faith and Message*]." Ward to Hall, 20 October 1962.

Baptist history in the early seventeenth century. There will be three major divisions in the chapter. The first division will focus on uses of confessions and covenants among English Baptists to about 1800. The second division will focus on the general relationship between confessions, covenants, and soul liberty. The third section will examine how Baptists in America used confessions and covenants up to 1900.

Chapter 5: Confessional Accountability and Soul Competency

With the publication of *The Axioms of Religion* in 1908 E. Y. Mullins inaugurated a new era in Baptist life. How did the principle of soul competency affect the role of confessions in Baptist life in the aftermath of Mullins's landmark publication? Baptists of the past sought to balance the concerns of individual rights and corporate responsibility by keeping clearly in view the voluntary, corporate relationship of believers to one another in churches and associations. As Enlightenment thinking gained ascendancy in Southern Baptist life so did individualism. Along with that, reason and/or personal experience became the arbiter(s) of truth for many. Beginning with the proposal and adoption of the BFM in 1925, Baptists were faced with two competing ideas of religious accountability. This chapter will examine the writings of Mullins, Conner, and other leading Southern Baptists of the early twentieth century and explore the tension that existed between these two competing ideologies. This will lead to an evaluation of how the Committee viewed the question in 1963.[34]

Chapter 6: The Work of the Committee on Baptist Faith and Message

This chapter will deal with some of the logistics of the Committee's work. It will begin with the proposal to call for the Committee's formation in 1962 and will trace out how the Committee organized itself. The subcommittee appointed by Hobbs and charged with preparing an initial draft will be examined first along with the early drafts it produced. Alongside that will be noted Hobbs's insistence on help from denominational agen-

---

34. Norman, *More than a Name*, 41. It is not my intention to make soul competency the primary focus of this book (see "Limitations"). The subject will be handled in terms of its historical development up to 1963. Much of this material will be based on a major seminar paper dealing with soul competency in the SBC from 1845–1925. Issues of soul competency that have developed since 1979 are beyond the scope of this document; however, a number of works relative to soul competency and confessionalism since 1963 have been included in the bibliography.

cies and state papers. The Committee enlisted the aid and advice of specific persons and the faculties of the seminaries generally. This chapter will examine the available data concerning those consultations. The roles of Wayne Ward, Mercer University's faculty, and James Leo Garrett in aiding the Committee will stand out as significant contributions to the final document.

Chapter 7: Substantive Changes in the Baptist Faith and Message

In this chapter Hobbs's goal for the Committee's work and four areas of doctrinal revision will be examined closely. These changes will be compared with available Baptist writings by Hobbs and others to determine the extent of continuity of thought or shifts in theological understanding. The areas of change to be examined will be Scripture, Ecclesiology, Anthropology, and Soteriology. Each of these areas were re-worded or revised in some significant way by the 1963 Committee.

Conclusion

The Conclusion will summarize the evidence and the argument. From there a final evaluation of the Committee's work will be given.

Appendix 1: The Ward Draft

This appendix will contain a copy of the draft sent by Dick Hall to Wayne Ward, along with his comments, both from within the text and in his letter to Hall.

Appendix 2: The Mercer Draft

This appendix will contain a copy of the draft sent by the Committee to the faculty at Mercer University, along with their comments on the draft. A careful examination of this draft and the Ward Draft shows how much Ward's comments influenced the Committee.

Appendix 3: Comparison of Ward and Mercer Drafts

This appendix presents, in parallel columns, the texts of the drafts received by Ward and the Mercer University faculty so as to demonstrate how the Committee incorporated the comments from Ward on the initial draft into the next draft of the BFM.

Appendix 4: A Declaration of Basic Beliefs

This appendix will contain a confession written by James Leo Garrett at the request of Nane Starnes. A significant portion of Garrett's article on eschatology found its way into the BFM 1963 under the heading of "The Kingdom."

2

Historical Crises Leading to the Formation of the Committee on Baptist Faith and Message

CONSERVATISM IN THE SOUTH

W HEN, IN 1962, THE Southern Baptist Convention voted to appoint a Committee to study the Baptist Faith and Message, it was not because a theological crisis had arisen from out of nowhere. Theological shifts had been taking place throughout the twentieth century that were beginning to surface with results that alarmed many average Southern Baptists. While the modernist-fundamentalist debate of the early twentieth century had brought division to Baptists in the North, their brethren in the South largely escaped the carnage because of the high degree of doctrinal homogeneity that existed in Southern churches. In the words of Nancy Ammerman, "There were simply not enough modernists around in the Convention to generate a good fight."[1]

Between 1925 and 1961 changes had come quickly to the SBC, especially in the academy. A cohesive system of beliefs began to give way to divergent views about the Bible and the doctrine of salvation. Indeed, some change in the doctrine of salvation had been anticipated by trends noted by James P. Boyce in the nineteenth century.[2] Ammerman argued that in the aftermath of the Great Depression and World War II population shifts radically altered the makeup of the South, displacing its religious

1. Ammerman, *Baptist Battles*, 48. Ammerman concedes that at this point the SBC was essentially a fundamentalist denomination. This is not to say there was no controversy in the SBC during the early twentieth century. J. Frank Norris led a divisive movement of Fundamentalists during this period, and the 1925 edition of the Baptist Faith and Message was approved by the Convention in response to modernist and liberal threats to traditional Baptist beliefs.

2. Boyce, "Three Changes in Theological Institutions," in *James Petigru Boyce*, 49.

homogeneity with a kind of pluralism that no longer allowed one form of evangelical expression to dominate.[3]

THE RISE OF PROGRESSIVE THOUGHT

Greg Wills traced the beginnings of progressive thought in the SBC back to the 1880s and names C. H. Toy as a specific case in point. Toy resigned from the faculty of SBTS in 1879 after having adopted the higher critical method of OT interpretation.[4] Wills noted that W. C. Lindsay, who served as pastor of the First Baptist Church, Columbia, S.C., from 1877 to 1910, began publishing liberal views two years before Toy's views became known. He further pointed out that from 1900 to 1940 numerous Baptist schools in the South experienced controversy over the promulgation of liberal views. Suspicions grew that the seminaries were the sources for liberal views that filtered down to the universities and the pulpits.[5]

Wills reported that the *BS* accused W. O. Carver, who taught at Southern, of denying the virgin birth in 1914. Others were suspected of holding to evolution or of embracing the ecumenical movement. James E. Dean was dismissed from New Orleans Baptist Bible Institute in 1931 for holding liberal views. Wills noted that institutional presidents tended to protect progressive thinking teachers as long as possible and then dismissed only those whose views became well known enough to pose a public relations problem for the institution.[6]

Writing on the issue of the doctrine of Scripture, Dwight A. Moody noted that for the first half century of Southern Baptist life the concept of revelation as espoused in the writings of Dagg, Boyce, Basil Manly Jr., and Carroll dominated Southern Baptist thought. For each of these men "the revelation was the Bible; the Bible was revelation."[7] Dwight Moody pointed out that with the writings and teaching of Mullins and Conner the locus of revelation shifted from the text of Scripture to the event of

3. Ammerman, *Baptist Battles*, 50–56.

4. Wills, "Progressive Theology and Southern Baptist Controversies," *SBJT* 7 (Spring 2003): 14.

5. Ibid., 14–15.

6. Ibid., 15–16.

7. Moody, "The Bible," in *Has Our Theology Changed?* 12. See also Bush and Nettles, *Baptists and the Bible*, chapters 9–17 for a more comprehensive survey of changing Baptist views on the Bible from the time of James P. Boyce down to the writing of the 1963 BFM.

God's self-disclosure. For Mullins the Scriptures were the "record of God's revelation of himself to his people." Moody noted that Conner echoed the sentiments of Mullins on this point.[8] Dwight Moody then discussed the thought of Dale Moody and Leo Garrett on the issue of revelation and Scripture. Here he saw an attempt to create a synthesis of the positions advanced by the first two generations of Southern Baptist leaders. Of special interest was Moody's observation that Scripture was both record and revelation. The Bible was first and foremost a record of God's revelation, but the recording and original interpretation of the revelatory events also constituted a part of God's revelation.[9]

Dwight Moody noted that the early leaders of the Convention held to a verbal and plenary view of inspiration but that Mullins considered the issue of inspiration a secondary one. The primary issue in his thought was "how the Bible is read and heard today."[10] Conner only affirmed in the most basic terms the inspiration of the Bible.[11] Dale Moody sought a view of inspiration broad enough to account for all the phenomenon of Scripture and embraced the best elements of the four principle views of inspiration prevalent among Protestant thinkers, both liberal and conservative.[12]

With regard to the doctrine of inerrancy, Dagg, Boyce, and Manly all believed in the infallibility of the Bible, which for them carried a commitment to inerrancy. This matter lay at the heart of the issue surrounding the Toy controversy. Toy taught that some parts of the Old Testament were not true, and this resulted in his dismissal from the faculty of Southern Seminary.[13] Dwight Moody argued that Mullins' language regarding inerrancy seemed to refer only "to the religious or spiritual content of the Bible" and not to the whole of the Bible.[14] Conner sought to avoid a defense of inerrancy because he saw any such defense as begging the question.[15] Dale Moody distinguished between infallibility, which for him dealt with

8. Mullins, *The Christian Religion in its Doctrinal Expression*, 142. See Moody's comments, "The Bible," 13.

9. Moody, "The Bible," 13.

10. Ibid., 17.

11. Ibid., 18.

12. Ibid., 19–20.

13. Ibid., 23–25.

14. Ibid., 26.

15. Ibid., 27.

what the Bible intended to teach, and inerrancy, which dealt with issues of factual accuracy. While he wrote that he had no serious conflict with the Chicago Statement on inerrancy, he sought to emphasize "the religious, moral, and/or doctrinal message of the Bible." In so doing he sought to avoid being identified with either the old Princeton orthodoxy or the new movement to affirm inerrancy.[16]

Those involved in educating Southern Baptist leaders in the seminaries were moving on a trajectory away from the historic and conservative position of the Convention's founders. By the 1950s and early 1960s events were approaching a watershed moment. Wills noted that McCall deliberately sought, by means of slow and careful education, to bring the Southern Baptist Convention in line with the thinking of contemporary scholarship. When a group of faculty members at Southern wanted to push the envelope in the late 1950s it resulted in the firing of thirteen, although one was re-instated when he broke ranks with the group.[17]

Not all those who taught in Baptist colleges and seminaries embraced the move to progressive thought on the Bible. The progressive element had introduced a diverse line of thinking into the Convention, but McCall's own approach highlights the fact that astute progressives understood the essentially conservative nature of the SBC at the grassroots level. At Baylor University, Old Testament Professor J. B. Tidwell stood for the traditional view of the Bible as God's inspired word. Tidwell unashamedly owned the Bible as "the word of God" and called for its teachings to be accepted on that basis.[18] He also devoted an entire chapter in *Thinking Straight about the Bible* to the Scriptures' own direct claims to be the very word of God.[19] Nettles and Bush demonstrated that A. T. Robertson held to the doctrine of the inerrancy of the biblical autographs, and he called for the submission of the human intellect to the revelation given by God in the Scriptures.[20]

---

16. Ibid., 28–29. Wayne Ward, who wrote his doctoral dissertation at Southern on the issue of the Bible and taught there along with Moody, claimed that the verbal plenary view of Scripture was not a biblical teaching but an aberrant outgrowth of Protestant rationalism. See Ward, "The Concept of Holy Scripture in Biblical Literature," 1.

17. Wills, "Progressive Theology," 16–17.

18. Tidwell, *Christian Teachings*, 17.

19. Tidwell, *Thinking Straight about the Bible*, 24. Tidwell did lay emphasis upon the spiritual or religious truths of the Bible and argues against using it as a book of science.

20. Bush and Nettles, *Baptists and the Bible*, 272–73.

In this context of developing theological pluralism within the SBC events took shape that resulted in the Convention forming a Committee to revisit the BFM and address the doctrinal concerns of Southern Baptists who represented both ends of the spectrum. On the one hand stood conservative pastors and lay members in the churches, and on the other hand stood advocates of progressive thought in the seminary classrooms.

According to James Hefley the Convention was managed carefully to insure that the conservative base remained convinced that all was right doctrinally, while at the same time professors remained free to pursue their studies in an environment of relative academic freedom. Denominational leaders chose presidential candidates known to be "cooperative and conservative." That is, they sought out individuals who could assure the constituency of the soundness of the Convention agencies without too much interference in the internal workings of those agencies.[21] All that it took to produce a crisis was for the content of progressive classroom teaching to become public knowledge.

THE APOSTASY CONTROVERSY AT SOUTHERN SEMINARY

Controversy first erupted regarding the doctrinal soundness of SBTS Theology Professor Dale Moody in 1961. Moody attended a preaching event in Oklahoma, and in the course of the event expressed views on the question of apostasy which some deemed inconsistent with traditional Southern Baptist views on the subject.

Moody's Life and Work Up to 1962

A Texas native, Dale Moody was born in Jones County on 27 January 1915. He was reared in Grapevine, Texas, on the present site of Dallas-Fort Worth International Airport. His home environment encapsulated a deep Baptist heritage. His conversion took place at about the age of twelve, under a grove of trees where he stopped while horseback riding. He was baptized and united with the Grapevine Baptist Church near the end of the summer of 1927. He studied at Baylor, where he displayed academic ability in both theology and science. After toying with the idea of attending Dallas Theological Seminary, he chose to enroll at Southern Seminary.

---

21. Hefley, *The Conservative Resurgence in the Southern Baptist Convention*, 25–26.

He received his Th.M. at Southern in 1941 and later entered into doctoral work under the direction of W. O. Carver.[22]

Moody also had opportunities to study under such noted twentieth century theologians as Paul Tillich, Emil Brunner (about whom he wrote his dissertation), Karl Barth, Oscar Cullmann, and Walter Eichrodt. He earned a second doctorate as a result of two years of study at Oxford.[23]

Moody, according to Stiver, sought to prove everything by the Scriptures, and he did not fear controversy. Stiver notes that even as a student pastor in Texas, Moody ran into trouble for advocating that the Bible taught the possibility that one truly saved could fall from the state of grace and lose his or her salvation.[24] While Moody became noted for his views on apostasy, he enjoyed a great reputation as one who sought to build his theology on the Scriptures.[25] Moody's position on eternal security eventually resulted in his leaving Southern Seminary in the 1980s.[26]

Moody and the Oklahoma Bible Conference

In 1961 Moody was a featured speaker at a state-wide Bible conference sponsored by the Baptist General Convention of Oklahoma. At this conference Moody made remarks that raised the suspicions of many attending pastors regarding his doctrinal soundness. They accused him of advocating that persons genuinely born again could fall away and lose their salvation. This led a group of pastors, among whom Herschel Hobbs was numbered, to sign a resolution sent to Southern Seminary calling for an investigation of Moody's doctrinal soundness. In a statement to BP Moody wrote that he believed there was a kind of faith that was temporary and transient and that there was saving faith that endured and persevered.[27]

Oklahoma Pastors Respond to Moody

Hobbs, in an article sent to the *BS*, explained the response of the Oklahoma County Pastors' Conference and his involvement in it. According to

22. Stiver, "Dale Moody," in *Baptist Theologians*, 539–40.

23. Ibid., 540.

24. Ibid., 541–42.

25. Ibid., 540: Stiver notes, "Always the reference point was Scripture."

26. Ibid., 542.

27. McGregor, "Moody Answers Charges of Oklahoma Resolution," *BS* (Dallas), 9 August 1961, 12.

Hobbs numerous persons at the Pastors' Conference also attended the Bible Conference where Moody spoke. They recounted the questionable doctrinal content they heard from Moody. Hobbs had been out of the country at the time and relied upon the eyewitness accounts of pastors whom he knew and trusted. A committee was formed which drafted a resolution that was presented for a vote and approved after Hobbs's return to Oklahoma City.[28]

Hobbs made it very clear in his article that he acted only as one pastor among all the pastors who attended the Pastors' Conference at the time the vote was taken. He did vote for the resolution, but he did not "sign" anything, and he did not act as president of the Convention. The resolution called for all the seminary presidents to ensure the competency and doctrinal integrity of their faculties, and it called on Southern Seminary to investigate specifically the doctrinal soundness of Moody's theology on the matter of apostasy.[29]

Moody's Defense of His Teaching on Apostasy

E. S. James interviewed Moody in August, 1961. In his report of the interview he noted that Moody believed in a spurious faith and a genuine, saving faith. Moody noted that one who renounced Christ was never actually saved. He argued that his position was consistent with that of A. T. Robertson and W. O. Carver.[30]

Southern Seminary's Handling of the Apostasy Controversy

After receiving the resolution from the Oklahoma County Pastors' Conference, Southern Seminary appointed a select committee composed of three trustees and chaired by C. Penrose St. Amant, dean of the School of Theology, to investigate the charges against Moody. The committee met with Moody on 1 February 1962, and at that meeting he affirmed that he was, in fact, in full agreement with the 1925 BFM on the issue of the security of the believer. The committee also reviewed transcripts of the messages Moody delivered at the Bible Conference in Oklahoma in the summer of 1961. The committee voted to clear Moody of the charges brought against

28. Hobbs, "Oklahoma Resolution: Hobbs Issues Statement to Clarify Actions," *BS* (Dallas), 23 August 1961, 15.

29. Ibid.

30. James, "Alien Immersion . . . Open Communion . . . Ecumenicity . . . Apostasy . . . An Interview with Dale Moody," *BS* (Dallas), 30 August 1961, 6.

him and passed that recommendation on to the full Board of Trustees, who approved of the committee's action.[31] Despite this action suspicions grew that doctrinal problems remained in the faculties of the seminaries of the SBC. A second controversy rocked the Convention before the end of 1961 which all but eclipsed the controversy surrounding Moody.

THE ELLIOTT CONTROVERSY AT MIDWESTERN SEMINARY

Ralph Elliott's book *The Message of Genesis* set off a fire storm of controversy over the theological soundness of the seminaries and the Sunday School Board of the SBC. The progressive leanings of professors in the classroom came into the spotlight for public consumption by the reading public of the SBC. The confidence of the people within the Convention took a hard hit, and rumors of doctrinal unsoundness in the seminaries turned into open distrust of the faculty. Elliott had published, and in so doing he revealed to the public the content and potential consequences of the higher critical method in the seminaries. Seminary professors initially rallied to his support, but in the end he faced the outcome in relative isolation.

Elliott's Career at Southern

Ralph Harrison Elliott was born 2 March 1925, in Danville, Virginia. He graduated from Carson-Newman College with an associate's degree in 1949 and received the bachelor of divinity degree from Southern Seminary in 1952. He completed his doctoral studies in Old Testament and received the Th.D. from Southern Seminary in 1956.[32] Elliott taught briefly at Southern before McCall recommended him to Berquist for appointment to the faculty of the new seminary in Kansas City, Missouri.[33] McCall notes that a number of those dismissed from Southern in 1958 also ended up at Midwestern, and that this turn of events did not prove helpful to Elliott during the controversy.[34]

31. "Seminary Trustees Approve Carver Merger; Deny Moody Violated Articles of Faith," *AlB* (Mobile), 12 April 1962, 4.

32. Biographical Data Sheet, courtesy of MBF. He served in the United States Army as an infantryman in World War II. On 14 October 1945, he married Virginia Ellen Case, also of Danville, Virginia.

33. McCall and Tonks, *Duke McCall: An Oral History*, 250.

34. Ibid.

Elliott's relationship to McCall requires some explanation. McCall considered Elliott a "conservative, evangelical Christian" in recommending him for Midwestern. There is nothing in McCall's recounting of the events that indicate he had anything but love and respect for Elliott and his potential as a Christian scholar in the service of the Convention.[35]

Elliott has a very different recollection of the situation at Southern Seminary and of the purge of 1958. Elliott recounts with great disappointment the treatment he and other faculty members received from McCall. McCall had asked them to provide him with some brain-storming advice for his work on an upcoming edition of *Broadman Comments*. According to Elliott, McCall used the faculty submitted ideas almost verbatim without giving any credit to any of the faculty members. This created an immediate firestorm on the campus.[36]

Elliott studied under Clyde Francisco, and the two became very close. Francisco, according to Elliott, wanted to join the new faculty at Midwestern. Berquist came to McCall wanting to interview Francisco. McCall told him he could do that if he wanted, but that he would never get Francisco. He would have a better shot at getting Elliott.[37] Elliott had no idea that McCall had recommended him when Berquist called him and asked him to come to the airport in Louisville for a meeting. The relationship between Francisco and Elliott suffered a serious blow as a result.[38]

According to Elliott "double speak" served as the basis for keeping the conservative elements in the churches from suspecting theological deviations in the seminaries. Good communication skills involved saying one thing while meaning something else. Professors carefully avoided publishing. As one professor told Elliott, "When you publish it, they will get you." Professors would teach in the classroom and speak among their learned colleagues one way, but when they went out to preach in the churches they would use traditional language. This language conveyed a conservative message to the hearers in the pews who had no idea that

---

35. Ibid.

36. Elliott, *"The Genesis Controversy" and Continuity in Southern Baptist Chaos*, 3–5.

37. McCall and Tonks, *Duke McCall*, 250.

38. Elliott, *"The Genesis Controversy,"* 3–5.

these men had redefined the terms to mean things other than what seemed to be said.[39]

Elliott and the Sunday School Board

One issue that vexed those who lost their positions in 1958 was this very issue of "double speak." They felt the time had come to publish the fruits of scientific biblical scholarship and "shock" the Convention forward.[40] During Elliott's time at Southern, William J. Fallis of the Sunday School Board came and asked for someone to publish a book intended to introduce Southern Baptists to the fruits of higher scholarship. Elliott, along with Francisco, accepted the task.[41]

The original plan had been a joint book project on Genesis that would, in a modest degree, employ the fruits of the higher critical method. Francisco found himself strapped with a heavy teaching load, and the responsibility for the initial draft fell to Elliott, who had some free time. In the end, at the insistence of Francisco, the book would be Elliott's work alone. Broadman Press published it and the Southern Baptist reading public got its first look on 1 July 1961.[42]

By this time Elliott had accepted the teaching position at Midwestern, a new seminary formed because Missouri Baptists suspected Central Baptist Seminary, an American Baptist school in Kansas, of disseminating liberal teachings. The stated intention of the trustees was that Midwestern would be "in the mainstream of conservative Baptist thought and doctrine."[43] In 1962 W. Ross Edwards, secretary to the Board of Trustees for Midwestern from its founding until June 1962, wrote a scathing critique of the school's administration and faculty. He commented, "We need a Seminary that will fit in with the conservative traditions that have made Southern Baptists great."[44] While Elliott saw his work as a modest, even conservative handling of the fruits of biblical scholarship, others did not.

---

39. Ibid., xvi.

40. Ibid., 8.

41. Ibid., 7.

42. Ibid.

43. Report of the Board of Trustees of Midwestern Baptist Theological Seminary, 25 October 1962, MBF.

44. Edwards, "Midwestern Baptist Theological Seminary," transcribed by A. J. Smith from the original, 11 January 2002, BFM file, folder 1, SBHLA.

Publication of The Message of Genesis

With the publication of *The Message of Genesis* Southern Baptists got their first real look at the teaching content of Old Testament faculties in the seminaries of the Convention. K. Owen White, pastor of First Baptist Church, Houston, responded to Elliott's book with a letter to the Baptist papers of the Convention. The *AIB* published the letter in the 11 January 1962 issue, along with a short editorial and a resolution adopted by the trustees of Midwestern Seminary.[45] In this letter White outlined his concerns regarding the book, utilizing extended quotes. He also took great pains to lay out how he believed the Convention should respond to the book.

Causes for Concern

Almost one half of White's letter consisted of extended quotes from Elliott's work. His concerns included Elliott's treatment of the first eleven chapters of Genesis as parable, his treatment of the longevity of the antediluvian patriarchs, his treatment of Abraham as a monotheist, the call to sacrifice Isaac, the allegation that Melchizedek was a priest of Baal, and Lot's wife turning to a pillar of salt. White proposed three actions in response to Elliott's book: (1) ask men who hold such views to seek teaching positions in denominations where their views will find a ready audience; (2) ask the trustees of the Southern Baptist seminaries to take seriously the threat of liberalism and exercise great caution in hiring faculty; and (3) insist that the Sunday School Board be sensitive to such teachings and not publish works tainted with liberal error.[46]

Elliott proposed to view Genesis "from a theological-religious standpoint." He emphasized the record of God's revelation in the text and saw in the text the "parabolic and symbolic nature of much of the Old Testament Scriptures." The earliest materials in Genesis (from the J and P sources, according to Elliott) sought to "convey deep religious insights" and did not aim for historical or scientific accuracy.[47]

---

45. White, "Houston Pastor Takes Stand on Liberalism in the Southern Baptist Convention: 'Death in the Pot,'" *AIB* (Birmingham), 11 January 1962, 5. Macon, "Midwestern Comes under Criticism, " *AIB* (Birmingham), 11 January 1962, 2. "Resolution. The Trustees of Midwestern Baptist Theological Seminary," *AIB* (Birmingham), 11 January 1962, 5.

46. White, "Houston Pastor takes Stand."

47. Elliott, *The Message of Genesis*, 15.

In his treatment of Abraham, Elliott took him to be a historical character. He rejected the notion that Abraham was a monotheist, however. Abraham, according to Elliott, came from a family that worshiped Yahweh, but that did not mean that Yahweh was the only God they believed to exist. For them Yahweh was the supreme God over all other gods. He stated, "To Abram and his clan, other gods might have existed. Perhaps they attributed to these other gods certain powers, but they were *as nothing* to the supreme."[48] Abram worshiped only Yahweh, and he sought to lead his family to the same practice.

In his treatment of Melchizedek, Elliott based his argument that he was a priest of Baal on a liturgical document uncovered at Ras Shamra which described the worship at Salem from 1800–1600 B.C., which Elliott maintained was the general period for Abraham and Melchizedek. According to this document the people of Salem referred to Baal as the "highest God" and "the 'possessor of all things,'" that were also terms used in Genesis. Hence, according to Elliott, Melchizedek was a priest of Baal. Abram offered the sacrifice and allowed Melchizedek a share of the booty as an act of courtesy. The speech of Abraham, then, became a witness to his belief that it was Yahweh, and not Baal, who was the most high God and the possessor of all things.[49] This interpretation raised serious questions about the handling of Melchizedek in Hebrews 7, which in turn led to questions about the inspiration of the Bible and the unity of its message.

White charged that Elliott, in his book espoused pure liberalism tainted with the teachings of Wellhausen. He stated, "The book from which I have quoted is liberalism, pure and simple! It stems from the naturalistic theology of Wellhausen and his school which led Germany to become a materialistic, godless nation." White then argued that Elliott's book failed to take seriously the Bible as God's written word. For White higher criticism, as demonstrated in Elliott's work, brought forth interpretations that did not square with the accepted Baptist belief of biblical inerrancy. This, he argued, constituted a departure from the theology of Boyce, Broadus, Robertson, Mullins, and others.[50]

---

48. Ibid., 93, emphasis his.

49. Ibid., 115–17.

50. White, "Houston Pastor Takes Stand."

Responses to the Crisis

Elliott's book sparked a crisis within the Convention which called into question the theological soundness of the seminaries whose responsibility it was to train the next generation of pastors, scholars, and Convention leaders. Responses to this crisis spanned the spectrum from solid support for Elliott to calls for his immediate dismissal from the faculty of Midwestern. Responses can be broadly categorized as coming from the seminaries, from pastors, and from the Baptist Sunday School Board.

Responses from the Seminaries

The best source of information regarding responses to Elliott's work is the Millard Berquist files. Berquist served as the first president of MBTS. His files are kept at Midwestern, and access is limited. Berquist himself sought to defend Elliott. In a letter to Malcolm Knight he asserted that Elliott's basic position was sound and defensible, and his effort was to square divine revelation with scientific investigation. According to Berquist, Elliott tried to defend and maintain an approach to interpretation that safeguarded the infallibility of the theological message of the Bible while making allowances for errors in the text based on a primitive cosmology or flawed knowledge of historical events found in the biblical record. In other words, the Bible communicated infallible theological truth within a potentially fallible package.[51]

On the other hand, Duke McCall, at SBTS, felt that to defend Elliott's book was a mistake. He personally refused to defend it. To many the whole debate centered on the issue of academic freedom, and friends told Elliott he would be viewed as a coward if he rewrote the book. McCall said Elliott allowed himself to get locked into an indefensible position by his colleagues. According to McCall, Elliott failed to communicate adequately what he meant in his writing.[52] Nonetheless, McCall said that whenever a seminary faced a problem all the seminary presidents closed ranks and sought to help out the institution in trouble. McCall tried to dissuade Berquist from defending the book and focus on defending a young professor's right to make a mistake on his first publication.[53]

---

51. Berquist to Knight, 5 September 1962, MBF.
52. See chap. 1, n. 28, for a brief discussion of "communicating."
53. McCall and Tonks, *Duke McCall*, 248–50.

Old Testament colleagues from the various seminaries also weighed in with their thoughts on Elliott's work. From Southern both Clyde Francisco and Marvin Tate expressed concern and support. Francisco set out to make his position regarding Elliott's book clear, noting areas of agreement and disagreement. He disagreed with Elliott's use of "liberal vocabulary" which he felt made Elliott's work something which could not be properly understood by most Southern Baptists. He also believed that Elliott went too far in trying to solve certain problems, leaning danger-ously to the left on certain matters. Specifically, Francisco thought Elliott went too far in treating all of Genesis 1–11 as parable. He disagreed with Elliott's conclusion that Melchizedek was a priest of Baal, and he dis-agreed with Elliott's treatment of Abraham's offering of Isaac as a sacrifice. He considered the term "folklore" to be "unfortunate." He considered the greatest failing on Elliott's part to be that he did not give a more evangeli-cal turn to his work. He wrote, "There is not too much difference between your conclusions and those of Richardson or Mowinckel. As you know, this type of emphasis is destroying our schools as training grounds for preachers in order to produce scholars."[54] These remarks, made after the firestorm began ought to be compared with Francisco's earlier remarks. At first Francisco congratulated Elliott on a well written work which he said would become the textbook for his class in the fall semester of 1961.[55]

Marvin Tate characterized the book as "significant" and "helpful." Tate assigned readings from the book and heartily recommended it to his students.[56] Southern Seminary Archeology Professor Jerry Vardaman noted how he once came under attack at Southwestern. He sympathized with Elliott and commended him for a well written book. Vardaman la-mented, "Have we spoon-fed our people so long that they are still unable to move on to scientific and mature Biblical study?"[57]

Other professors from Southern, as well as those who had prior con-nections to the school, wrote to Elliott regarding his work. Dale Moody wrote to Elliott and encouraged him to answer E. S. James of the Texas *BS* directly.[58] Henley Barnette, ethics professor at Southern, wrote to ex-

54. Francisco to Elliott, 5 October 1961, MBF.

55. Francisco to Elliott, 17 July 1961, MBF.

56. Tate to Elliott, 9 November 1961, MBF.

57. Vardaman to Elliott, 16 February 1962, MBF.

58. Moody to Elliott, 16 January 1962, MBF.

press his distress over Elliott's article being dropped from the seminary magazine, *The Tie*, in the aftermath of the controversy over his book. He encouraged Elliott to take courage in suffering for his honest convictions.[59] Samuel Southard, associate professor of Psychology of Religion at Southern, wrote to voice his support for Elliott. He noted, "The significance of the book is that you as a seminary professor are now saying for everybody that which was formerly said only for a privileged few in a Southern Baptist seminary."[60] John D. W. Watts wrote from Switzerland, were he was professor of Old Testament and dean, to encourage Elliott and give his support.[61]

Support also came from Southwestern and Southeastern. In a letter to Elliott, Boyd Hunt (who taught at SWBTS) admitted that all the seminaries taught essentially what Elliott had written in his book, but he also noted that they have been "turning out fundamentalist preachers" and that the day of reckoning for that had come upon them unawares. He indicated that they must all find the maturity to stand together.[62]

On the other hand Elliott had his critics at Southwestern. Leslie Carlson taught Biblical Introduction and Semitic Languages. He wrote to Mack Douglas to note that he did not and would not endorse Elliott's book or agree with him "regarding the integrity and authorship of Genesis." Carlson noted that Elliott was "following a strictly liberal viewpoint."[63]

Numerous letters of support came from Southeastern Seminary. In a letter dated 9 April 1962, John Steely, professor of Historical Theology wrote to express his support for Elliott.[64] Marc Lovelace, professor of Archeology wrote to commend Elliott for his very helpful book.[65] Stewart Newman, professor of Philosophy of Religion, wrote to encourage Elliott in his work with the hope that knowledge and learning would prevail over well-intentioned ignorance.[66]

Students who had studied under Elliott also expressed their opinions concerning his character and his work. A letter by Truett Baker ex-

59. Barnett to Elliott, 6 March 1962, MBF.

60. Southard to Elliott, 19 February 1962, MBF.

61. Watts to Elliott, 14 March 1962, MBF.

62. Hunt to Elliott, 17 January 1962, MBF.

63. Carlson to Douglas, 10 October 1961, MBF.

64. Steely to Elliott, Kansas City, 9 April 1962, MBF.

65. Lovelace, to Elliott, Kansas City, 29 March 1962, MBF.

66. Newman to Elliott, 28 April 1962, MBF.

pressed the thoughts of many students from this turbulent period. Baker expressed great appreciation for the presence of the seminary and for the work of such men as Elliott, Morris Ashcraft, and Roy Honeycutt.[67] A former student from Elliott's days at Southern read the book and wrote to comment on it as well. Lovina Fly served as director of the BSU at Middle Tennessee State College. While not claiming to understand all that he wrote in his book, she noted that her faith was deepened, not destroyed, by it.[68] After Elliott's dismissal students at Midwestern adopted a resolution calling upon the trustees to reconsider their decision.[69]

Midwestern's trustees responded to the crisis with a certain degree of patience and concern for all parties involved. In December 1961 the Board adopted a resolution which recognized that the seminary desired "to be in the mainstream of conservative Baptist thought and doctrine." It further affirmed the 1925 BFM. While noting differences of interpretation between members of the Board and Elliott, the Board found no cause for considering Elliott to be anything other than "a consecrated Christian, a promising scholar, a loyal servant of Southern Baptists, and a dedicated and warmly evangelistic preacher of the Gospel."[70]

In June 1961 the SBC affirmed by standing vote its belief "in the entire Bible as the authoritative, authentic, infallible Word of God." The Convention also condemned any teaching in the seminaries or colleges that undermined that belief in students.[71]

A special committee was formed by the Trustees of Midwestern to study the problem further. They recommended that the full Board adopt a statement that included an acknowledgment of the need for a "pre-set framework of doctrinal beliefs by which its teachers must be tested" as Boyce had laid out in the founding of Southern Seminary. "It is recognized that each seminary teacher has the obligation to carry on his work within the framework of the fundamentals of Baptist doctrine." Allowances were made for differences of interpretation and the necessity for teachers to continue to search for a more complete understanding of

67. Baker to Berquist, 17 May 1962, MBF.

68. Fly to Elliott, 21 June 1962, MBF.

69. "Resolution Concerning the Dismissal of Dr. Ralph Elliott by the Midwestern Baptist Theological Seminary," submitted by the Baptist students of North Carolina, 3 November 1962, MBF.

70. Report of the Board of Trustees, MBTS, 25 October 1962, MBF.

71. Ibid.

the text. The trustees acknowledged that the higher critical methods had a place in this search for understanding. The trustees, however, expected teachers to approach their work from the given perspective that the Bible was God's word, and it did not depend on external verification from historical or scientific research. They affirmed plenary inspiration. The task of the teacher was "to strengthen the faith of the student and help him prepare to present [the Bible's] message." Various views of interpretation should be presented in the classroom. They soundly rejected the concept that the Bible is "myth" and "folklore." The real bone of contention with Elliott at this time became the question of the republication of his book. The special committee asked him not to republish it "at this time." He refused to comply with this request, and as a result they dismissed him from the faculty for insubordination.[72] In a letter from Elliott to Malcolm Knight, Elliott affirmed that if the entire Board of Trustees requested it he would refrain from republishing his *Message of Genesis* so long as he was a faculty member at Midwestern Seminary.[73]

Responses from Pastors

Pastors also entered the fray in the controversy over *The Message of Genesis*. In a letter to Conrad Willard, Newman Antonson, pastor of Dumas Avenue Baptist Church, stated that if a preacher stood in a Baptist pulpit and proclaimed what Elliott had written he would be barred from the pulpit. He wrote, "If [Elliott] wants to hold and teach liberal views that is his prerogative, but for him to accept the salary which comes from Cooperative Program money from people that believe in the inerrant, infalible [sic] authority of the Bible is certainly out of line."[74] W. E. Cook, pastor of Downtown Baptist Church, Oklahoma City, wrote to Berquist to ask that Elliott's book not be used as a textbook in the seminary, noting that motions were being made to send money elsewhere until the matter was cleared up.[75] Pastor C. Murray Fuquay of First Baptist Church, Midwest City, Oklahoma, warned of dire consequences for Midwestern should Elliott's views continue to be propagated.[76] Numerous such let-

---

72. Ibid.
73. Elliott to Knight, 20 October 1962, MBF.
74. Antonson to Willard, 19 December 1961, MBF.
75. Cook to Berquist, 20 December 1961, MBF.
76. Fuquay to Berquist, 20 March 1962, MBF.

ters came from churches in Oklahoma.[77] Harold Warner, pastor of Palm Avenue Baptist Church, Tampa, Florida, laid the charge that neo-orthodoxy was being taught at MBTS and propagated by Broadman Press. He mentioned neither Elliott nor his book in the letter.[78]

Elliott had supporters in the pastorate also. In an editorial, Pastor Sterling Price of Third Baptist Church argued against calling Elliott a liberal and said that the issue amounted to a matter of differences of interpretation first and foremost. Secondly, he argued for personal liberty on the basis of the priesthood of the believer against "credal definitions." He called for a spirit of diversity within the Convention.[79]

Several letters expressed a general concern for the direction of the SBC and the seminaries without naming specifically either Elliott or Moody. Charles Skutt, pastor of LaBelle Place Baptist Church, Memphis, Tennessee, wrote to inform the Committee on Baptist Faith and Message that the church had voted unanimously in opposition to the liberalizing tendency "in our Convention-supported Seminaries" and affirmed a solid belief in the supernatural inspiration of the Bible.[80] In the aftermath of the 1962 Convention in San Francisco, Pastor Millard Box wrote to Hobbs expressing his church's sense of concern over the seminaries and the need for a complete and wholesale house cleaning that would involve not only the seminaries but also the Sunday School Board.[81] In a letter written in early 1963, Woodrow Robbins warned Hobbs that "Modernists have a

---

77. The Berquist Files contain three folders of letters from concerned lay church members throughout the SBC. There are fifteen folders of letters from pastors, generally divided by state conventions. There are at least four folders of resolutions regarding Elliott's book. There is one large folder each devoted to K. O. White and Douglas Mack. Numerous other folders contain materials from state convention officials and state paper editors throughout the Convention. The file contains a large amount of material that needs to be better arranged. There is much reduplication of documents, and they are scattered throughout the file in various folders. The file consists of two drawer boxes approximately two feet long by one foot wide. Many documents are preserved as negative images. These, along with many others, are in a state of deterioration, and there is a great need for someone who specializes in archival preservation to catalog properly and protect these rare and important documents.

78. Warner to Maquire, 27 April 1962, MBF.

79. Price, "Liberals versus Conservatives," The Third Baptist Visitor 26, no. 26 (28 June 1962): 1.

80. Skutt to The Committee on Study of Theological Interpretation, 27 June 1962, BFM file, folder 1, SBHL.

81. Box to Hobbs, 13 June 1962, BFM file, folder 1, SBHL.

two-fold attack." Their plan involved first taking the schools, and then putting key persons in positions of leadership in the Convention who would protect modernists in the various denominational institutions.[82]

Responses from Denominational Leaders.

Leaders from both the state conventions and the SBC responded to the crisis created by the publication of *The Message of Genesis*. These leaders included editors in state papers and state convention heads. The responses included both supporters and those who sought Elliott's removal.

In a letter to Berquist, Harold Sanders, executive secretary-treasurer of the Kentucky Baptist Convention alleged that people of "ill will" were promoting the controversy.[83] In a letter written in July 1962 John Maquire, executive secretary-treasurer for the Florida Baptist Convention noted that it might be necessary for the unity of the Convention to persuade Elliott to step down of his own choosing, at least until the controversy subsided.[84] In an earlier letter Maquire lamented that the Convention could be split between conservatives and liberals over the Elliott affair, the workings of K. O. White and the editorial reviews published by Leon Macon (*AIB*) and E. S. James (*BS*).[85]

Opponents of Elliott's views included John Havlik of Louisiana, and N. J. Westmoreland of Kansas. Havlik, secretary for the Department of Evangelism for the Louisiana Baptist Convention, wrote a short article to defend the traditional Baptist belief regarding Mosaic authorship of the Pentateuch. He cited John Broadus, John R. Sampey, A. T. Robertson, and J. B. Tidwell, as well as Clyde Francisco.[86]

In a letter to Berquist, Westmoreland, executive secretary-treasurer for the Kansas Convention of Southern Baptists, expressed his belief that the teachings of *The Message of Genesis* "are wrong and dangerous." He further challenged the notion that all the seminaries taught the same thing, noting that "Dr Francisco did not teach what Dr. Elliott teaches in his book at Southern when I attended."[87]

---

82. Robbins to Hobbs, 23 January 1963, BFM file, folder 6, SBHLA.

83. Sanders to Berquist, 14 July 1962, MBF.

84. Maquire to Berquist, 23 July 1962, MBF.

85. Maquire to Berquist, 15 January 1962, MBF.

86. Havlik, "Southern Baptists and the Old Testament," *BD*, 30 December 1961, 4.

87. Westmoreland to Berquist, 26 October 1961, MBF.

Reuben Alley, editor of the *RH* of Virginia, wrote to Berquist to assure him that the *RH* would always stand on the side of freedom in the classroom.[88] Wayne Barton, who authored the column "Gleanings from the Greek New Testament" that appeared in most state papers, wrote to Elliott to encourage him, to condemn the outcries against his book, and to offer his sympathy for Elliott's plight.[89] Erwin L. McDonald, editor of the *ArkB*, wrote to Mack Douglas denouncing the San Francisco Convention's actions against Elliott as outside the purview of the Convention. He believed any accusation against a seminary faculty member should be handled by the trustees of the seminary.[90]

Leon Macon wrote that while Elliott was a sincere man, "his interpretations of certain passages are not true to Baptist interpretations."[91] E. S. James, wrote in January 1962, against Elliott's book as setting forth views about Genesis that undermined traditional Baptist beliefs. He noted the responsibility of seminary professors to write with future generations in view. While noting that he found much in the book commendable, it contained so much dangerous material that it should not have been written and should not be used as a text in any Southern Baptist seminary.[92]

Denominational leaders found it necessary to address the issue raised by Elliott's book by forming a Committee to revise the BFM. According to Garth Pybass, one of only three members of that Committee still living in 2004, the intention of the "criterion" statement in the article on Scripture was "to convey biblical infallibility based on Christ's testimony of it in the gospels."[93]

After the formation of the Committee, leaders corresponded frequently with Hobbs to ascertain his sense of how best to proceed in dealing with the controversy at Midwestern regarding Elliott. Convention Executive Secretary Porter Routh wrote to Hobbs with concerns about

88. Alley to Berquist, 2 November 1961, MBF.

89. Barton to Elliott, 22 November 1961, MBF.

90. McDonald to Douglas, 26 June 1962, BFM file, folder 1, SBHLA.

91. Macon, "Midwestern Comes Under Criticism," *AlB* (Birmingham), 11 January 1962, 2.

92. James, "Baptist Theologians and Their Books," *BS* (Dallas), 10 January 1962, 4-5.

93. Pierce, "Elder Baptist says '63 BF&M intended to clarify Bible belief," BP 8 January 2002. The other two members alive in 2004 were Verlin Krutschwitz, and Walter Davis. As will become clear, this interpretation of the "criterion" statement would take on differing interpretations within the Convention.

a letter from Berquist which Routh believed would work at odds with Berquist's intent. He also raised the question of whether Elliott's adversaries' motives came from a desire for power more than orthodoxy.[94]

C. Z. Holland, who served on the Committee from Arkansas, sent a draft letter for Berquist to Hobbs first for his input. In this letter he expressed his conviction that Berquist would find it quite difficult to retain Elliott on the faculty "without formenting [*sic*] an attitude of mind among the run of the mill preachers that will, in the course of time," get out of control.[95] Hobbs responded to Holland that he felt that there would be "an unwholesome reaction to the form letter which [Berquist] and Hester sent out." He further noted that one state editor wrote to Malcolm Knight demanding that both Berquist and Hester step down.[96]

Reaction from Baptist Colleges and Universities

Reactions from the colleges and universities varied as did the responses from pastors and editors of state Baptist papers. Some saw no problem with the position Elliott had staked out, while others, like K. Owen White, saw his position as dangerous and heretical.

Charles Trentham, dean of the School of Religion at the University of Tennessee and pastor of First Baptist, Knoxville, wrote a commendation of Elliott's book noting that he preserved the spiritual values of the Book of Genesis.[97] Likewise voices of support came from Furman and Ouachita. At Furman University, H. J. Flanders Jr. wrote to express his appreciation for Elliott's book and to encourage him.[98] Wayne H. Peterson, who taught at Ouchita, commended Elliott for a "splendid job" in his treatment of Genesis.[99]

On the other side voices from smaller schools condemned the work. B. A. Copass, director of curriculum development at San Marcos Academy, in San Marcos, Texas, wrote to E. S. James to commend him on his "restraint" in dealing with Elliott's book, which Copass character-

94. Routh to Hobbs, 25 July 1962, BFM file, folder 2, SBHLA.

95. Holl to Berquist, [19?] July 1962, BFM file, folder 2, SBHLA; see also the accompanying letter to Hobbs, 19 July 1962, BFM file, folder 2, SBHLA.

96. Hobbs to Holland, 24 July 1962, BFM file, folder 2, SBHLA.

97. Trentham to Berquist, 15 January 1962, MBF.

98. Flanders to Elliott, 11 June 1962, MBF.

99. Peterson to Elliott, 21 October 1961, MBF.

ized as "rank heresy."[100] Rufus R. Crozier, dean and registrar at Hannibal-LaGrange College Extension Center, wrote criticizing Elliott's work as evidence of liberal tendencies at Midwestern. He commented that "the deep convictions which we hold have been greatly disturbed" by Elliott's book. He attached to the letter a six page document written on legal size paper critiquing the work.[101]

Responses from the Sunday School Board

At the Southern Baptist Convention meeting in San Francisco in 1962, Ralph F. Powell of Missouri presented a motion calling for the Sunday School Board "to cease from publication and printing the book, The Message of Genesis [sic], by Dr. Elliott, and that they furthermore recall from all sales this book which contradicts Baptist convictions."[102] Powell, upon request, later withdrew his motion, but if any doubt had remained, the Sunday School Board could now see that many had great concerns regarding Elliott's work.[103]

In a letter to Elliott, James Sullivan admitted that he had pushed for the publication of The Message of Genesis without reading the manuscript because he believed it was intended only to be used as a seminary text-book.[104] William Fallis, an editor at Broadman, noted prior to publication that he expected the book to receive "vigorous criticism" but pushed for its publication and wrote to Berquist, requesting that he prepare an endorsement of the work to strengthen the case for its publication[105] In the aftermath of the controversy the Sunday School Board decided not to reprint the book. In a letter to Elliott, Joe Green Jr., general book editor at Broadman, expressed his disappointment that Elliott's book would not be reprinted by Broadman and also noted that he found Elliott's approach consistent with Mullins's and Conner's view of biblical authority. He believed the survival of the Christian faith depended upon such recognition of the human element in the Bible as Elliott had brought to the fore.[106]

---

100. Copass to James, 13 January 1962, MBF.

101. Crozier to Berquist, 20 September 1961, MBF.

102. Merrit, ed., *Annual of the Southern Baptist Convention Nineteen Hundred and Sixty-Two*, 65.

103. Ibid., 69.

104. Sullivan to Elliott, 24 January 1962, MBF.

105. Fallis to Berquist, 2 November 1960, MBF.

106. Green to Berquist, 27 September 1962, MBF.

Response of the 1962 Convention

When the messengers assembled in San Francisco in 1962, the Convention responded to the controversy sparked by Elliott in two clear actions. First, the Convention adopted a motion prepared by an ad hoc committee and presented by J. Ralph Grant of Texas that a new Committee be formed to study the BFM 1925 and present a report to the Convention meeting in Kansas City in 1963. Herschel Hobbs chaired this Committee and the presidents of the various state conventions constituted the body.[107] Secondly, the Convention adopted by standing vote a motion brought by K. Owen White which read as follows:

> I move that the messengers of this Convention, by standing vote, reaffirm their faith in the *entire* Bible as the authoritative, authentic, infallible Word of God, that we express our abiding and unchanging objection to the dissemination of theological views in any of our seminaries which would undermine such faith in the historical accuracy and doctrinal integrity of the Bible, and that we kindly but firmly instruct the trustees and administrative officers of our institutions and [other] agencies to take such steps as shall be necessary to remedy at once those situations where such views now threaten our historic position.[108]

Hobbs himself responded in the Convention Sermon, "Crisis and Conquest," by denouncing liberalism, materialism, and modernism in his introductory remarks, and then focused the force of his sermon on showing how neo-orthodoxy, for all its attempts to return to the Bible, failed to accomplish what it intended. According to Hobbs this failure prevailed because "it still tends to make the Bible subservient to the autonomy of physical science."[109]

In the end the controversies surrounding Moody and Elliott propelled forward a call for action. Hobbs responded in the fall of 1961 with an extensive writing project entitled "Baptist Beliefs" that became weekly features in the state papers and continued to run into 1963. Each week Hobbs took on a different doctrinal issue and gave a brief exposition of

---

107. Merrit, *SBC Annual*, 64.

108. Ibid., 65. White later amended the motion somewhat, and it was adopted. See page 68 of the *SBC Annual* for the amended version.

109. Hobbs, "Crisis and Conquest" in *Annual of the Southern Baptist Convention Nineteen Hundred and Sixty-Two*, 83.

that particular doctrine.[110] These matters also raised the question of how confessional statements should function in Baptist life, especially at the denominational level, and along with that, the place of soul competency in relation to doctrinal accountability. Chapter three focuses on other concerns the Committee faced and concludes with a brief summary of Hobbs's view of Baptist confessionalism and soul competency.

CONCLUSION

Examining the Apostasy Controversy and the Elliott Controversy reveals that the SBC in the early 1960s consisted of at least two distinct groups. One group stood solidly in the conservative tradition. Examples of pastors that opposed Elliott's work as heretical or dangerous include Newman Antonson, W. E. Cook, C. Murray Fuquay, Harold Warner, and K. Owen White. One seminary professor who opposed Elliott's work was Leslie Carlson of Southwestern. B. A. Copass of San Marcos Academy and Rufus Crozier of Hannibal-LaGrange College expressed deep concerns regarding Elliott's work.

More "progressive" voices also sought to influence the direction of the Convention. As noted above, the Sunday School Board solicited the work from Elliott with the intention of exposing the Southern Baptist reading public to the fruits of modern biblical scholarship. Students and seminary professors wrote to Elliott with letters of support, encouragement, and appreciation, though Francisco did note disagreement at certain points. Charles Trentham of Knoxville, Tennessee, occupied both the role of academic and pastor. He fully supported Elliott, as did professors from Furman and Ouachita.

When Moody voiced sympathies for the ecumenical movement and spoke in ways which appeared to challenge the doctrine of eternal security he set off an alarm in the Convention. When Elliott published a treatment of Genesis which challenged the traditional understanding of the book he set off more alarms concerning the doctrinal soundness of the seminaries of the SBC. Many Southern Baptists sensed a distinct division between the academics and the churches.

White's motion at the Convention voiced the desire of the messengers to check the excesses expressed by Moody and Elliott and demonstrated

---

110. The first of these articles appeared in the *B&R* on 5 October 1961.

the intent of the churches, through the Convention, to set boundaries for the exegetical and theological tasks of seminary professors.

As president of the Convention, Hobbs found himself faced with a monumental task. He had to find a way to preserve the organic unity of the Convention. He also had to satisfy the conservative base that sound doctrine would be taught in the schools and published by the Sunday School Board. Furthermore, he had to ensure members of the academy that they would enjoy intellectual and academic freedom. These competing demands led to the formation of the 1962 Committee on Baptist Faith and Message. These competing demands, as will be seen in chapter 7, also resulted in a doctrinal statement which allowed for wider latitude of interpretation among Southern Baptists.

3

Concerns Faced by the Committee

AFTER THE CONVENTION APPROVED the formation of the Committee on Baptist Faith and Message, concerned Southern Baptists wrote to Hobbs to express their particular concerns. Furthermore, the state papers since at least 1961, had chronicled a number of concerns which faced the Convention other than the doctrine of apostasy and the interpretation of Genesis. The civil rights movement claimed a great deal of attention in the South, as did concerns about President Kennedy and the Catholic Church, the growing materialism of the age, and communism. Other doctrinal concerns related primarily to the nature of the church and the ecumenical movement. The Elliott and Moody controversies also raised the question of the relationship between academic freedom and confessional standards for denominational institutions. The Committee had to do more than simply re-state for their generation the essence of Baptist beliefs. They had the task of charting a course that would preserve the unity of the denomination, determine what societal concerns to address and how, and balance the rights and responsibilities of denominational employees.

SOCIETAL CONCERNS

Southern Baptists had no claim to immunity from the societal trends that swept the nation in the late 1950s and early 1960s. Efforts by Martin Luther King Jr. to bring to reality true equality for African Americans had serious implications for the South. The election of a Roman Catholic as President of the United States also raised great fears for the largest Protestant denomination in the nation. Growing prosperity brought its own consequences to church life as people focused more on entertainment and material possessions in this life rather than eternity. During this time people feared communist and socialist sympathizers in the United States as well as nations such as the Soviet Union, the Peoples' Republic of China, and Cuba (the first communist state in the Western Hemisphere).

Racism

For Southern Baptists the question of desegregation did not concern only public schools and other public services.[1] The question came to include private, Baptist owned colleges as well as local congregations.[2] As will be demonstrated, reactions in Southern Baptist papers and churches covered the spectrum from maintaining the segregated status quo to calls for complete desegregation. That the SBC owed its birth, in part, to the controversy over slavery over one hundred years prior left its mark on both white and black Baptists in the South.[3]

Desegregation in Baptist Schools and Churches

The key concern at this point was not the issue of desegregation of the public schools, but how the arguments for and against desegregation played out in Baptist colleges and congregations. The actions of school administrators and trustees, student groups, local associations and

1. McIver, "The Cry for Freedom," *BS* (Dallas), 11 January 1961, 6. McIver quotes a missionary who told him, "Some of the most mission-minded Southern Baptists would be astonished to know the extent to which racial prejudice at home neutralizes the financial and spiritual support of foreign missions."

2. Kasten, "Baptist Education for Negroes," *BS* (Dallas), 1 February 1961, 2. Kasten's short paragraph appeared on the "Letters to the Editor" page. Kasten noted that Baptist schools should lead the way in providing "unsegregated" educational opportunities and asked whether Southern Baptist schools were open to students regardless of race. "Two Waco Groups Pass Motion on Integration," *BS* (Dallas), 15 February 1961, 16. Both the Executive Board of the Waco Association and the Pastors' Conference passed motions calling for racial desegregation in Baptist schools in Texas. BP, "Union Association Pastors' Group Suggests Racial Integration of Baptist Schools," *BS* (Dallas), 15 February 1961, 22. BP, "Warnings Prevalent on Segregation, Church State Relations at Convention," *BS* (Dallas), 31 May 1961, 7. Josephine Skaggs, a missionary to Nigeria, called on Southern Baptists to reevaluate their professed love for Africans when they, in reality, would not admit them into their own church services. She recounted an incident in which she was invited to speak at a church while on furlough, but when she requested permission to bring a Nigerian with her, she was told it would be best if she did not come.

3. Copeland, *The Southern Baptist Convention and the Judgment of History*, 4–5. Copeland overstates the role of slavery in the formation of the SBC, but his argument that the relationship of slavery to the beginnings of the SBC did influence the mentality of later generations with regard to the race issue is valid.

churches, as well as the opinions of editors at state papers reflected a variety of opinions on the question, though clearly the momentum favored desegregation.

In 1961 the Tennessee Baptist Convention instructed its Christian Services Committee to oversee the racial desegregation of the state's three hospitals. In an article from the 23 November issue of the B&R report on the progress of desegregation showed a marked move toward racial integration at all three hospitals. At the Nashville hospital African American nurses found employment as part of the hospital staff. The only hospital that had any potential for difficulty was located in Memphis, as its trustees came from Tennessee, Arkansas, and Mississippi, and yet here the move toward integration kept pace with the other two hospitals.[4]

In Union Association, Houston, Texas, a motion passed unanimously calling all Texas Baptist schools to admit intellectually qualified African-American applicants to their student bodies. At that time only Wayland Baptist, located in Plainview, Texas, admitted African-American students. The action came following a sermon at the Pastor's Conference by James A. Walker of Forest Oaks Baptist Church, in which Walker preached on the equality of all men before God.[5] By November of 1961 three Texas Baptist schools had opened their doors to receive African-American applicants. Corpus Christi College began receiving African-American students, and the trustees of Hardin-Simmons University voted to instruct administrators to begin accepting applications from African-Americans as well.[6]

Perhaps Mrs. A. C. Pratt, of Floydada, Texas, best expressed the conflicted feelings of many Southern Baptists in her letter to the editor of the *BS*, dated 1 February 1961. She wrote, "I find myself unable to endorse

---

4. Christian Services Committee, "Progress Reports on Desegregation," *B&R* (Nashville), 23 November 1961, 9.

5. BP, "Houston Baptists Act on Integration Issue," *AIB* (Birmingham) 23 January 1961, 14. See also "Waco Baptist Association Adopts Race Resolution," *AIB* (Birmingham), 9 March 1961, 16, where it was reported that the Waco Baptist Association also adopted a resolution calling for the desegregation of Texas Baptist schools (this was also reported in the *BS*, 15 February 1961, 16); and "Baptist College Opens Door to Negro Graduate Students," *AIB* (Birmingham), 18 May 1961, 5, where it was reported that Wake Forest College had opened its graduate school program to African-American students. It is curious that the *AIB* reports these trends but never writes about them on the editorial page. See also Don McGregor, "Fund Raising, Doctrinal Emphasis, Integration Demand Attention," *BS* (Dallas), 15 March 1961, 10–11.

6. "Hardin-Simmons May Admit Negroes," *BS* (Dallas), 22 November 1961, 13.

either integration or segregation." She then reflected on the problem of knowing people as individuals versus perceptions about persons as members of a group, the problem of a sense of "belonging" that would attend a child born into a racially mixed family, and the reality of the dignity of all persons as created in the image of God.[7]

Martin Luther King Jr. at Southern Seminary

Perhaps the most volatile event, racially, for the Convention, came about when the civil rights activist Martin Luther King Jr. preached in a chapel service at SBTS on 19 April 1961. King was invited, along with several others, to speak during the Gay Lectures, and at his chapel appearance the turnout was estimated at fourteen hundred students. The response from Alabama was swift and to the point. Dean Fleming, secretary of the Baptist Laymen of Alabama, Inc., issued an immediate call for Duke McCall's termination as seminary president if pro-integration teaching continued at Southern Seminary.[8]

Highland Avenue Baptist Church, Montgomery, Alabama, overwhelmingly approved a resolution from the deacons on 25 June 1961, instructing the executive secretary of the Alabama Baptist Convention not to allocate any part of the Cooperative Program dollars from Highland Church to Southern Seminary.[9] A sufficient number of churches in Alabama followed a similar course to motivate the seminary trustees and McCall to issue a carefully written apology for King's appearance at Southern. The apology stated in part, "The Executive Committee of the Board of Trustees, together with President Duke K. McCall, wishes to express regret for any offense caused by the visit of the Rev. Martin Luther King Jr., to the campus of the seminary."[10]

Hobbs and the Committee faced the question of race relations, and Hobbs advocated a "gradualist" position. In a letter to Robert L. Lee, Hobbs wrote, "We must not allow ourselves to be torn apart by radicals on either side of the theological issue. The same is true relative to the

---

7. Pratt, "Integration . . . Segregation," *BS* (Dallas), 1 February 1961, 3.

8. BP, "King's Seminary Talk Draws Alabama Critic," *B&R* (Nashville), 4 May 1961, 5.

9. Morgan et al., to the Members of Highland Avenue Baptist Church, 29 July 1962, BFM file, folder 2, SBHLA.

10. "Southern Baptist Seminary Trustees and President Duke McCall 'Regret' King Visit," *AlB* (Birmingham), 31 August 1961, 6. The article notes that "the resolution . . . will do much to relieve the resentment toward that seminary in many churches in Alabama."

other problems you mentioned, particularly that of race. In my judgment the 'gradualist' position is the proper one in race relationship."[11] Hobbs believed it would take time to educate rank and file Southern Baptists and bring them to an acceptance of racial integration. A first step in this direction came about in the Committee's work on the 1963 statement. What appears to be the first draft of the 1963 statement upholds racial equality, stating in Article V. Man, "As [created in the image of God] he possesses dignity and is worthy of respect and Christian love regardless of race or class." A later draft sent to Mercer University omits the reference to race or class.[12]

Catholicism

With the election of John F. Kennedy to the office of President of the United States, the nation took a new turn in its political and religious identity. Kennedy became the first Roman Catholic elected President in the history of the nation. Prior to his election professing Protestants of one denomination or another dominated the national political landscape. The presence of a Catholic president raised concerns over the relationship between church and state for Baptists.

President Kennedy and Southern Baptists

Writing in the *BS*, James commended President-elect Kennedy for his choice of men of active religious life for his cabinet. He noted, especially, that Kennedy chose only one Roman Catholic, his brother, Robert, as attorney general. The others were Presbyterian, Methodist, Episcopalian, Jewish, Mormon, or Unitarian.[13] Kennedy drew more favorable reporting from BP with his appearance before the Seventeenth Annual International Christian Leadership Conference in Washington, D. C. At this conference he appeared along with Billy Graham, and he upheld the principle of freedom of religion and the need for a strong faith in God in America's political leaders. He quoted frequently from the Bible, and along with

11. Hobbs, to Lee, 10 July 1962, BFM file, folder 2, SBHLA.

12. See Appendix 3. Evidence indicates that Wayne Ward suggested dropping the specific reference to race and class; see Appendix 1.

13. James, "President-Elect Nominates Churchmen for New Cabinet," *BS* (Dallas), 11 January 1961, 4.

vice-President Johnson emphasized the need for spiritual devotion in the turbulent times in which the country found itself.[14]

James Cole wrote in the *BM*, encouraging Louisiana Baptists to support President Kennedy and take him at his word when he pledged in his campaign to uphold the separation of church and state. In a state dominated by the Roman Catholic Church, Louisiana Baptists showed a special concern for issues related to the separation of church and state during the Kennedy administration, as will be seen below.[15]

Federal Aid for Parochial Schools

One area that particularly concerned Southern Baptists related to attempts to gain federal funding for parochial schools. With Kennedy in the White House, Roman Catholic leaders believed the time had come to push for federal aid for Catholic schools. Baptists in New Mexico, another state with a substantial Catholic population, feared that some form of federal aid would eventually pass congress and land on the President's desk. The question remained whether he would sign it. A BP article appeared in the *BNM* noting that in the opening days of the eighty-seventh congress, twenty-three education bills had been submitted, some of them proposing some form of federal aid for parochial schools. The reporter expressed a concern that President Kennedy might sign into law a bill allowing tax deductions for school expenses regardless of what school a student attended.[16]

The *BM* reported on 2 February 1961 that Francis Cardinal Spellman, archbishop of New York, and the primary advocate of federal funding for private schools, criticized the Kennedy administration for failing to provide financial assistance to private schools. He considered the move an unfair taxation on those who would not benefit directly from the public

---

14. Baptist Press, "Kennedy, Graham Pay Tribute to Liberty," *BS* (Dallas), 15 February 1961, 16.

15. Cole, "The New President," *BM* (Alexandria), 26 January 1961, 2.

16. BP, "Education is Prominent in Bills before Congress," *BNM* (Albuquerque), 19 January 1961, 16. Similar concerns were expressed in the *BM*. The greatest amount of press coverage on parochial school aid and Catholicism can be found in these two state papers. The 19 January 1961 issue of the *BM* carried a lengthy article on page 3 regarding the use of public school buses for transporting students to parochial schools in a case which appeared before the Supreme Court.

school system because their children attended private schools, and so he considered the action discriminatory in nature.[17]

On 9 February 1961, the *BM* reported that the *Washington Post* called for a rejection of the Catholic plan for federal funding for parochial schools,[18] and in another front page article alongside it appeared a BP article on Kennedy's state of the union address. In his address Kennedy soundly rejected the Catholic proposal that Cardinal Spellman recommended. Kennedy stood firm in his address for the separation of church and state.[19]

In response to the challenge of Catholicism and the cry for federal funding for parochial schools the Committee kept its focus on the essential Baptist principle of "a free church in a free state." In every draft of the 1963 document the article on Religious Liberty emphasized this fundamental aspect of Baptist life.

Materialism

In the post World War II era the United States experienced economic growth. Automobiles, labor-saving inventions, and entertainment vied for the people's attention. Convention leaders recognized a growing spirit of philosophical materialism in the prevailing naturalism of modern science and increasing godlessness in the form of practical materials—an increasing obsession with material possessions and entertainment.

Societal Affluence and Spiritual Decline

In January of 1961, President Eisenhower spoke at The National Conference of Catholic Charities. He, rather optimistically, said, "The 'tragedy' of a materialistic nation will never befall America as long as churches and synagogues 'and people who believe in God and in themselves continue to give of their spirit, their time, and their substance, that they may be

17. BP, "Carlson Scores Cardinal's Public Education Stand," *BM* (Alexandria), 2 February 1961, 1, 4.

18. BP, "Washington Paper Urges Church-State Separation: Cardinal's Statement on Aid Opposed," *BM* (Alexandria), 9 February 1961, 1.

19. BP, "JFK Rejects Catholic Bid For Support," *BM* (Alexandria), 9 February 1961. Despite Kennedy's repeated actions upholding the separation of church and state, Baptists during this period continued to demonstrate fears of the growing power of the Roman Catholic Church in America, as is evidenced from the ongoing press coverage of Catholic efforts during this period. See bibliography for listings of state paper articles.

secure and their fellow man may have faith, hope, and courage.'"[20] At the same time the *BS* published comments by a leading Lutheran on how to safeguard Christian colleges from secularism and materialism by ensuring denominational ownership, securing only professing Christians as faculty, and providing adequate funding for the schools.[21]

Southern Baptist Convention vice-presidents Roland Q. Leavell and W. Herschel Ford wrote for the *BS* on the pressing issues facing the Convention in the coming year. Leveall said, "The fundamental problems of Baptists are spiritual: selfishness, materialism, worldliness, sensuality, prayerlessness, laxness in worship and service."[22] His main concern focused on how distracting such things can be from the main task of evangelism. He feared theological minimalism in the interest of ecumenicity. He also noted that extreme want and extreme prosperity tend to have a negative impact on evangelism.[23]

Writing a devotional column in the *CI*, Mrs. L. G. Hardman Jr. noted the danger of every day responsibilities crowding out spiritual devotion, which caused the soul to "dwindle" through neglect. She warned, "Our days fill with legitimate things and God is crowded out unintentionally. Our soul perishes through neglect." Hardman addressed the more subtle aspect of practical materialism—the pace of life and the danger of letting expediency determine priorities.[24] The Scriptures themselves warn of the dangerous effects of affluence on spiritual health (Deut 32:15).

In response to the rising tide of practical materialism and affluence, the Committee chose to leave Article XIII. Stewardship, virtually unchanged. In this article the BFM lays great stress on the proper perspective toward worldly possessions as things held in sacred trust and used for the glory of God.[25]

---

20. "In the World of Religion," *AIB* (Birmingham), 5 January 1961, 7.

21. "Safeguards Against Secularization," *BS* (Dallas), 22 February 1961, 5.

22. Leavell and Ford, "Report from the Vice-Presidents: Principle Problems Facing Southern Baptists in the Coming Year," *BS* (Dallas), 12 July 1961, 11.

23. Ibid.

24. Hardman, "Devotional: Busy People, Dying Religion," *CI* (Atlanta), 4 May 1961, 2.

25. See Appendix 3. The only change involved the use of the third person plural pronoun in several places and its corresponding verb tense.

Communism

In the aftermath of World War II the nations of Western Europe and the United States found themselves involved in a new kind of warfare–the cold war. Communism in Russia and mainland China posed serious threats to the stability of Western democracy. Communism managed to get a foothold in the New World when Fidel Castro came to power in Cuba, just ninety miles off the cost of Florida. Like their fellow citizens, Southern Baptists were not immune to the fear of communism.

From Amarillo, Texas, Mrs. W. A. Breining wrote to Hobbs expressing concerns about Fabian Socialism[26] getting a "toehold" in the Convention. She pointed to materials in New Frontier's literature that spoke of co-existing with communists in Southeast Asia, and argued that this would jeopardize mission work in that region. She complained that the May 1962 Adult Teacher Manual played down patriotism and cited a specific passage from pages 26 and 27.[27]

In January of 1961 Joe T. Poe, missionary to Chile, wrote an article for the *BS* entitled "What Alternative to Communism." In the article Poe noted that some nations seemed unable to escape Catholicism without going into communism, while others escaped communism by embracing Catholicism. He noted that because evangelical Christians took a stand against materialism and naturalism, that did not make them guilty of compromise with the Catholic Church. On the other hand, because evangelicals rejected medieval dogmas and other facets of Catholicism, it did not make them sympathetic toward communism. Evangelical Christianity offered a way out of the polar extremes of both.[28]

In the 25 January issue of the *BS*, Charlotte E. Wright wrote in from Midland, Texas, asking that the *BS* spend the next four years highlighting and exposing the threat of international communism.[29] Mrs. J. L. Guffey, of

26. *Webster's Third New International Dictionary of the English Language*, vol. I, (1961), s.v., "fabian." Fabian Socialism: "being or belonging or relating to a society of socialists organized in England in 1884 to spread socialistic principles gradually."

27. Breining, to Hobbs, 23 May 196[2], BFM file, folder 1, SBHLA. Breining displays the very real fear of her time. She anticipates a "double meaning" to what is written. The paragraph she cites draws a distinction between God's kingdom purposes and the American way of life, which the writer of the article condemns as "secular, materialistic, pleasure-bent and unwilling to except [sic] the gospel demands for brotherhood."

28. Poe, "What Alternative to Communism?" *BS* (Dallas), 4 January 1961, 7.

29. Wright, "Letters to the Editor: Communism in America," *BS* (Dallas), 25 January 1961, 2.

Abilene, Texas, wrote in to express her dissatisfaction with the *Standards'* handling of questions about communism in its 8 March issue.[30] In the 29 March issue James took on directly the challenge that Baptist editors had not dealt sufficiently with the communist threat. All Baptist editors opposed communism. James agreed that, globally, communism could be the greatest threat facing the world. He also noted attempts by the Roman Catholic Church to extend its power in the United States through parochial school funds from the United States Treasury and its dominance of the chaplaincy program in the United States military. Baptist editors, he said, would not be drawn into the McCarthy-like panic that swept the nation in the 1950s. "When we see evidence of communist activity we will warn against it without failure, but we refuse to label every effort at human betterment with the badge of communist sympathies," he said.[31]

Richard Owen, writing in the *B&R*, outlined how Christians in America, by spiritual neglect, fear and hate, could hand the world over to the communists in Krushchev's lifetime. He concluded the article by pointing out that communism never won out in a free election and that its failure can be demonstrated by the way in which its leaders continually mask the true state of their nations with propaganda. He predicted that communism would fail in the end.[32]

Ongoing concerns about the threat of communism prompted the *B&R* to run a series entitled "Searchlight on Communism," by Paul Geren.[33] Geren proposed to examine communism as a doctor would examine a malignant tumor. He noted its extensive reach over various nations and its open hostility to any theistic world view.

In addressing the concern over communism and socialism, the Committee modified only slightly Article XV. The Christian and the Social Order. In this article the Committee addressed the responsibility of Christians to use their resources for the relief of the poor and needy, and "to work with all men of good will in any good cause, . . . without compromising their loyalty to Christ and his truth." To protect against the

---

30. Guffey, "Letters to the Editor: Communist Threat," *BS* (Dallas), 8 March 1961, 2.

31. James, "Baptist Editors and the Communist Threat," *BS* (Dallas), 29 March 1961, 4.

32. Owen, "Handing the World Over to Communism," *B&R* (Nashville), 1 June 1961, 4.

33. The first of this series appeared in the 22 June 1961 issue of the *B&R* on page 2. It was subtitled, "Cancer of Communism Requires Closer Study." This series, a total of four articles, ran in other state papers as well and was produced by the Christian Life Commission of the Southern Baptist Convention.

accusation of promoting only a "social gospel" the Committee inserted, at Ward's suggestion, the statement, "Means and methods used for the improvement of society and the establishment of righteousness among men can be truly and permanently helpful only when they are rooted in the regeneration of the individual by the saving grace of God in Jesus Christ."[34]

DOCTRINAL CONCERNS

Southern Baptists expressed concerns about doctrinal trends in both letters to the members of the Committee on Baptist Faith and Message and articles in the state Baptist papers. These concerns focused on the doctrine of Scripture, security of the believer, and the nature of the church in light of the growing ecumenical movement sweeping through the nation.[35]

Doctrine of Scripture

Throughout their history Baptists have exhibited a marked devotion to the Bible as the basis for faith and practice. Consequently, one's views about the Bible carry great weight, and can easily become a cause for great concern. The rise of liberalism in American religious institutions created alarm as early as the Toy Controversy at Southern Seminary in the 1870s.[36] With the publication of Elliott's *The Message of Genesis* the controversy over the nature of Scripture and the inspiration of the Bible erupted again.

Southern Baptists voiced concerns in letters to the Committee and in the state papers regarding what seminary professors and denominational workers believed about the truthfulness of the Bible. In short, did these people truly believe in the inerrancy of the Bible, and would Hobbs and the various trustees of the Convention hold denominational employees to that standard?

A resolution passed by the Indian Creek Association meeting in Savannah, Tennessee, on 14 September 1962, commended the Sunday

---

34. "The Baptist Faith and Message, Article XV. The Christian and the Social Order," in *Baptist Confessions of Faith*, rev. ed., ed. W. L. Lumpkin, 399. See also Appendix 1.

35. For a detailed treatment of the place of Elliott and Moody in these controversies, see chap. 2.

36. See Bush and Nettles, *Baptists and the Bible*, 208–20.

School Board for not reprinting Elliott's book. The resolution also urged that the BFM 1925 not be changed but "that it be left as is."[37]

Marjorie Dockery wrote to Hobbs to complain on the one hand about the dangers of Elliott's book, and on the other about the dangers of supplanting the authority of the Bible with a man-made "declaration of faith." In her assessment both avenues represented a turning away from God's wisdom given in his word to the wisdom of men.[38]

Hobbs wrote back to Dockery and gently instructed her in the time-honored Baptist practice of writing confessional statements. He assured her that the work of revising the BFM 1925 would not entail a change in the faith of Southern Baptists, nor would the Bible be supplanted as the sole authority for faith and practice.[39]

In response to a letter received from C. L. Snyder, Hobbs in June of 1963 affirmed the inerrancy of the Bible in Hebrew and Greek. He went on to say, "I do not believe that there are errors in the English versions if we properly understand them." Hobbs explained the problem of a lack of understanding about parts of the Bible and affirmed that when all the facts were known the Bible would be substantiated as accurate.[40]

Hobbs wrote in July of 1962 to Robert L. Lee about the Convention that met in June. He noted that "The grass roots people needed to know that the Convention voted unanimously the reaffirmation of our faith in the Bible as the Word of God. Others needed to know that the Convention expects its agencies to operate within that framework."[41]

In an attempt to help Kentucky Baptists understand the issues surrounding the scientific approach to biblical studies Ray Summers wrote a piece entitled "Historico-Critical Interpretation" which appeared in the *WR*. In this article Summers argued that the goal of interpretation "is the meaning of that printed page to the writer, the original reader, to us in

---

37. Lewter et al., "Resolutions Concerning the Current Theological Problem Southern Baptists Face in These Days," Savannah, Tennessee, 14 September 1962, BFM file, folder 3, SBHLA.

38. Dockery to Hobbs, n.d., BFM file, folder 3, SBHLA.

39. Hobbs to Dockery, 13 September 1962, BFM file, folder 3, SBHLA.

40. Hobbs to Snyder, 10 June 1963, BFM file, folder 8, SBHLA. See also Hobbs comment to W. E. Peeples, "I do not believe there is a single error in the Bible." Hobbs to Peeples, 5 July 1962, BFM file, folder 1, SBHLA.

41. Hobbs to Lee, 10 July 1962, BFM file, folder 2, SBHLA. See also Hobbs to Breining, 9 July 1962, BFM file, folder 1, SBHLA.

our day and need. 'What is this writer saying to me through these words?' This is the quest of interpretation." According to Summers this approach allows the Scriptures to determine doctrine rather than doctrine setting the basis for interpreting Scripture.[42]

Thomas Austin wrote to K. Owen White in the aftermath of the 1962 Convention to contest his resolution on the Bible. He argued that Baptists had never voiced an affirmation of the Bible in such sweeping terms as White proposed. Austin posed his question:

> I publicly challenge you to go to the annuals of the Southern Baptist Convention and produce evidence that it has previously and officially affirmed "faith in the entire Bible as the authoritative, authentic, infallible word of God."[43]

Austin pointed to the wording of the 1925 BFM, noting that the Bible was not called the "word of God" in the Preamble. He further noted the 1946 Convention report on Baptist Principles which stated that "the one and only authority in faith and practice is the New Testament as the divinely inspired record and interpretation of the supreme revelation of God through Jesus Christ."[44]

After addressing White in a most insulting and condescending manner, Austin bemoaned, "Your resolution would apparently have us believe that the entire Bible is the authoritative, authentic, and infallible revelation itself."[45] Austin focused his basis for his response solely on the recorded actions of the Convention over its history vis-á-vis the Bible. He did not take into account the accepted way in which confessions of faith used the Bible. Neither did he consider how leading voices in the Convention throughout its history—voices such as B. H. Carroll, Basil Manly Jr., and John A. Broadus among others—(whose writing had been broadly received by Southern Baptists as reflective of their own views) wrote in defense of the Bible as God's word.[46]

---

42. Summers, "Historico-Critical Interpretation," WR (Louisville), 23 March 1963, 3.

43. Austin to White, 9 June 1962, BFM file, folder 1, SBHLA.

44. Ibid., See also, *Annual of the Southern Baptist Convention, Nineteen Hundred and Forty-Six*, 38. More will be said about this "Statement of Principles" in chap. 5.

45. Ibid.

46. For a full treatment of how previous generations of Baptists viewed the Bible see Bush and Nettles, *Baptists and the Bible*.

William E. Hull, on sabbatical in Europe, received a copy of an early draft of the revised BFM. He noted his overall appreciation for the document, not only for what it said, but for what it did not say: "There is equal appreciation for what is *not* said, such as sweeping statements on the infallible character of those aspects of the Bible that have nothing to do with its divine truth, or an effort to tie us to some particular scientific theory of creation."[47] Hull fell into the category of those who sought to differentiate between the kernel of truth the Bible seeks to communicate and the husk in which it is encapsulated.

These correspondences reflect a dichotomy of thinking among Southern Baptists. On the one hand rank and file Southern Baptists reflected conservative thinking in regard to the nature, authority, and inspiration of the Bible. On the other hand many "educated" Southern Baptists reflected a more progressive approach to the Bible informed by the scientific approach to interpretation. A sampling of the state papers further reinforces the position that rank and file Southern Baptists held deeply the conservative view of the Bible and feared anything they perceived as "liberal," while leading Southern Baptist educators put forth what might be considered more sophisticated positions.

Robert Torbet wrote an article in the *AkB* in which he dealt with the issue of the Bible's authority in the life of the Christian. Torbet argued, in essence, that the true, primary authority in the life of the believer is Jesus Christ, and that the Bible, confessions, interpretations, and personal conscience are, to a greater or lesser extent, secondary. "He alone is the final norm for truth. In this sense our ultimate authority is not a book, nor an institution, nor a creed, but a living Person, the incarnate Son of God."[48] Torbet's position clearly made the Bible something less than the authoritative word of God.

Hobbs, in the aftermath of the Elliott Controversy, wrote a series of articles entitled "Baptist Beliefs." In the article on "Inspiration" he avowed that the Bible is the Spirit-inspired word of God. The two main views of inspiration he dealt with were the verbal and dynamic views. Of each he stated, "Both positions hold to the inerrancy of Scripture." He further noted that while disagreement as to the manner of inspiration existed,

---

47. Hull, to Hobbs, n.d., BFM file, folder 6, SBHLA.

48. Torbet, "Baptists and Biblical Authority," *AkB* (Little Rock), 24 May 1962, 14.

"Upon the 'result' there is general agreement that the Bible is the inspired Word of God."[49]

Macon, writing in the *AlB*, decried any tendency to lessen the authority of the Bible as the written word of God. "All religions require an authority which is outside of the self. If we so teach the Bible and interpret it in a manner which casts any reflections upon its being the revealed word of God, then people begin to live by their opinions and not by 'thus saith the Lord.'"[50]

Many Southern Baptists feared liberal and neo-orthodox views of the Bible specifically. In fact, rank and file Southern Baptists may not have made a distinction between the two, though one would hope that pastors with a seminary education could tell the difference. Pastor Woodrow Robbins of Lexington Avenue Baptist Church, High Point, North Carolina, wrote to Hobbs to express his concerns about modernism taking hold in the Convention: "The Modernists have a two-fold attack. One, to take over the schools. Second, to put men in the key places in the leadership of the convention." He cited an article which appeared in *The Christian Century* by S. S. Hill Jr. as his source.[51]

Pastor Millard Box of Longpoint Baptist Church, Houston, Texas, wrote to Hobbs expressing his sense that a complete house cleaning might be in order for the Convention schools and agencies (he names the Sunday School Board specifically). He spoke of many pastors whom he knew who felt that liberalism and neo-orthodoxy thrived east of the Mississippi more than in the western states.[52] Charles Skutt, writing on behalf of his entire congregation, stated

> that this church does, by unanimous vote, deplore the present trend toward liberalism in our Convention supported Seminaries and that, moreover, this church rejects the possibility of liberalising [*sic*] of the traditional Baptist position on the divine inspiration of the scriptures as a result of any study by this Committee.[53]

49. Hobbs, "Baptist Beliefs: Inspiration," *AkB* (Little Rock), 16 August 1962, 7.

50. Macon, "Religion Requires an Authority," *AlB* (Birmingham), 15 February 1962, 3.

51. Robbins to Hobbs, 23 January 1963, BFM file, folder 6, SBHLA.

52. Box to Hobbs, 13 June 1962, BFM file, folder 1, SBHLA.

53. Skutt on behalf of LaBelle Place Baptist Church to the Committee on Baptist Faith and Message, 27 July 1962, BFM file, folder 1, SBHLA.

Hobbs, in responding to the "Resolutions Concerning the Current Theological Problem Southern Baptists Face in These Days"[54] stated, "Let me assure you that should any changes be made in the 1925 Statement they will not be toward liberalism."[55] A few months earlier Hobbs wrote to Boyd Hunt at Southwestern and stated that he did "not know of a single 'liberal' seminary professor," and also commented that the Convention had cast itself in a conservative mode at the 1962 meeting. The problem, as Hobbs saw it, lay in steering a middle course between liberalism and fundamentalism.[56]

Security of the Believer

Not only Dale Moody,[57] but more openly, Robert Shank advocated the view that true believers could fall away and lose their salvation.[58] His book, *Life in the Son*, contained three hundred twenty-nine pages of text plus five appendices. A well indexed work, it set forth a scholarly, biblical study of the doctrine of apostasy from an Arminian perspective.

Shank's book brought forth a clear response from James Hodges, pastor of Southside Baptist Church of Taladega, Alabama. Hodges critiqued Shank's work on four key grounds. First of all, Shank denied that any true comparison could be made of the new birth to natural birth because of the metaphysical nature of the new birth. Secondly, Shank denied the impartation of the divine nature in any sense that left the redeemed sinner with a struggle between an "old nature" and a "new nature." Thirdly,

54. See n. 35.

55. Hobbs to Lewter, 5 October 1962, BFM file, folder 3, SBHLA.

56. Hobbs to Hunt, 3 July 1962, BFM file, folder 1, SBHLA. Numerous letters to and from Hobbs and/or the Committee reflect on the one hand the concerns of Southern Baptists that liberalism is taking hold in the Convention, and on the other hand Hobbs insistence that it has not and/or will not happen on his watch. For a full treatment of how the Committee addressed this concern see chap. 7.

57. For a discussion of Moody and the Apostasy Controversy, see chap. 2. For a full treatment of how the Committee addressed this concern, see chap. 7.

58. Shank, *Life in the Son: A Study in the Doctrine of Perseverance*; see especially chapter 4, "Can Eternal Life be Forfeited?" Commenting on Luke 8:12–13, Shank writes: "The use of the word [*pisteuousin*] in verse 12 establishes its meaning as it is employed in the parable. It is clearly believing unto salvation: . . . No warrant is present for assigning a different meaning to the word as it appears in verse 13. . . . Those who 'for a while believe' are depicted by Jesus as making a sincere beginning in the life of faith." Their subsequent fall does not obviate the fact that their believing, while it continued, was actual saving faith" (32–33).

Hodges accused Shank of holding and advancing Arminian views of salvation. Lastly, Hodges noted that Shank failed to do justice to the concept that true believers had no desire to depart from Christ.[59]

Ecclesiology

Since the rise of the Landmark movement in the mid-nineteenth century Southern Baptists routinely faced questions related to ecclesiology. Does the Bible speak only of local congregations, or is there a sense in which it speaks of a universal church? Should communion be restricted, and if so, to whom? Should believers immersed in other fellowships be received into the membership of Baptist churches without requiring their being immersed again? Under the headings of the ecumenical movement, the ordinances and church membership some of these questions came to resurface in Southern Baptist life in the early 1960s.

In January of 1961 James Singleton sounded the alarm against the ecumenical movement in an article in the *B&R*. He cited three reasons proponents of the ecumenical movement advanced for their position: (1) the world situation demands that Protestants speak with a unified voice in the face of communism, atheism, and dialectical materialism; (2) the unity and numerical strength of the Roman Church demands the response of a united Protestantism; and (3) the prayer of Jesus in John 17:22 lays upon his disciples the imperative to seek unity. Singleton pointed out, however, that some in the then Federal Council of Churches viewed the ecumenical movement as a means for healing the breach between Protestants, Catholics, and Greek Orthodox Christians. The result would be a restored single Catholic Church. He then pointed out that Southern Baptists voted in 1950 to reject any "artificial union" of churches.[60]

Singleton set aside for the sake of argument key Baptist distinctives and offered four reasons for rejecting the ecumenical movement. First, he noted that the mainline denominations had become infested with liberalism, resulting in a message that was less than true to the gospel of Christ. Secondly, he noted that many of the churches involved in the ecumenical movement received state support in other countries, and this clearly violated the Baptist concept of separation of church and state. Thirdly, he noted that this would create a "super church" that would, in turn, con-

---

59. Hodges, "Hodges Answers Dr. Shank," *AlB* (Birmingham), 2 March 1961, 7.

60. Singleton, "Church Unity: Good or Bad?" *B&R* (Nashville), 5 January 1961, 5.

trol the outlet for the gospel. Fourthly, some leaders of the movement envisioned an eventual reunion with Rome which would necessitate the compromise of Protestant beliefs.[61]

Richard Owen weighed in on the issue in March 1961 in an editorial. In this article he captured something of the tension that existed at the time. He noted that Southern Baptists received harsh criticism for their unwillingness to join the National Council of Churches. Yet he maintained, in the spirit of Christian charity, "that there is a spiritual fellowship among all true followers of the Lord Jesus Christ." This spiritual unity he prized highly, but he warned against the dangers to individual and congregational liberty that organizational unity would ultimately bring.[62]

Nonetheless, some Southern Baptists showed signs of uneasiness with the prevailing Landmarkist tendency of Baptist ecclesiology. Article 12 of the BFM 1925 spoke of the church only in the sense of a local congregation. It contained no reference to the larger Christian community as in any sense a "universal" church. While this wording suited the Landmarkist faction, others desired to see Southern Baptists embrace a broader vision of the nature of the church.

Winn T. Barr, a Kentucky pastor, wrote to Kruschwitz, Kentucky's representative on the Committee on Baptist Faith and Message about this issue. Barr saw Southern Baptists divided into two camps: (1) ecumenical Southern Baptists, and (2) Landmark Southern Baptists. "The ecumenical Baptist, believing in the universal church as a present reality, ignores the valid use of generic language." He believed this could only lead to "unionism" and compromise. "But the landmark Baptist, believing that only Baptists have churches, ignores Christ's own broad definition of what a church is." This could only result in isolation from the larger Christian community. Barr sought a statement on the church which avoided both pitfalls.[63]

Later Barr wrote again to Kruschwitz and sent him a document entitled "Universal Churchhood," which he had written.[64] Kruschwitz

---

61. Ibid., 13.

62. Owen, "Church Mergers," *B&R* (Nashville), 16 February 1961, 4. Numerous articles from the early 1960s reflect a desire on the part of some that a reunification of some kind be effected between Southern and American Baptists during the planned Jubilee Celebration jointly undertaken by both bodies.

63. Barr to Kruschwitz, 13 December 1962, BFM file, folder 5, SBHLA.

64. Barr to Kruschwitz, 28 December 1962, BFM file, folder 5, SBHLA.

forwarded this document on to Hobbs.[65] In this article Barr drew from lectures by W. O. Carver, building on the concept of the indwelling of Christ in the believer. Carver asked the question, "How can the one body as presented in the transcendent concepts of Ephesians 4 be restricted at any point to a local church?" Barr answered that Christ indwells all who assemble in his name.[66] From this Barr concluded "that there are different types of churches with varying degrees of permanence."[67] In response to the question, "Why be a Baptist?" Barr pointed to the Great Commission as the "obligation of maximum obedience" and argued that Baptist churches "are simply churches that have come very close to the Apostolic model." Barr concluded then, that any gathering of believers in the name of Christ was, broadly speaking, a church, yet the best model of a church was that which most closely approximated the apostolic model. In the final analysis Barr stated: "Maybe He (Jesus) was teaching *universal churchhood, the churchhood of each Christian assembly.*"[68]

Confessionalism and Accountability

In the wake of the Elliott and Moody controversies the question of confessional accountability and Christian liberty of thought rose to the surface. Many conservative voices rose up and called for the strict enforcement of confessional standards in Southern Baptist schools. Some saw confessional statements as an ineffective way of holding faculty accountable while others saw them as counter-productive.[69] Others, on the basis of liberty of conscience and the principle of academic freedom decried such actions as "creedalism."

McDonald, in an editorial entitled "The Seminary Controversy," wrote generally in favor of holding seminary professors accountable to a doctrinal summary. He complained, however, that some in the Convention

65. Kruschwitz, to Hobbs, 8 January 1963, BFM file, folder 5, SBHLA.

66. Barr, "Universal Churchhood," unpublished article, BFM file, folder 5, SBHLA.

67. Ibid.

68. Ibid., emphasis his. For an extended discussion of the Committee's response to this issue see chap. 7.

69. Hubbard to The Committee on Baptist Faith and Message, 24 July 1962, BFM file, folder 3, SBHLA. Hubbard wrote: "That fact is a liberal will sign the Transcript with his tomgue [sic] in his mouth and go right on teaching his liberal doctrines." He also called the "Transcript of Principles" "nothing more than a wall of defense for liberal teachers to hide behind."

sought to bypass the proper channels of accountability. McDonald argued that the seminary trustees have the responsibility to determine whether or not a professor had deviated from an acceptable interpretation of the doctrinal standards of the Convention or the school in question. Once the trustees ruled on a matter their ruling should be accepted and the Convention should move forward. He also warned and complained of anticipated attempts to stack the trustee boards with members of a particular theological persuasion as an act beneath the dignity of Southern Baptists.[70]

C. DeWitt Matthews, who taught preaching at Midwestern, wrote an article which appeared in the *AkB* advocating that Baptists not move into a rigid application of a confession and stifle personal interpretation. "Baptists," he said, "have fled from creeds. Some have died rather than submit to them. For them the Bible was creed enough." He then called for Baptists to resist the urge to turn a confession into a binding creed "that all other Baptists must believe or be called 'heretic, rebel, a thing to flout.'"[71]

A key concern at this point is how Hobbs viewed confessions of faith in Baptist life. Dockery comments on Hobbs's view of confessions as follows:

> he nevertheless was hesitant to acknowledge the place of doctrinal confessions as normative for the Christian community. His emphasis on individualism and the comptency of the soul in each believer moved him to a false dichotomy between a "living faith" and a "confessional or creedal faith." In the preamble to the 1963 Baptist Faith and Message, Hobbs claimed that the confession has "no authority over the conscience."[72]

Hobbs wrote in 1978 that the 1925 BFM anchored Southern Baptists to a position of progressive conservatism while leaving them free from the constraints of a creed.[73]

---

70. McDonald, "The Seminary Controversy," *AkB* (Little Rock), 1 March 1962, 4. In this editorial McDonald even allows that the term "creed" might legitimately be used to describe the function of the "Abstract of Principles" or the *Baptist Faith and Message*, 1925.

71. Matthews, "No Creed but the Bible," *AkB* (Little Rock), 2 August 1962, 16.

72. Dockery, "Herschel H. Hobbs," in *Theologians of the Baptist Tradition*, 221.

73. Hobbs, "The Baptist Faith and Message–Anchored but Free" *BHH* (13 July 1978): 34. See also Hobbs, "Southern Baptists and Confessionalism: a comparison of the origins and contents of the 1925 and 1963 confessions" *R&E* 76 (Winter 1979): 55–68.

In the Preamble to the 1963 BFM Hobbs and the Committee sought to protect the right of private interpretation on the basis of soul competency,[74] yet in Article XII. Education, the Committee spelled out the confessional boundaries of those serving the denomination in educational institutions:

> In Christian education there should be a proper balance between academic freedom and academic responsibility. Freedom in any orderly relationship of human life is always limited and never absolute. The freedom of a teacher in a Christian school, college, or seminary is limited by the pre-eminence of Jesus Christ, by the authoritative nature of the Scriptures, and by the distinct purpose for which the school exists.[75]

Southern Baptists in the early 1960s held differing views on the role of confessions of faith in Baptist life. This factor required the attention of the Committee as they worked to revise the 1925 statement. The next two chapters will address how Hobbs and the Committee understood the historic role of Baptist confessions in relation to personal responsibility in biblical interpretation. This investigation necessitates a look at how the use of Baptist confessions relates to the principles of soul liberty and soul competency. Chapter 4 will concern itself with confessionalism and soul liberty. Chapter 5 will address confessionalism and soul competency.[76]

---

74. Hobbs, *My Faith and Message: An Autobiography*, 241–42.

75. "Baptist Faith and Message, Article XII," in Lumpkin, *Baptist Confessions of Faith*, 398.

76. For a fuller discussion of the philosophical differences between soul liberty and soul competency, see Norman, *More Than Just a Name*.

4

Confessional Accountability and Soul Liberty

INTRODUCTION

QUESTIONS OF AUTHORITY AND the bases for unity and church fellowship re-emerge in the SBC whenever a need arises for confessional expression or revision. A case in point is the recent debate over the adoption of the BFM 2000. With this action by the Convention the debate over the place of confessions moved again to center stage in the life of the denomination. Indeed, what role the BFM should play in the life of the SBC raised concerns in 1925 which prompted that committee to attach an explanatory preface to the document explaining how it might serve the denomination.[1]

In 1962 the Committee wrestled with the need to protect the right of private interpretation while at the same time it sought to ensure some form of Baptist confessionalism. In the end the Committee lifted the essential matter from the 1925 Preamble and used it as the foundation for the Preamble to the revised BFM. In so doing it preserved continuity with the previous version and demonstrated an acceptance of Mullins's interpretation of the role of Baptist confessions of faith, apparently without questioning that interpretation or looking further back into Baptist history to see how confessions functioned prior to 1900.

Writers spilt a great deal of ink after 1963 in an effort to define and understand the proper role of confessions of faith in Baptist life. Almost the entire Winter 1979 issue of the *R&E* contained articles dealing with

---

1. *Annual of the Southern Baptist Convention Nineteen Hundred Twenty-Five*, 71. This explanation is repeated in BFM 1963, 4, and BFM 2000, 4–5.

Baptist confessionalism. Glenn Hinson wrote on the subject of creeds and confessions as generally used in Christianity.[2] W. L. Lumpkin wrote on "The Nature and Authority of Baptist Confessions of Faith."[3] Bill Leonard wrote on the types of confessions found among Baptists in America.[4] Leo Garrett wrote on the nature of biblical authority in Baptist confessions.[5] Hobbs contributed an important article comparing the 1925 and the 1963 BFM.[6] Walter Shurden examined how Southern Baptists responded to the 1925 and 1963 versions of the BFM.[7] John Hurt, in his article, took the position that Southern Baptists should have no creeds or confessions, while Joe Odle took the opposite position and supported the role of confessions in Southern Baptist life.[8]

Between the early 1970s and the mid 1980s several articles dealing with Baptist confessionalism appeared in *BHH*. Davis Woolley wrote a short editorial in 1970 entitled "Baptist Aversion for all Creeds" to complement James Carter's "Southern Baptists' First Confession of Faith," which appeared in the same issue.[9] In 1978 Hobbs contributed an article on the BFM which argued that Southern Baptists could have a confession without its becoming a binding creed.[10] Garrett contributed an article on Baptists and sources of authority.[11] In 1984 several articles appeared re-

2. Hinson, "Creeds and Confessions in the Christian Tradition," *R&E* (Winter 1979): 5–16.

3. Lumpkin, "The Nature and Authority of Baptist Confessions of Faith," *R&E* (Winter 1979): 17–28.

4. Leonard, "Types of Confessional Documents among Baptists in America," *R&E* (Winter 1979): 29–42.

5. Garrett, "The Concept of Biblical Authority in Historic Baptist Confessions of Faith," *R&E* (Winter 1979): 43–54.

6. Hobbs, "Southern Baptists and Confessionalism: A Comparison of the Origins and Contents of the 1925 and 1963 Confessions," *R&E* (Winter 1979): 55–68.

7. Shurden, "Southern Baptists Responses to the 1925 and 1963 Confessions," *R&E* (Winter 1979): 69–84.

8. Hurt, "Should Southern Baptists Have a Creed/Confession?—No!" *R&E* (Winter 1979): 85–88. Odle, "Should Southern Baptists Have a Creed/Confession?—Yes!" *R&E* (Winter 1979): 89–94.

9. Woolley, "Baptist Aversion for all Creeds," *Baptist History and Heritage* (January 1970): 1–2. Carter, "Southern Baptists First Confession of Faith," *BHH* (January 1970): 24–28, 38. Both of these articles display a decided aversion for confessions and creeds.

10. Hobbs, "The Baptist Faith and Message—Anchored but Free," *BHH* (July 1978): 33–40.

11. Garrett, "Sources of Authority in Baptist Thought," *BHH* (July 1978): 41–49.

lated to the authority of the Bible in the July issue of *BHH*. An article by Lumpkin dealt specifically with the role of the Bible in early confessions of faith.[12]

In the context of the revision of the BFM in 1962–63 and the role of confessions in establishing denominational unity, it seemed useful to explore the role of confessions and covenants as bases for unity among Baptists in England and the United States from the seventeenth through the nineteenth centuries.[13] Pool argued that the Preamble to the 1963 BFM "constitutes the chief article among doctrinal articles of this confessional statement."[14] His argument rests on the contention that the SBC, in approving this Preamble set forth the legitimate uses of confessions for Southern Baptists in a manner consistent with Mullins's concept of soul competency.[15] This chapter explores the use of confessions in Baptist life prior to Mullins and examine whether the limits set forth in the Preamble are consistent with prior Baptist practice.

For the purposes of this chapter it seemed best to focus on the primary source data from early English and American Baptist churches and associations. This chapter demonstrates that early Baptists had three bases for unity: (1) a commonly shared view of Scripture, (2) churches (at least to some extent) gathered on the basis of a covenant, and (3) associations united around confessions. Within the context of the discussion of confessions and covenants the relationship between these instruments of accountability and soul liberty will also be noted.

CONFESSIONAL ACCOUNTABILITY AND SOUL LIBERTY AMONG EARLY ENGLISH BAPTISTS

Soul liberty among believers assumes access to the Bible and the right to read and interpret the Scriptures. This was no less true for early English Baptists than for Baptists today. The first question to answer is, "How did

12. Lumpkin, "The Bible in Early Baptist Confessions of Faith," *BHH* (July 1984): 33–41.

13. Since Baptists in the United States are descended from English Baptists who settled in America, and many practices and traditions have come down from English Baptists a certain level of commonality of practice is expected between the two groups.

14. Pool, "Chief Article of Faith: The Preamble of *The Baptist Faith and Message* (1963)," in *Sacred Mandates of Conscience: Interpretations of* The Baptist Faith and Message, ed. Jeff B. Pool, 37.

15. Ibid., 37–38.

Scripture and its interpretation fit into the developing pattern of confessionalism and soul liberty?"

Scripture and Soul Liberty Among English Baptists

Several approaches for evaluating English Baptists' views on Scripture present themselves. A person may examine the confessional material to see what they said about the Bible in those documents.[16] One may look at the location of the article on Scripture within the confessional document.[17] Another approach notes how Scripture references are used to support doctrinal claims in the various extant documents.[18] One fact stands out: early Baptists placed the Bible at the center of their lives: "One would have difficulty raising a dispute among Baptists about this personal aspect of biblical authority. Exhortations to the regular and frequent reading of Scripture are a part of any catechetical instruction given to Baptist converts."[19] As will be shown, however, the mere affirmation that one believed the Bible did not always guarantee the privilege of fellowship within a church or association. Questions about how a person understood the Bible became paramount as rationalist influences impacted theological formulation. These influences led many to affirm heterodox teachings regarding Christ and the Trinity.

Scripture as the Word of God

Baptist placed a premium on the Bible because they saw in it the very words of God. Early Baptists saw the Bible as the key to knowing and understanding God, as can be seen in the opening articles of "A Short Confession of Faith," which affirmed, "We believe, through the power and instruction of the Holy Scriptures that there is one only God."[20] Thomas

16. Bush and Nettles, *Baptists and the Bible*, 32ff.

17. Hendricks, "God, the Bible, and Authority in The Baptist Faith and Message (1963)," in *Sacred Mandates of Conscience: Interpretations of the Baptist Faith and Message*, ed. Jeffrey Pool, 106ff. See also Estep, "The Nature and Use of Biblical Authority in Baptist Confessions of Faith, 1610–1963," *BHH* 22 (October 1987): 12.

18. Steely, "Biblical Authority and Baptists in Historical Perspective," *BHH* 19 (July 1984): 9.

19. Ibid., 7.

20. "A Short Confession of Faith," in *Baptist Confessions of Faith*, ed. McGlothlin, 54. McGlothlin notes that this confession, drawn up by de Ries while Smyth was attempting to unite with the Mennonites, may not be representative of General Baptist views regarding "oaths, war, civil magistracy, etc," Ibid.

Helwys believed that whatever the Christian believed ought to be proved by Scripture. His work, "A Declaration of Faith of English People Remaining at Amsterdam in Holland" has Scripture references in the text of each article as supporting evidence for the doctrinal claims of the confession.[21] Helwys affirmed a high view of Scripture when he stated in Article 23:

> That the scriptures off the Old and New Testament are written for our instruction, 2. Tim 3.16 & that wee ought to search them for they testifie off CHRIST, Io. 5.39. And therefore to bee vsed withall reverence, as conteyning the Holie Word off GOD, which onelie is our direction in al things whatsoever.[22]

Like General Baptists, Particular Baptists also affirmed the Bible as God's written word, as demonstrated both in how they used Scripture proofs and in what they wrote about the Bible in their various documents. William Kiffin, writing in 1645, referred to the Scriptures as "the Word of God."[23] Hanserd Knollys, in a debate about the validity of separating from the established church, wrote of taking "the Word of God" and sitting down like the Bereans to study and see if what either side said conformed to the Scriptures.[24] The Second London Confession calls the Scriptures "the Word of God written."[25] Early Baptists did not use the term "Word of God" merely as a polite euphemism for the Bible.

Scripture as the Authoritative Standard

Because early English Baptists saw the Bible as the written word of God, they viewed it as the authoritative standard in all matters of faith and practice. Proof of this lies in the fact that, solely on the basis of their read-ing the Bible, early English Baptists made the dangerous and decisive

---

21. "A Declaration of Faith of English People Remaining at Amsterdam in Holland," in *Baptist Confessions of Faith*, ed. McGlothlin, 85ff.

22. Ibid., 91.

23. Kiffin, *A Briefe Remonstrance of The Reasons and Grounds of those People Commonly Cllaed Anabaptists, for their Separation , etc. Or Certaine Queries Concerning their Faith and Practice, Propounded by Mr. Robert Poole; Answered and Resolved* (London: n.p., 1645), 5.

24. Knollys, *A Moderate Answer vnto Dr. Bastwicks Book; Called Independency not Gods Ordinance* (London: Iane Coe, 1645), 2.

25. "Confession of Faith Put Forth by the Elders and Brethren of Many Congregations of Christians (baptized upon Profession of their Faith) in London and the Country (London: n.p., 1677, 1689)," in *Baptist Confessions of Faith*, ed. Lumpkin, 249.

step to separate from the established Church.[26] In his written debate with Poole, Kiffin asked, "I pray you shew me what Gospel Institution have you for the Baptizing of Children, . . . what can you finde for your practise therein, more then [sic] the durty puddle of *mens Inventions* doth afford."[27] Kiffin saw Christ's teachings in the NT as having final authority for the life and practice of the church. The Second London Confession emphasized this when it opened with the statement: "The Holy Scripture is the only sufficient, certain, and infallible rule of all saving Knowledge, Faith, and Obedience."[28] Early English Baptists staked everything on what the Bible said, and risked imprisonment and death, because they saw it as the only authoritative standard in all matters of faith and practice. While affirming the Bible as the ultimate authority, many also saw the need to set down in clear terms what they understood the Bible to teach.

A mere claim to believe the Bible lacked sufficient clarity. Many groups claimed to follow the Bible. Both Particular and General Baptists claimed to base their teachings on the Scriptures, yet expressed differences separated them for years. Other factors came into play as foundational to Baptist unity.

THE COVENANT, THE LOCAL CHURCH AND SOUL LIBERTY

Charles Deweese noted that the first English Separatists organized "gathered or covenanted congregations."[29] Deweese pointed out that Separatists usually signed written covenants which spelled out the individual member's commitment, and that such practice commonly took place in forming new churches. Early English Baptists inherited this practice from their Separatists predecessors.[30]

Not all the early Particular Baptists followed this pattern, however. Knollys stated that the only conditions of which he knows are repentance, faith and baptism.[31] He states:

> This hath been the practice of some Churches of God in this City, without urging or making any particular covenant with Members

26. Steely, "Biblical Authority," 12–13.

27. Kiffin, *A Moderate Answer*, 5 (emphasis Kiffin's).

28. Lumpkin, *Baptist Confessions*, 248.

29. Deweese, *Baptist Church Covenants*, 22.

30. Ibid.

31. Knollys, *A Moderate Answer*, 19.

upon admittance, which I desire may be examined by the Scriptures cited in the Margent [*sic*], and then compared with the Doctors three conclusions from the same Scriptures, whereby it may appear to the judicious Reader, how near the Churches some of them come to the practice of the Apostles rule, and practice of the primitive Churches, both in gathering, and admitting Members.[32]

Kiffin also implied that the only basis for membership was a credible profession of faith and baptism. He wrote, "that being thus baptized upon profession of Faith, they are then added to the church"[33] Nowhere in the document did Kiffin make mention of a covenant, although there is an implied understanding that once one came into the membership of the church the congregation had a responsibility to watch over that one in love.[34] One can see, then, that covenants were not uniformly employed among Particular Baptists at the outset. Nevertheless, ample evidence exists that they used covenants and that they came into wider usage as time passed.

Covenantal Commitments

Perhaps no other leader in the area of covenanted churches stands out more than John Spilsbury. In *A Treatise Concerning the Lawfull Subject of Baptisme*, Spilsbury devoted a great deal of space to the concept of the eternal covenant of grace by which the Son redeemed the elect before going into a discussion of what constituted a church. Spilsbury isolated two necessary components, which he called "matter and form." Believers who desire to unite and have been properly baptized according to the NT pattern compose the matter. The form is the covenant. He uses "covenant" in two senses–the eternal covenant of grace and the formal covenant of the gathered church.[35]

32. Ibid., 20. Haykin argues that the London Confession of 1644 stipulates only that the local church is composed of baptized believers. After quoting Article XXXIII, he writes, "In other words, the local church should consist only of those who have professed faith in Christ and have borne visible witness to that faith by being baptised." It appears, however, that the end of the article implies a covenant, for it states, "joined to the Lord, and each other, by mutual agreement." Haykin, *Kiffin, Knollys and Keach: Rediscovering Our English Baptist Heritage*, 35.

33. Kiffin, *A Briefe Remonstrance*, 13. See also "The Kiffin Manuscript," in McBeth, *A Sourcebook for Baptist Heritage*, 26–27.

34. Ibid.

35. Spilsbury, *A Treatise Concerning the Lawfull Subject of Baptism*, 40–41. Spilsbury's name is spelled in various ways. The spelling followed is that employed by Torbet, *A*

Spilsbury writes,

> The forme is that by which these are united and knit up together in one fellowship, and orderly body, and that is the covenant of grace that lies between God and his people, by which God visibly becomes the God of such persons, and they his people above all other. That this forme of a Church is not Baptisme, I prove thus; that by which God and a people become each others apart from al other people, that is the forme of them; but the covenant is that by which God owns a people for his, and they him for their God, there the covenant is the forme.[36]

In this passage Spilsbury argued that the covenant of grace between the Father and the Son constituted the form of the church. Later, however, he used the word covenant to denote that compact between the several members of a gathered congregation:

> But for the last, namely, the outward administration of Baptisme, that ever follows the Saints joyning in fellowship, by mutuall faith & agreement in the doctrine, *wherein consists the stating of the Church in her conjoyning in covenant,* which ever goes before the administration of Baptisme, and gives power and authoritie for the same.[37]

Spilsbury argued from the eternal covenant of grace for the employment of the written covenant within the local, gathered, congregation.

History of the Baptists, 42. John Gill uses this same language in discussing the constituent elements of the church; see Gill, *A Body of Doctrinal and Practical Divinity*, 854. Burrage has an extended discussion on the differences between Knollys and Spilsbury on the issue of covenants. See Burrage, *The Church Covenant Idea: Its Origin and Its Development,* 113ff.

36. Spilsbury, *A Treatise*, 41.

37. Ibid., emphasis mine. Spilsbury further notes on 42 that there are four constituting causes in God's organizing of a church: (1) the word of God, (2) the confession of faith, and (3) the covenant (free and mutual consent to obey the truths affirmed), and (4) the Spirit of Christ binding the people together. At the bottom of 42 Spilsbury explains what he means by "confession of faith" in such a way as to indicate an oral testimony of faith in Christ: "which confession of faith is produced by the power of the Gospel, shining into the heart of man, and drawes away the same after that by which the gospel is revealed." Compare Blackwell, "A Particular church or churches, which is no other then [sic] a company of saints in profession, explicitly or implicitly consenting together, as worship God in the Word, Sacraments, and Prayer, and all other duties of Religion." Blackwood, *The Storming of Antichrist, In His Two Last and Strongest Garrisons; of Compulsion of Conscience, and Infants Baptisme,* 7.

Also, the covenant entered into by the members of the church should spell out certain key doctrinal commitments.

Spilsbury was not the only Baptist in England who approved of the use of a covenant during the 1640s and 1650s. In Bristol the Broadmead Church constituted on the basis of a short covenant in 1640,[38] while in 1656 the Baptist Church in Leominster constituted on the basis of a covenant.[39] Burrage argued that Keach, in 1694, believed in at least a verbal covenant commitment from the baptismal candidate,[40] and George reproduced a lengthy covenant authored by Benjamin and Elias Keach in 1697.[41] Indications are that, though not uniformly accepted in the 1640s, church covenants early on enjoyed common usage and gained acceptance toward the end of the seventeenth century.

Two essential elements appear in these early church covenants. The first element is the desire to follow Christ. The Broadmead Covenant stated that the purpose of the persons thus united was to "come forth of the world and worship the Lord more purely, persevering therein to their end."[42] The Leominster Covenant stated that the persons united to "give up themselves to the Lord."[43] In 1675 the church at Amersham (a Six-Principle Baptist Church) covenanted "to bee walking vp to and keeping & according to the worde of god."[44] The desire to follow Christ meant to follow the precepts laid down in his written word.[45]

Secondly, members of the church covenanted to watch over one another in love. Noting again the Leominster Covenant, the members there covenanted to "give up themselves . . . to each other to walk together in all the ordinances of Jesus Christ."[46] Keach's covenant stated even more strongly this concept of familial watch-care:

38. George and George, eds., *Baptist Confessions, Covenants, and Catechisms*, 173.

39. Ibid., 175.

40. Burrage, *The Church Covenant Idea*, 120.

41. George and George, *Baptist Confessions*, 177–79.

42. Ibid., 173.

43. Ibid., 175.

44. Deweese, *Baptist Church Covenants*, 117.

45. Spilsbury, *A Treatise*, 40. Spilsbury writes, "The Scriptures remaining in the place of the Apostles for us to have recourse unto, and serve as the mouth of Christ to all beleevers, as the Apostles did before they were written."

46. George and George, *Baptist Confessions*, 175. See also Raymond Brown, *The English Baptists of the 18th Century*, in *A History of the English Baptists*, ed. B. R. White (London: The Baptist Historical Society, 1986), 19.

2. We do promise to watch over each other's conversations, and not to suffer sin upon one another, so far as God shall discover it to us, or any of us; and to stir up another to love and good works; to warn, rebuke, and admonish one another with meekness, according to the rules left us of Christ in that behalf.[47]

Watching over one another in Christian love formed an essential element of the life of these churches. Sharp disciplinary measures usually befell one who deviated from the precepts of the covenant.[48]

Covenantal Expressions of Doctrine

While not all covenants gave a clear and definite expression of the beliefs of the church, they did entail a commitment to uphold the teachings of Christ as set forth in the Scriptures. As time passed, however, and confessions became longer, certain doctrinal tendencies emerged. It may be asked how this squared with the Baptist emphasis on religious liberty and liberty of conscience.

Watts noted that one of the key features in Separatist life was the idea of "a free community bound together by voluntary agreement to a covenant."[49] This concept of a church gathered by voluntary consent, which the Baptists took over from the Separatists, made possible doctrinal uniformity through a covenant. No one compelled another to unite with a Baptist church by anything other than persuasion of the conscience. If one dissented from the views of a particular congregation, he had freedom to leave it for another or start his own.

While covenants did not contain detailed doctrinal expositions such as those found in the confessions of the same era, nonetheless, certain covenants reflect a tendency toward upholding and defining core doctrinal concepts. The Amersham Covenant, for instance, stated, "Furst to walk in and kepe pure all the prinsiples of the doctrine of Christ viz heb the 6: 1:2 and not to haue Communion at the Lords tabell with Any that doe not keep them in purity Acording to the word or that shall Alow them selves

47. Ibid., 178.

48. Deweese, *Baptist Church Covenants*, 117. The Amersham Covenant stated very specifically, for instance, that those who took communion at any church that held contrary principles were not to be received into fellowship until they had demonstrated repentance.

49. Watts, *The Dissenters: From the Reformation to the French Revolution*, 3.

so to doe."[50] In the reference to Heb 6:1-2, one can see a reference to the doctrinal limits prescribed by Six-Principle Baptists.

Likewise, in Keach's Covenant, references to the everlasting covenant and the free grace of God in Christ underscored the strong Calvinistic convictions which constituted the backbone of his theology.[51] The Covenant also affirmed that members of the church will "strive together for the truths of the gospel and purity of God's ways," all the while seeking to maintain the unity of the Spirit.[52] These documents imply certain limits on private interpretation in order for one to remain within the church. Deviation too far one way or another could result in exclusion from the fellowship. Precisely what doctrines required clear affirmation will be the subject of the next major section of this chapter.[53]

THE CONFESSIONS, THE ASSOCIATION AND SOUL LIBERTY

Among the earliest confessions were the private, or personal confessions produced by Barrow and Greenwood,[54] Smyth,[55] Helwys,[56] and others. However, the dominant and most influential confessions (First London, Midland, and Second London) came about through the efforts of several

50. Deweese, *Baptist Church Covenants*, 117.

51. George and George, *Baptist Confessions*, 177. For a fuller treatment of Keach's theology, see Nettles, *By His Grace and For His Glory: A Historical, Theological, and Practical Study of the Doctrines of Grace in Baptist Life*, 62–65; and Vaughn, "Benjamin Keach," in *Baptist Theologians*, ed.George and Dockery, 49–76.

52. Ibid., 178.

53. Mauldin, *The Classic Baptist Heritage of Personal Truth: The Truth As It Is In Jesus*. In this work Mauldin seeks to argue that early English Baptists focused on "personal" truth grounded in experience with Christ. The argument is set forth that the truth of Scripture must be viewed through the lens of Christ in order to be perceived properly. Jesus Christ is set forth as "personal truth." Mauldin says, "With their minds fastened upon this cardinal yet scandalous trust in the singular light of Jesus Christ, who is both 'the truth [and] the Word of truth,' English Baptists first intend to build only upon Jesus Christ as the cornerstone of personal truth" (25). Mauldin takes his cue for this concept of "personal truth" from the writings of Paul Hobson.

54. Lumpkin, *Baptist Confessions*, 80.

55. Ibid., 97–99. Strictly speaking, Smyth's confession was written by him to represent his group to the Mennonites. Nevertheless, it is the production of a single mind, and so could be termed a personal confession.

56. Ibid., 114–15. Helwys' confession is similar in nature (though not content) to Smyth's in that it is the product of a single mind designed to represent a congregation of believers.

churches which sought to present a unified witness to the world in which they found themselves. Torbet listed five uses for confessions among early English Baptists:

> "(1) to maintain doctrinal purity; (2) to clarify and validate the Baptist position; (3) to serve as a guide to the General Assembly or local association in counselling [sic] churches; (4) to serve as a basis for fellowship within local churches, associations, or a General Assembly; (5) to discipline churches and members."[57]

Estep mentioned what he considers to be a more important use: "to publish before the world a true and correct summary of Baptist faith and practice."[58] (Estep's point is well taken, for both the First and Second London Confessions were written, at least in part, as defenses of Baptist orthodoxy and pleas for toleration.) The main focus here will be the issues of doctrinal purity and a basis for fellowship.[59]

Confessions as Doctrinal Safeguards

Associational doctrinal statements can be seen as doctrinal safeguards from two angles. First of all, one may look at what happened to churches, associations, or national bodies which forsook doctrinal standards in the name of liberty of conscience or which pursued a course of latitudinarianism with regard to doctrinal formulation. On the other hand, one may look at what happened in those cases where churches and associations maintained and required confessional subscription. Both approaches will be incorporated here, beginning with the anti-confessional party.

Among those who abandoned confessional subscription a tendency toward doctrinal decline which also led to spiritual decline prevailed. McBeth noted that tendency toward doctrinal decline particularly among the General Baptists. Beginning in the early 1690s consistent attacks upon the deity of Christ developed. The Salters' Hall Controversy showed the real extent of the progress of Unitarian views among General Baptists,

---

57. Torbet, *History of the Baptists*, 46.

58. Estep, "The Nature and Use of Biblical Authority," 4.

59. For a fuller discussion of the role of the association in maintaining doctrinal purity, see Griffith's "The Power and Duty of an Association," reprinted in *BHH* 2 (January 1967): 48ff.; May, "The Role of Associations in Baptist History," *BHH* 12 (April 1977): 69–74; and Carter, "Dealing with Conflict in Associational History," *BHH* 17 (April 1982): 33–43.

Anglicans, and Presbyterians.[60] Some during this period advocated Arian views while other set forth the more radical Socinian viewpoint. According to Watts, the Socinian view began attracting followers as early as the 1640s.[61] Within a century of the Salters' Hall meeting "most Presbyterian meetings and many of the General Baptists churches related to the General Assembly had become Unitarian."[62] Torbet argued that the General Baptists lacked evangelistic zeal, and he attributes this, in part, to constant doctrinal controversy.[63] The controversy over the deity of Christ and the doctrine of the Trinity raged throughout the eighteenth century, as the writings of Andrew Fuller on the subject shows.[64]

Several examples could be cited illustrating how the use of confessions maintained doctrinal fidelity during turbulent times. Watts noted that the denominations who subscribed to the creed at Salters' Hall continued to hold to orthodox doctrines and a strong Calvinism one hundred years later.[65] Among General Baptists, the New Connection, which required doctrinal subscription, became the dominant evangelistic force for Baptist Arminianism.[66]

In 1855 William Stokes, a Midland Association pastor, compiled *The History of the Midland Association of Baptist Churches, From Its Rise in the Year 1655 to 1855*. The work begins with "A Brief Essay on Creeds." In this essay Stokes argued for the appropriateness of voluntarily subscribed creeds. He stated:

> It is not enough, therefore, that a man declares that he believes the Bible. Christian communities have a right, for the sake of truth and peace, to ask of him, "In what sense do you believe the Bible? Do you believe it as a Socinian? or as an Arian? or as a Pelagian? or as a Rationalist? or as a broken hearted sinner who depends

60. McBeth, *The Baptist Heritage: Four Centuries of Baptist Witness*, 155.

61. Watts, *Dissenters*, 372.

62. Ibid., 376. The majority of those attending the Salters' Hall conference refused to subscribe to any doctrinal standard. These were predominantly General Baptists and Presbyterians. A minority of members composed mostly of Particular Baptists and Congregationalists subscribed to a trinitarian creed.

63. Torbet, *History of the Baptists*, 63. It is possible that other factors contributed to the lack growth among General Baptists during this time.

64. See Fuller, *The Complete Works of Andrew Fuller*, vol. 2.

65. Watts, *Dissenters*, 376.

66. McBeth, *Baptist Heritage*, 158–59. Torbet, *A History of the Baptists*, 76.

on a crucified Redeemer for life and salvation? When you say you believe the Bible, *what* is it that you really believe?"[67]

Stokes traced the history of Baptist confessions, down to the 1689 Confession, which still exerted a dominant influence in his day.[68]

Stokes saw the Midland Confession (adopted at its founding in 1655) as the basis for the 1689 London Confession.[69] Furthermore, he affirmed that the blessing of God on the usefulness of the association stemmed from the doctrinal fidelity of the association:

> this Association has held fast the form of sound words to the present day. The solid scriptural doctrines professed by our fore- fathers, now two centuries since, are the very doctrines avowed at the present moment; and the continued existence and usefulness of the Association have been owing, under the Divine blessing, to the consistent maintenance of the faith for which our predecessors suffered.[70]

According to Stokes, confessional fidelity played a major role in the life of the association. It served as a check against doctrinal declension and a basis for the churches to unite in the work of God's Kingdom.

Confessions as Expressions of Catholicity

Employed by associations, confessions served not only to distinguished Baptists from other professing Christians but highlighted points of uni- ty within the Baptist family. There is a hint of this in the First London

---

67. Stokes, *The History of the Midland Association of Baptist Churches*, 10. Compare to Fuller, "Creeds and Subscription," in *The Complete Works of Andrew Fuller*, vol. 3, 449–51, in which Fuller defends the practice of subscription in similar terms.

68. Stokes, *History of the Midland Association*, 13.

69. Ibid., 15, 34–35. It is worth noting that Stokes claims that the two doctrinal state- ments are in agreement on every essential doctrine: "And it is here proper to remark that it (the 1689) accords in every great particular of doctrine and practice with the Sixteen Articles of Faith originally adopted by this Association in 1655." Those who would claim that the placement of the articles on God and Scripture demonstrate some kind of shift in Baptist theology ought to take notice of such statements as this, for the Midland Confession of 1655 places the articles on God first and the article on Scripture in the third place, while the Second London moves the article on Scripture to the first heading. Notwithstanding, Stokes claims no change in doctrine. Compare, Hendricks, "God, the Bible, and Authority," (116–17).

70. Ibid., 36.

Confession's articles on the church (Articles XXXIII-XLVII). Note especially Article XLVII:

> And although the particular Congregations be distinct and severall Bodies, every one a compact and knit Citie in it selfe; yet are they all to walk by one and the same Rule, and by all meanes convenient to have the counsell and help one of another in all needfull affaires of the Church, as members of one body in the common faith under Christ their onely head.[71]

The beginning of an associational structure and consciousness premised upon a common understanding of the faith began to emerge at this point.

The Somerset Confession (1656) Article XXVIII noted also the duty of churches to "communicate each to [the] other, in things spiritual, and things temporal."[72] The most catholic statement in any Baptist confession, however, appeared in the Second London Confession, Article XXVI, which stated that there is a universal Church made up of all the elect. Section fifteen stated the associational principle of churches holding communion together through the sending of messengers, especially in settling difficulties, to "consider, and give their advice in, or about that matter of difference, to be reported to all the Churches concerned."[73] Congregational government and local church autonomy did not mean that each church lived in isolation with no responsibility to or connection with the larger Christian community. Associational confessions served to reinforce the larger aspect of Christian unity.

Brown noted that associations played a large role in the life of English Baptists in the eighteenth century. Associational meetings served as occasions for settling doctrinal and pastoral issues. Disciplinary issues sometimes appeared before the association, and pastors even sought the advice of the association when called to another church.[74]

Stokes noted that the Midland Association acted to promote "a *high state* of personal piety" among the members of the churches.[75] The associational circular letter served as the normal organ for this task. In one

---

71. Lumpkin, Baptist Confessions, 168–69.

72. Ibid., 211.

73. Ibid., 289.

74. Brown, *English Baptists*, 40–41.

75. Stokes, *History of the Midland Association*, 39.

instance the association rebuked the church at Bewdley for the manner in which they ordained one "Bro. Thompson." The association contended "that 'the advice and help of the ministers of their sister churches' on such an occasion are expedient, and would 'make the matter much more beautiful.'"[76] In 1718 the same church received a commendation from the association for excluding "Mr. Thompson" after he lapsed into Socinianism.[77]

Stokes summarized his view of the role of the association in these words:

> From these and a few similar allusions, it is evident that the Association watched over the affairs of the churches with affectionate concern, and deemed it a duty to give *special* advice whenever any passing exigency appeared to require it. Indeed, apart from this Christian sympathy and co-operation, it is difficult to determine of what good an Association can possibly be.[78]

Just as the church collectively had a responsibility to watch over the individual members with loving care, so too, the association had a responsibility to watch over the member churches. In this way unity was promoted, and doctrinal and moral integrity were maintained.

In describing the purpose of the Midland Association, Stokes listed five crucial elements: (1) the association served in an advisory capacity to the churches on matters of practice and discipline; (2) the association sent gifted preachers into those areas where churches needed pulpit supply; (3) the association aided impoverished churches in times of financial hardship; (4) the association served as a means whereby the churches could carry on the Kingdom's work through joint efforts; and (5) the churches of the association exercised watch-care over each other's doctrines and practices so as to maintain the unity of the faith.[79]

SOUL LIBERTY AND BAPTIST CONFESSIONALISM IN NORTH AMERICA

Soul liberty among Baptists in England did not conflict with the use of confessions as instruments of accountability because of the voluntary,

76. Ibid., 46.
77. Ibid., 47.
78. Ibid., emphasis his.
79. Stokes, *History of the Midland Association*, 27–28.

covenanted relationships of church and associational membership. From colonial beginnings down to the Civil War Baptists in North America, and especially in the Southern States, continued to follow the path laid down by their English Baptists forefathers. After the Civil War increasing trends toward individualism began to undermine doctrinal accountability in the name of soul liberty.

Soul liberty does not stand alone as a doctrine in American Baptist life. It must be understood in relation to other doctrines of the faith. One must understand soul liberty in relation to the doctrines of Scripture, salvation, the priesthood of all believers, religious liberty in general, and the role of the church in discerning truth from error. One must have a definition of soul liberty rooted in Baptist history. A look at historic, representative Baptist writers provides a window into how Baptists historically understood soul liberty.

Definition of Soul Liberty

In a book edited by Charles Jenkens, Thomas Armitage defined soul liberty to mean "that a man is responsible to God, and to him only, for his faith and practice, so far as the infliction of any [civil] punishment for disobedience to God is concerned."[80] The Second London Confession, embraced by Baptists in America from earliest times, speaks of soul liberty:

> God alone is Lord of the Conscience, and hath left it free from the Doctrines and Commandments of men which are in any thing contrary to his Word, or not contained in it. So that to Believe such Doctrines, or obey such commands out of Conscience, is to betray true liberty of Conscience; and the requiring of an implicit Faith, and absolute and blind Obedience, is to destroy Liberty of Conscience, and Reason also.[81]

Soul liberty, then, did not stand as a kind of *carte blanche* to believe anything and everything one found pleasing. The Second London

---

80. Armitage, "Baptist Faith and Practice," in *Baptist Doctrines*, ed. Charles A. Jenkens, 36.

81. "Second London Confession," in *Baptist Confessions of Faith*, ed. Lumpkin, 279–80. Evidence indicates that William Screvens' congregation at Kittery, Maine, held to the Second London Confession when it was organized in 1682, see Baker, *A Baptist Source Book*, 1–2. The first mention of the Second London Confession as used by an association is in the minutes of the Philadelphia Association for the year 1724, in which it is spoken of as "owned by us," as if it had been established for some time as a doctrinal standard in that association. See Gillette, *Minutes of the Philadelphia Baptist Association*, 27.

Confession noted that Christian liberty of conscience meant the freedom to believe and obey whatever the Bible taught and the obligation to resist whatever teachings have purely human origin. Soul liberty did not function as a cloak for sin or the perversion of the Bible's clear teachings.[82] Soul liberty carried with it accountability to the larger community of faith and the responsibility to maintain logical consistency in working out this doctrine in relation to other doctrines.

Relation to Other Doctrines

Any responsible treatment of soul liberty, then, must take into account the Baptist view of the Scriptures. Here again, one meets another hotly debated subject in Baptist life today. Have Baptists historically believed that the Bible is God's fully inspired word or merely a record and witness to God's revelation to humanity?

In a book published after his death, B. H. Carroll noted: "When you hear the silly talk that the Bible 'contains' the word of God and is not the word of God, you hear a fool's talk."[83] Wallace represented Baptist thinking in his time when he wrote that God's divine inspiration of the biblical writers "prevented [them] from introducing errors which would have misrepresented the thought of God."[84] The vast majority of Baptists near the turn of the twentieth century stood committed to the belief that the Bible, as given in the autographs, contained no errors.

The earliest Baptists on American soil anticipated the views of Carroll and Wallace. Thomas Memminger, writing the circular letter for the Philadelphia Association in 1797 referred to the Bible as that "which alone is truth."[85] The way in which Baptist writers in America used the Bible from the very beginning shows their confidence in its divine inspiration. Writing in the first circular letter for the Philadelphia Association, Abel Morgan said of the Bible,

> These holy writings are of God, divinely inspired, 2 Tim. iii. 16; the word of God, John x. 36; 1 Cor. xiv. 36, 37; the mind of Christ,

82. Ibid.

83. Carroll, *Inspiration of the Bible*, comp. and ed. J. B. Cranfill, 20. See also Manly, *The Bible Doctrine of Inspiration*.

84. Wallace, *What Baptists Believe*, 15.

85. Memminger, "Circular Letter, 1797," in Gillette, *Minutes of the Philadelphia Baptist Association*, 329.

1 Cor. ii. 26; of Divine authority, Isa. xl. 8; the infallible ground of faith and certain rule of obedience, Isa. viii. 20; full and complete in all its parts, historical, doctrinal, and prophetical; every way useful and profitable: e. gr. to obtain the saving knowledge of the one only living and true God, Father, Son, and Holy Ghost, 2 Tim. iii. 15.[86]

Such a view of inspiration did not make the Bible a holy relic, a mere object of worship. On the contrary, Baptists saw the Bible as a book to be studied and obeyed. R. B. C. Howell spoke of the responsibility of the church, not to legislate, but to execute that body of divine legislation already given in God's word.[87] In the work which he edited, Jenkens gave an extended treatment of the importance of obedience to the word of God. The believer had to submit willingly to the clear meaning of the biblical text. Refusal to submit was not an option.[88]

Baptists in the nineteenth century viewed the Bible as the very word of God. Furthermore, they viewed it as the ultimate and final authority in all religious disputes. J. L. Dagg linked the authority of the Bible directly to the divine authorship of the Bible. It contained God's commands, promises, and testimony. "Whether, as a rule of faith, of duty, or of hope, the authority of the Bible is supreme."[89] The church, then, had a responsibility to enforce the precepts of Scripture, and the individual believer had a responsibility to learn God's will as given in the Bible and follow it without question.

Similarly, an article appearing in the *TB* on fundamental Baptist principles noted ten basic principles related to religious liberty. The article pointed out that Baptists believed no human government should seek to control the individual's conscience, and quoting from Thomas Jefferson stated, "Error of opinion may be tolerated where reason is left free to combat it." However, the article also asserted: "Liberty of thoughts, liberty of speech, only limited by God's will as represented in His Word" stood as an essential Baptist belief.[90] It appears that prior generations of Baptists un-

---

86. Morgan, "Circular Letter, 1774," in Gillette, *Minutes of the Philadelphia Baptist Association*, 137.

87. Howell, *The Terms of Communion at the Lord's Table*, 29–30.

88. Jenkens, "Introduction," in *Baptist Doctrines*, ed. Charles A. Jenkens, 11–24. See also Van Ness, *The Baptist Spirit*, 34.

89. Dagg, *Manual of Theology*, 40.

90. W. C. C. "Fundamental Principles," *TB*, 20 March 1879, 2. No citation is given for the quote from Jefferson except to attribute it to him.

derstood religious liberty differently in different contexts. For unbelievers, religious liberty extended to the right to persist in erroneous views, while for church members the Bible's clear teachings became the means for checking error. Baptists, then, developed multiple levels of application for the principle of soul liberty depending upon whether or not a person professed faith through believer's baptism and church membership.

Soul Liberty and the Believing Community

Within the context of the church, soul liberty did not afford the right to assert and believe whatever one wished. Likewise, churches did not have the liberty to assert or cast off doctrines apart from the approbation of the local association without consequences. These relationships carried with them certain inherent limitations on soul liberty.

Greg Wills noted that churches often disciplined members for deviating from the accepted doctrinal norms usually expressed in confessions, covenants, or both. He noted that a pure right to religious liberty belonged to a person as a member of society at large, but not as a member of the local church. Religious liberty protected the individual from civil punishment over religious opinions, "but churches had every right to inflict spiritual penalties for erroneous beliefs."[91] Purity of morals and unity of doctrine constituted necessary components of the church's ability to fulfill its God-ordained mission in the world. These two pillars of the church could only be upheld if the church had the power to discipline its members. So Wills concluded, "Baptists submitted both their behavior and their beliefs to the authority of the congregation."[92]

Just as individual members were expected to submit their views to the judgment of the local church, so too the church was expected to subject its views to the judgment of the local association. In 1885 the Sweetwater Baptist Association organized as a body in Sweetwater, Texas. The founding constitution stipulated that the association could refuse to seat messengers from any church which held to unsound doctrine.[93] In 1892 the association adopted "Articles of Faith" composed of twenty articles.[94]

---

91. Wills, *Democratic Religion*, 87–88.

92. Ibid., 88.

93. Smith, "A History of the Sweetwater Baptist Association 1885–1957," 41ff. Special thanks to Louis Johnson of Abilene, Texas, for obtaining this material for me.

94. Ibid., 47–48.

Wills cited an incident where an association moved to discipline a church for casting off the associational confession in 1851. In the same association in 1852, a controversy arose involving a minister who rejected the association's confession on the grounds of soul liberty. This minister influenced three churches to follow his lead, and accused the association of exerting illegitimate powers. In 1853 the association excluded from fellowship all three churches.[95] Wills noted: "This power to exclude any church that deviated from 'the orthodox principles of the Gospel' gave the association an effective authority over the doctrine and practice of member churches." When the church objected, accusing the association of meddling in the internal affairs of the church, the association withdrew fellowship from the church on the basis of its disorderly conduct.[96]

Soul Liberty and Church Discipline

Some attention has been given to church discipline in matters of doctrine. However, more needs to be said, lest there be left some misunderstanding of how the churches perceived their powers in this regard.

In 1748, the Philadelphia Association noted the limits of personal conscience in relation to erroneous doctrines. The question before the association centered on God's foreknowledge and whether a person who denied foreknowledge had the right to church membership on the basis of personal conviction. The association first rejected the denial of God's foreknowledge as "repugnant to Scripture," and then said, "We judge such worthy of the highest censure; because a church is to proceed against a person who is erroneous in judgment, as well as against one who is vicious in practice, notwithstanding they may plead conscience in the affair."[97]

Joseph Carter wrote in 1883 that Baptists do have "Articles of Faith" but that these doctrines are not forced upon the consciences of the people. These documents contained short compendiums of what a church or association believed the Bible to teach on key doctrines. Final appeal, however, was always to the Bible.[98] Such flexibility owed its existence to the fact that a Baptist church was a voluntary body. The church could not inflict physical punishment upon one who deviated from the faith, nor

---

95. Wills, *Democratic Religion*, 98–99.

96. Ibid., 101.

97. "Circular Letter, 1748," in *Minutes of the Philadelphia Association*, 58.

98. Carter, *Distinctive Baptist Principles*, 8–9.

could it compel the state to do so. But the church retained the voluntary power to reject someone from its membership as well.

Carter further noted in regard to private interpretation:

> We do not mean that men are at liberty to think of the Bible what they please, and obey or disobey its precepts as they choose. But that each man is bound to use his judgment, and to govern it according to the teaching of the Bible as he understands it. The right to investigate the truth for himself does not carry with it the right to disobey it or to doubt it.[99]

Carter then affirmed that the church had the responsibility to excluded from its membership those who fell into heresy.[100]

Discipline, then, did not compel one to believe something of which he or she was not fully persuaded, but it did establish the boundaries within which one might believe certain things and still retain membership in the local church. One could not believe anything and still call himself a Baptist. Nineteenth century and earlier Baptists saw such a view of soul liberty as the seed bed for doctrinal anarchy and the loss of any basis for church purity, unity and fellowship.

CONCLUSION

Seventeenth and eighteenth century English Baptists made the study of Scripture a central feature in their daily lives. They took the Bible as God's written word and believed what they found in it. Whatever did not accord with the clear meaning of the text they rejected. While this did not solve all doctrinal problems, it did create a climate in which two Baptist groups achieved a high level of unity within their respective camps for some time.

Baptists demonstrated that they took the Bible seriously by their willingness to part with tradition wherever tradition parted with the Bible. Therefore they shed the cloak of the state church and infant baptism, exchanging it for the cloak of a gathered church and believers' baptism. This principle led them to embrace the concept of covenanting together as one body in Christ. The principle of a church covenant they derived from the covenant of grace by which Christ saved the believer. The covenant provided the necessary form for the existence of the church, while baptized

99. Ibid., 13.
100. Ibid., 14.

believers provided the matter, or substance of the church. The covenant established minimal doctrinal guidelines and a code of conduct to which all members conformed. These provisions insured church unity.

Church unity at the level of the local congregation proved inadequate to answer to the needs for fellowship within the larger Christian community. Baptist churches, therefore, organized associations, based on doctrinal confessions, as an expression of the larger, universal church. Associations provided a means whereby the local churches held each other accountable and encouraged one another in the Lord's work. The confession served as the point of unity and sustained doctrinal orthodoxy in turbulent times. Where the confessional principle was abandoned doctrinal declension led to a loss of evangelistic power.

Early English and American Baptist unity and strength revolved around four principles: (1) a firm commitment to the inerrancy and complete authority of the Bible as the written word of God; (2) the church as constituted by voluntary mutual consent, usually through a covenant (3) the accountability of the believer to the local congregation manifested in the church's covenant; and (4) doctrinal accountability to the larger Christian community through the acceptance and sincere adherence to a confessional standard based on the Bible as God's written word.

In the final draft of the BFM 1963 the Committee reproduced the essential limitations on confessional use set forth by Mullins and the 1924 Committee. Five specific affirmations about the historic Baptist use of confessions were affirmed in both documents: (1) confessions constitute a "consensus of opinion" of a given Baptist body and do not add to what must be believed for salvation; (2) they are never viewed as complete statements of all that Baptists believe; (3) all Baptist groups have the right to write their own confessions; (4) the sole and final authority for Baptist beliefs is the Old and New Testament Scriptures; and (5) they are affirmations of religious conviction and should not hamper intellectual "investigation in other realms of life."[101]

Hobbs and the Committee further modified the fourth affirmation above with the additional comment that "the sole authority for faith and practice among Baptists is Jesus Christ whose will is revealed in the Holy Scriptures." The Preamble further defined the Baptist use of confessions as non-binding documents of consensus that allows for "the soul's

---

101. Hobbs, et. al., "Report of the Committee on Baptist Faith and Message" in *Annual of the Southern Baptist Convention 1963*, 269.

competency before God, freedom in religion, and the priesthood of the believer."[102]

In other words, the confession served the denomination as a guide to inform, but it was quite limited in its function as an instrument of doctrinal unity or accountability. In this chapter, however, it has been demonstrated that Baptist churches and associations prior to 1900 routinely used confessions, not only to tell the world what Baptists believed, but also to check doctrinal departures on the part of churches, church members, and pastors. At this point the question arises as to how Baptists came to have this alternate view of the historic use of confessions. Chapter 5 will address that question in exploring the development of the concept of soul competency as expounded by Mullins and those who came after him.

102. Ibid., 270.

5

Confessional Accountability and Soul Competency

UNDERSTANDING THE 1963 COMMITTEE's concept of Baptist confessionalism requires taking a look back at the period surrounding the development of BFM 1925.

Early in the twentieth century, American Protestant Christianity found itself embattled from within over liberal theological trends coming out of Europe. Behind these new theological trends stood the Enlightenment, which promised to free the mind from superstition and myth. Confidence in the powers of reason and the autonomous self stood as a key feature of Enlightenment philosophy.[1] Scientific investigation posed serious challenges to Christianity in such areas as natural science, behavioral science, and most alarming of all, biblical studies.[2] At the same time American Christianity enjoyed the influence of the spirit of rugged individualism. Baptists enjoyed no special immunity:

> The older Baptist pattern of church order was much more seriously eroded than the thought of either Strong or Weston would indicate. The radical individualism of Jeffersonian democracy, which had found expression in Backus, Leland, and Wayland, had deeply penetrated Baptist life and had been reinforced by the general temper of Evangelicalism.[3]

1. Solomon and Higgins, *A Short History of Philosophy*, 192. See also Hudson, *Religion in America*, chap. 11.

2. González, *The Story of Christianity, Vol. 2*, 283–85. See also Hudson, "Shifting Patterns of Church Order in the Twentieth Century," in *Baptist Concepts of the Church*, 197–98.

3. Hudson, "Shifting Patterns of Church Order," 140. Hudson is writing specifically of Northern Baptists in the early twentieth century, but the spirit of individualism pervaded all parts of American society without regard to geographical location.

In this context Baptists looked to a new generation of leaders. The old ways and ideas seemed out of step with the times. Among Southern Baptists one leader rose above the rest and paved the way into the early twentieth century—Edgar Young Mullins. Within this context Mullins found a new rationale for the Baptist way. Mullins identified what he called "soul competency" as the defining theological contribution of Baptists to Christian thought: "The sufficient statement of the historical significance of the Baptists is this: The competency of the soul in religion."[4] This concept, which Mullins intended to use as an overarching concept for a number of Baptist distintinctives, ultimately altered the fragile balance between confessionalism and soul liberty.

BAPTIST CONFESSIONALISM IN THE EARLY TWENTIETH CENTURY

As a result of the advancement of individualism in Baptist life, a decline in the exercise of church discipline took root.[5] Wills argued that the decline in church discipline began after the Civil War and advanced most quickly in urban churches. By 1900, church discipline in the Baptist South had experienced a marked decline due to a number of influences.[6] Signs of a weakening of Baptist confessionalism already loomed on the horizon. Mullins arrived on the scene during this period of transition.

Edgar Young Mullins

Biography

Born 5 January 1860, the son of a Mississippi Baptist pastor, E. Y. Mullins's early childhood came under the shadow of the Civil War and Reconstruction. During the turbulent years of Reconstruction the Mullins family moved to Corsicana, Texas. The young Mullins demonstrated an

---

4. Mullins, *The Axioms of Religion*, 53.

5. Wills, *Democratic Religion*, 139–40.

6. Ibid., 116–38. See also Wills, "Southern Baptists and Church Discipline," *SBJT* 4 (Winter 2000): 9–10. Wills notes several contributing causes to the decline of church discipline after1870, and then states, "Commitment to an expansive individualism grew in response to such cultural trends and undermined the traditional Baptist commitment to the authority of the congregation. Belief in the authority of the congregation is foundational to discipline. Its lapse meant the loss of discipline" (10).

early gift for learning and took a job at age eleven as a typesetter for a local newspaper. He also worked as a telegraph operator while a teenager.[7]

At sixteen he entered Texas A&M's first cadet class. Here he learned both discipline and the skills of leadership which would serve him well later. After graduation he again took up the job of a telegraph operator to earn money to attend law school. Mullins was converted under the preaching of Maj. William E. Penn in a revival meeting in Dallas, Texas, in 1880. He was baptized soon after at his father's church in Corsicana, Texas, and within a few months sensed a call to the gospel ministry. He moved to Louisville, Kentucky, to enter into formal preparation at the Southern Baptist Theological Seminary in 1881.[8]

Concerning Southern Seminary in Mullins' day, R. Albert Mohler wrote:

> The Southern Seminary of Mullins's student experience was a school with clear theological convictions and a much-respected faculty, which included the school's founder and faculty chairman, James Petigru Boyce. Boyce, later appointed the school's first president, was the most formative figure in the seminary's establishment and early development.[9]

Boyce, a Southerner by birth, embraced with firm conviction a Calvinistic theology. His influence on Mullins was "powerful" according to Mohler. Mullins arrived at Southern shortly after its first theological conflict—a conflict that foreshadowed events to come in the Southern Baptist Convention. Crawford Howell Toy resigned from the faculty in 1879 because he had embraced concepts of higher biblical criticism which undermined a firm belief in the inspiration and authority of the Scriptures.[10]

---

7. Mohler, "Baptist Theology at the Crossroads: The Legacy of E. Y. Mullins," *SBJT* 3 (Winter 1999): 4. The entire Winter 1999 edition of *SBJT* is devoted to E. Y. Mullins. Also the entire Winter 1999 edition of *R&E* is devoted to Mullins but written from a different standpoint. See also Humphreys, "E. Y. Mullins," in *Baptist Theologians*, ed. George and Dockery, 330–50; and Humphreys, "Edgar Young Mullins," in *Theologians of the Baptist Tradition*, ed. George and Dockery, 181–201.

8. Mohler, "Baptist Theology at the Crossroads," 4–5. See also Mullins, *An Intimate Biography*, 13.

9. Mohler, "Baptist Theology at the Crossroads," 5.

10. Ibid. See also Bush and Nettles, *Baptists and the Bible*, 205–6 and 208–20 for a thorough discussion of Broadus's view of Scripture and the Toy Controversy.

Mullins graduated in 1885 and entered into the pastorate of the Baptist church in Harrodsburg, Kentucky. While serving in Harrodsburg he married Isla May Hawley of Louisville.[11] Mullins had hoped to serve as a missionary with the Foreign Mission Board, but first financial constraints at the mission board, and later his own health concerns prevented it. In 1888 he accepted the call to Lee Street Baptist Church, Baltimore, Maryland.[12] Here his sense of social responsibility grew. He received an appointment as associate secretary to the FMB in 1895. Mullins designed a program to promote missions education in Baptist schools, but according to his wife, he soon realized his work interfered with R. H. Willingham's effectiveness. He quietly stepped back into the role of office work which did not suit him. Mrs. Mullins devoted herself to prayer that he would find a more suitable place of service. One day a letter came from Newton Centre inviting him to become their pastor. Though reluctant at first, he accepted the call as pastor at Newton Centre Baptist Church, located in a suburb of Boston, Massachusetts.[13]

Life in Massachusetts brought Mullins into contact with philosophical and theological influences rarely encountered in his native South. He lived in near proximity to Harvard College, Newton Theological Institute and Boston University.[14] He explored the writings of German theologians such as F. D. R. Schleiermacher and Albrecht Ritschl and the philosophical systems of William James and Borden Parker Bowne. James championed pragmatism and Bowne led in the philosophical school of personalism. Through Mullins the effects of Enlightenment philosophy came to have a place in Southern Baptist life and thought, with a new emphasis on the individual and human experience in religion.[15]

11. Mullins met Isla May Hawley in the third year of his studies at Southern. Her family had recently moved to Louisville from Selma, AL. Mullins, *An Intimate Biography*, 15.

12. While at Baltimore Isla gave birth to two children, the second of whom died in infancy due to a pharmacist's error in preparing a prescription. Ibid., 50–58.

13. Mohler, "Baptist Theology at the Crossroads," 5–6. Mullins had accepted a call to the pastorate of First Baptist, San Antonio, Texas, in 1887, but news of Mrs. Mullins's pregnancy and the doctor's warnings against moving for several months prompted him to withdraw his acceptance of the call. Mullins, *An Intimate Biography*, 45–46.

14. Mullins, *An Intimate Biography*, 72–80, Mohler, "Baptist Theology at the Crossroads," 6.

15. Mohler, "Baptist Theology at the Crossroads," 8. More will be said concerning this below.

William Whitsitt came to the presidency of Southern Seminary while Mullins served in the North. Whitsitt's career as president of Southern came to an abrupt end because of a controversy over his views of Baptist origins which contradicted accepted Landmarkist beliefs. Whitsitt resigned in 1899, after serving only four years as president. Mohler notes that "the trustees sought a leader who would, if possible, be untouched by the Whitsitt controversy. The trustees turned to E. Y. Mullins, who had been outside the mainstream of Southern Baptist life during his years at Newton Centre."[16]

Mullins served Southern Seminary from 1899 until his death in 1928. He also served as president of the Southern Baptist Convention, 1921–24, and was the key architect of the BFM, 1925. He played a pivotal role in establishing the Baptist World Alliance and served as its president from 1923–28.[17]

Philosophical Paradigm Shift

Mullins impacted Southern Baptist life throughout the twentieth century with the publication in 1908 of *Axioms of Religion: A New Interpretation of the Baptist Faith*. According to Humphreys, Mullins claimed that the most important Baptist contribution to Christian thought "is the belief in 'soul competency,' that is, in the freedom, ability, and responsibility of each person to respond to God for herself or himself."[18] While Mullins treats soul competency as a universally accepted given among Baptists, in reality he appears to be the first to use this expression.[19] He treats it as an umbrella concept which includes the right to private interpretation of Scripture, soul freedom, regenerate church membership, priesthood of believers, and separation of church and state.[20] Norman argues that Mullins engaged in a philosophical paradigm shift from Reformation thought forms to Enlightenment thought, focusing on the autonomous

16. Ibid., 6.

17. Ibid., 7.

18. Humphreys, "Edgar Young Mullins," 187.

19. Skevington uses the expression in a 1914 work but never refers to E. Y. Mullins. See Skevington, *The Distinctive Principle of the Baptists*, 9. Skevington speaks of "the competency and sovereignty of the soul to deal directly with God."

20. Mullins, *Axioms of Religion*, 56–57.

individual's experience of God in Christ. This became the new locus of Baptist identity in the twentieth century.[21]

Soul Competency

Soul competency concerns the personal nature of the individual's relationship with God. It also, according to Mullins, "embraces the capacity for action in social relations as well."[22] Soul competency begins with the individual before God, but it does not end there. Freedom entails responsibility to others. Also, Mullins noted that his concept of soul competency ought not to be equated with human self-sufficiency. The issue of sin and depravity had to be faced. God's authority stands over the competency of the soul. Mullins further argued that soul competency was not the sum and substance of "the Baptist creed." His argument concerned the historical importance of the Baptist faith.[23]

Mohler noted that soul competency stood as Mullins' most enduring contribution to Baptist life and thought. Mullins sought by it to emphasize the necessity of personal repentance and faith as the foundational experience of the Christian faith expressed in conversion toward God.[24]

Incoherent Theological Methodology

Mullins led Southern Baptists at a time of great intellectual upheaval, and he sought a way to preserve on the one hand the historic beliefs of past Southern Baptists while on the other hand he recast them in a new philosophical system. Instability resulted from this. Mohler noted,

> Mullins's attempt to forge a mediating theological paradigm for Southern Baptists eventually failed because mediating positions are inherently unstable. Delicate compromises established in one generation are often abandoned in short order as new generations assume leadership.[25]

Moore and Thornbury noted that "even though most persons want to lay claim to at least some portion of the Mullins's legacy, no one achieves consensus by looking to Mullins's thought." A lack of internal

---

21. Norman, *More than Just a Name*, 35–36, 41–42, 46–47.

22. Mullins, *Axioms of Religion*, 54–55.

23. Ibid., 53.

24. Mohler, "Baptist Theology at the Crossroads," 19.

25. Ibid.

coherency in Mullins's theological method contributed to this failure of consensus. Casper Wistar Hodge noted that Mullins's system contained mutually exclusive claims to religious authority. Moore and Thornbury commented, "In any case, Hodge observed, Mullins's theology possessed no thoroughgoing methodological principle, his resulting method is quite 'impossible.'" Mullins failed to hammer out the relationship between personal experience and revelation. He sought to incorporate the pragmatism of James in some places while utilizing Bowne's personalism in others. Mullins, in the end, is often viewed "as a theologian who made peace with modernity."[26]

The Impact of Soul Competency as a Concept in Southern Baptist Life

Mullins's concept of soul competency worked itself like leaven throughout Southern Baptist life and thought. In *Sacred Mandates of Conscience*, Jeff Pool argued that the Preamble to the 1963 BFM stood as the preeminent article of faith for Baptists.[27] The Preamble to the BFM 1963 delineated the limits inherent in a Baptist confessional statement in relation to the principle of soul competency.[28]

William Tuck developed a similar line of thought in his understanding of soul competency. The present experience of Christ was primary for Tuck, not what can be read in a book (whether it be the Bible or the history of the Church).[29, 30]

26. Moore and Thornbury, "The Mystery of Mullins in Contemporary Southern Baptist Historiography," *SBJT* 3, no. 4 (Winter 1999): 52–54. See also, Mohler, "Baptist Theology at the Crossroads," 10–11.

27. Pool, "Chief Article of Faith" in *Sacred Mandates of Conscience*, 37.

28. Ibid., 44-45 (Pool's emphasis). For Pool and other moderate Baptists, a confessional statement contains not so much a compendium of fundamental biblical teachings but an expression of the professing Christian's experience of religion. When Pool asserts that "Christian confessional statements express Christian *understanding* of Christian experience . . ." one is left to wonder what role Scripture plays in confessional formulation. Interestingly, Roger Olson isolates experience as a form of religious authority as an essential component of Christian liberalism. See Olson, *The Story of Christian Theology*, 580.

29. Tuck, *Our Baptist Tradition*, 7. Tuck begins, rightly, by arguing for a regenerate church membership and the importance of experiential religion in Baptist life. However, from that starting point he argues that the way to experience God in Christ is not by looking back into the past (because one cannot really know the past with any certainty) but to look to the present work of God in one's life and in the church. "The Lord is not confined to the past. He goes before us to meet us in the present here and now."

30. Tuck goes on to argue that conservatives have made it necessary for one to under-

In the Winter 1999 edition of *R&E* James Dunn wrote that "the concept of 'soul competency' or 'soul freedom' is as timely as today's newspapers."[31] Dunn cited Campolo as defining soul competency as the individual's ability "to find in the Bible the answers he is seeking."[32] Dunn also pointed to Mullins's student, W. T. Conner, as affirming that Mullins rooted religious knowledge in the direct experience of God on the part of the person.[33]

Moore argued that soul competency concerned the individual believer before God in light of the authority of Scripture. In this view, experience stands under the judgment of the teachings of the Bible; therefore religious experience must conform to the teachings of the Bible.[34]

Norman argued that the concepts of soul liberty and soul competency are different concepts rooted in different philosophical traditions. He argued that, from the perspective of how Baptists gain religious knowledge, one met two competing approaches: the Bible and experience.

Biblical authority is the notion that the Bible in some way serves as the authoritative basis for the theology of Baptist distinctives. Christian experience is the idea that an individual religious experience of God is the foundation for the unique doctrines of Baptists.[35]

Norman pointed to E. Y. Mullins as the one who most prominently demonstrated the early shift to experience based belief. "The argument is that a Christian cannot have a valid understanding of the Bible and conversion without first having experienced God."[36] While it is true that

stand and accept a set of propositional belief statements in order to be saved. He includes in his list the inerrancy of Scripture and the substitutionary view of Christ's atonement. This, he alleges, destroys the doctrine of salvation by grace and sets up a works based system of salvation because propositional truth takes the place of the living experience the believer has with Christ. Ibid., 8–9.

31. James Dunn, "Church, State, and Soul Competency," *R&E* 96, no. 1 (1999): 61. Dunn equated soul competency with soul liberty. This confusion of the two concepts Norman convincingly refuted in *More Than Just a Name*.

32. Dunn, "Church, State and Soul Competency," 61, cited from Kenneth L. Woodward, "The Road to Repentance," *Newsweek*, 28 September 1998.

33. Ibid., 63.

34. Moore, "For the Bible Tells Me So," *The Tie* 68, no. 4 (2000): 6–7.

35. Norman, *More than just a Name*, 15. Norman notes that Baptists reject the external enforcement of creedal standards by governmental coercion. He also notes that such a view of creeds "is not the same as a 'voluntary, conscientious adherence to explicit doctrinal statements'" (17).

36. Ibid., 18.

one must have the Spirit in order to understand spiritual things (1 Cor 2:14–16), it is also equally true that religious experiences must have an external standard by which they are judged. As Machen pointed out, not all religious experiences are valid Christian religious experiences.[37] Machen argues strongly for the importance of the individual's experience of grace, but he warns against placing too much emphasis on personal experience:

> But at this point a fatal error lies in wait. It is one of the root errors of modern liberalism. Christian experience, we have just said, is useful in confirming the gospel message. But because it is necessary, many men have jumped to the conclusion that it is all that is necessary. Having a present experience of Christ in the heart, may we not, it is said, hold that experience no matter what history may tell us as to the events of the first Easter morning? May we not make ourselves altogether independent of the results of Biblical criticism? No matter what sort of man history may tell us Jesus of Nazareth actually was, no matter what history may say about the real meaning of His death or about the story of His alleged resurrection, may we not continue to experience the presence of Christ in our souls?[38]

W. O. Carver examined Machen's work and found it lacking. Carver reviewed *Christianity and Liberalism* in 1924. He faulted Machen for failing to give sufficient development to the internal aspects of the Christian life, and especially the work of the Spirit in the believer: "so far as the book goes, he [the reader] might reply if one asked him of the Holy Spirit, 'I had not so much as heard that there is a Holy Spirit.'"[39]

In the aftermath of Mullins's writings the emphasis shifted away from Scripture as the objective standard toward individualism and personal experience. Mullins himself sought to hold these elements in balance, but in the hands of later theologians the fragile balance was lost. By 1960 Hobbs asserted that personal experience stood as the final and strongest evidence for the inspiration of the Bible: "The Bible is experientially affirmed. The ultimate test of anything is that of experience."[40]

---

37. Machen, *Christianity and Liberalism*, 71.
38. Ibid.
39. Carver, "Christianity and Liberalism, A Review," *R&E* 21 (July 1924): 346.
40. Hobbs, *Fundamentals of Our Faith*, 12.

Building on his argument that Mullins inaugurated a significant paradigm shift in Baptist thought, Norman identified two distinct approaches to the volitional element in Baptist identity: religious liberty and soul competency. Mullins joined these two concepts in his *Axioms of Religion* by linking responsibility and freedom. Because of the image of God in man every person was "competent, responsible, and accountable to deal personally with God." Religious liberty, for Mullins, was one aspect of the volitional component of Baptist life.[41]

Norman wrote that early Baptists made religious liberty a key element of Baptist identity because their doctrine of salvation required "a free and voluntary response to God."[42] This view of religious liberty falls short of presenting what early Baptists considered foundational to the voluntary response of faith: the sovereignty of God in salvation. This can be demonstrated in the Second London Confession's emphasis on God's sole place as Lord of the conscience. The argument contained in the writings of early Baptists focused on the necessity of God's sovereign work in conversion, and hence the impotence of any human power to coerce religious faith and obedience. The principle of liberty of conscience in the writings of John Leland and Isaac Backus had its roots in their Calvinistic theology. Backus argued the necessity of human government because of man's sinful, fallen condition. At the same time he argued that true liberty only comes through the efficacious working of God's grace.[43] On this basis Backus argued for two spheres of government—civil and church. The civil government had responsibility for man's temporal affairs, while the government of the church held responsibility for man's eternal state. The church operated under the rule of Christ and had only spiritual weapons designed to effect spiritual ends.[44]

John Leland argued that each person enjoyed religious liberty because each person would one day stand before God in judgment: "Every man must give an account of himself to God, and therefore every man ought to be at liberty to serve God in a way which he can best reconcile to his conscience."[45] Yet he also noted that sin defiled the conscience, there-

41. Norman, *More than Just a Name*, 20–21.

42. Ibid., 22.

43. Backus, "An Appeal to the Public for Religious Liberty," in *Isaac Backus on Church, State and Calvinism*, ed. McLoughlin, 311.

44. Ibid., 315

45. Leland, "The Rights of Conscience," in *The Writings of John Leland*, ed. Greene, 181.

fore a radical change had to take place within the individual in order for a person to comply with God's law.[46] Furthermore, government did not have the power to effect this necessary change. Only the power of God's sovereign grace could change a sinful heart.[47]

In the "Circular Letter" of the Philadelphia Association for 1797, Thomas Memminger, commenting on Article 21 of the Second London Confession "Of Christian Liberty, and Liberty of Conscience," notes that only the individual and God have a right to access the individual's conscience:

> The all-wise Jehovah has given unto all men an equal freedom and liberty of conscience, the court of which is sacred, and wherein none have a right to tread but the individual himself and the blessed God by his word and Spirit, those only being the judges, who have authority to decide all matters concerning it.[48]

Mullins objected precisely to this view of divine sovereignty. In *Axioms of Religion* he redefines God's sovereignty in paternalistic tones:

> Men have ever stumbled at the doctrine of God's sovereignty, chiefly because they have not understood it. They have thought it meant that God was merely a predestinating omnipotence, that he is capricious lightning, a meteor God, moving across the heavens of man's hope in a lawless manner, smiting one and saving another, without regard to moral law. They have thought of him as sovereign omnipotence or as sovereign omniscience instead of sovereign fatherhood, as he is.[49]

Two things stand out at this point in Mullins's discussion. First, he allowed the general caricature of Calvinism to stand unchallenged and used it as a straw man. Secondly, he shifted the focus toward "the fatherhood of God." This shift re-envisioned at the foundational level the relationship between a sovereign God and morally responsible sentient creatures.

46. Leland, "The Virginia Chronicle," in *The Writings of John Leland*, ed. Greene, 123.

47. Leland, "Speech in the Massachusetts House of Representatives," in *The Writings of John Leland*, ed. Greene, 356–67.

48. Memminger, "Circular Letter," in *Minutes of the Philadelphia Association: 1707-1807*, 329. Article XXI, section 2, opens with "God alone is Lord of the Conscience" Building on their Calvinistic understanding of God's sovereign power in grace, early Baptists understood that only God had the power and the right to alter the human heart and frame it to worship him aright. No external power of man could accomplish this.

49. Mullins, *Axioms of Religion*, 79.

Human freedom, for Mullins, was essential to human responsibility, and a sovereign God must take that freedom into account and allow for it in his providential workings.[50] Mullins asserted, "any doctrine of divine sovereignty must safeguard man's freedom."[51] Furthermore, in tones quite distinct from previous generations of Baptist theologians, Mullins argues that

> neither prevenient nor regenerating grace, nor grace in any of its forms acts upon the will by way of compulsion, but always in accordance with its freedom. The will responds and man chooses for himself God's freely offered gift of salvation. Grace conforms to the structure of the will, pursues its windings, inflates but never forces it, fills it out as a human hand fits or fills a glove, the two forever distinct and separate, yet identical in shape and united in destiny.[52]

For Mullins, grace consisted not so much in God's loving exertion of his power to save from ruin the object of his affections as God's co-operation with his free creature in the hopes of securing the salvation of the individual. Soul freedom, under the concept of soul competency, underwent a radical redefinition. In fact, in the overall outworking of salvation in Mullins's scheme man achieved by grace his own righteousness in addition to that which God imparts.[53]

Norman, then, is correct insofar as he notes that there are two competing streams of thought in determining what it means to be "Baptist." One stream flows from the "Reformation tradition" which emphasizes the sole rule of Scripture as the determinative authority for faith and practice. The second stream, coming down from the writings of Mullins, flows from the philosophical currents of the Enlightenment, which focuses on Christian experience as the primary source of religious authority.[54] By the early 1960s Mullins's "new interpretation of Baptist beliefs" began to undermine Baptist confessionalism.[55]

50. Ibid., 80.

51. Ibid., 83.

52. Ibid., 84.

53. Ibid., 86.

54. Norman, *More than Just a Name*, 41. Norman rightly identifies the two disparate streams but fails to identify sufficiently the foundational role of God's sovereignty in relation to the individual in his treatment of the Reformation stream.

55. This will be demonstrated later in the chapter.

Soul Competency and Related Issues

Soul competency does not stand alone as a doctrine in Baptist life. Mullins understood soul competency in relation to the doctrines of Scripture, salvation, the priesthood of all believers, religious liberty, and role of the church in discerning truth from error. While other doctrines could be examined in relation to soul competency (and Mullins does so in his *Axioms of Religion*), the doctrines of Scripture and salvation occupy a central position for the purposes of examining the work of the 1963 Committee. Mullins and Carroll both demonstrated a great concern to connect the concept primarily to salvation through personal faith in Jesus Christ.

Definition of Soul Competency

Soul competency, in *Axioms of Religion*, stands for the individual's responsibility under God to come to Christ for salvation and interpret and obey the Scriptures without interference by the state, or by the church resorting to the civil magistrate for the enforcement of religious duty.[56]

Relation to Other Doctrines

Any responsible treatment of soul competency, then, must take into account the Baptist view of the Scriptures. In chapter 4 it was demonstrated that the leading Baptist writers and leaders down to the early twentieth century held to the full inspiration and final authority of the Bible as God's written revelation.

As previously noted, Carroll states: "When you hear the silly talk that the Bible 'contains' the word of God and is not the word of God, you hear a fool's talk."[57] Wallace represents Baptist thinking when he writes that God's divine inspiration of the biblical writers "prevented [them] from introducing errors which would have misrepresented the thought of God."[58] The vast majority of Baptists near the turn of the twentieth century were

56. Mullins, *The Axioms of Religion*, 53–58. Mullins argues that soul competency is not intended to state that the individual has a natural, unaided ability to come to God. The doctrine does not deny the effects of the fall or the doctrine of total depravity. It is interesting that in this section Mullins flatly denies that the doctrine of soul competency is "the Baptist creed" (53) although Pool seems to treat it as just that.

57. Carroll, *Inspiration of the Bible*, comp. and ed. by Cranfill, 20. See also Manly, *The Bible Doctrine of Inspiration Explained and Vindicated*.

58. Wallace, *What Baptists Believe*, 15.

committed to the belief that the Bible, as given in the autographs, contained no errors.[59]

While soul competency relates to the Bible on the matter of religious authority, Mullins and Carroll related it more frequently to the matter of salvation. In dealing with this aspect Carroll painted a powerful word-picture as he described a sinner alone with the Bible in front of him:

> His conscience is free to decide without embarrassment or hindrance from all external forces or influences. By the Spirit, through the book, his free conscience leads him to an opening in the circle which leads him to salvation. Conviction, changing his mind, giving of faith on the Spirit's part; the exercise of contrition, repentance, and faith on man's part. These are the constituent elements of regeneration from divine and human sides.[60]

In *Axioms of Religion*, Mullins argued that the doctrine of the priesthood of all believers and the democratic principle in religion flowed from the doctrine of soul competency.[61]

Mullins also argued that, because saving faith was a personal matter, soul competency led naturally to the doctrine of religious liberty. The conscience could not be coerced. No merely human priesthood or sacrament could come between the individual and God. Furthermore, no state church could enforce upon someone the fulfillment of his or her religious duty, or conformity to a set body of beliefs. The individual made free, responsible choices in the matter of religion. The believing individual, then, freely chose his or her church affiliation according to the dictates of God's word and his or her own conscience.[62]

59. See Bush and Nettles, *Baptists and the Bible,* for an extended discussion of representative views of Baptist theologians on the inspiration, nature and sufficiency of the Scriptures.

60. "Distinctive Baptist Principles," a sermon of B. H. Carroll before the Pastor's Conference at Dallas, Texas, [November 3, 1903], courtesy BCL.

61. Mullins, *Axioms of Religion*, 53. One should note that Mullins expressed this doctrine as the priesthood of *all* believers and not the priesthood of *the* believer. Historically Baptists have expressed the doctrine as Mullins stated it, giving a proper place to the community nature of the doctrine. Believers do not exercise their priesthood in isolation but in relation to one another through the local church. The latter expression dominates today and focuses on the role of the individual, often to the neglect of his or her reciprocal responsibility within the larger community of faith.

62. Ibid., 54–55. Prior to Mullins, Baptists developed multiple levels of application of the principle of religious liberty. For unbelievers, religious liberty extended to the right to persist in erroneous views, while for those who were members of the church, the Bible's

Soul Competency and the Authority of Scripture

As already noted, Baptists in the nineteenth century viewed the Bible as the very word of God. Furthermore, they viewed it as the ultimate and final authority in all religious disputes. When the Committee on Baptist Faith and Message brought its report to the 1925 Convention, it stated that the confession being presented was composed of "statements of religious convictions, drawn from the Scriptures."[63] Furthermore, the BFM 1925 began by asserting the full authority of the Scriptures in settling all religious disputes.[64]

How, then, did such Baptists as Mullins, Carroll, and others of their day use the Bible in settling disputed points of doctrine or practice and maintain a unity of the faith? The answer resides in the hermeneutical principle Baptists used as they read the Bible. They shared a common principle of interpretation which they inherited from the Puritans via the Second London Confession: Scripture interprets Scripture.[65]

That Baptist leaders at the beginning of the twentieth century continued to follow this line of interpretation can be demonstrated from an address given by E. Y. Mullins before a group of Disciples of Christ ministers in Indianapolis, and the subsequent exchange of letters between Mullins and L. R. Scarborough. At this point Mullins's rose above his own theological methodology of experiential personalism and exercised sound exegetical practice by making Scripture its own best interpreter.

Upon request Mullins presented a paper on the New Testament teaching of baptism in relation to the remission of sins and the new birth to a conference of Disciples ministers in Indiana. The paper was later published in *CI*. Mullins proposed to address the matter by dealing with all the significant passages of Scripture which most closely tie baptism to remission of sins and the new birth. His method of presentation looked at all the relevant New Testament data, and then from it derived an interpretation which did not create conflicts or contradictions between the various passages. In other words, by comparing Scripture to Scripture,

---

clear teachings served as the means whereby error was kept in check. Confessions of faith served as compendiums of essential beliefs to which all church members were expected to agree. See chap. 4.

63. *Annual of the Southern Baptist Convention Nineteen Hundred Twenty-Five*, 71.

64. Ibid.

65. "The Second London Confession of Faith," in *Baptist Confessions of Faith*, ed., Lumpkin, 251.

Mullins believed one could arrive at a harmonious interpretation, and that interpretation stood as the correct interpretation.[66]

After the address appeared in *CI* Mullins asked other key leaders in the SBC to give their appraisal of the paper. Several letters between Mullins and Scarborough ensued as a result of this request. Two things stand out as one reads these letters. First of all, one notices the level of respect and civility demonstrated by both men. Secondly, and more importantly, each appeals to the same principle of interpretation.

Scarborough, in his first letter, writes very approvingly of Mullins address in terms of its overall effect and defense of the traditional Baptist understanding of baptism's relationship to forgiveness and the new birth. However, he made several suggestions which he hoped would give greater strength to Mullins' argument. Scarborough felt that Mullins failed to include certain texts and so left some holes in his argument that, if filled, would strengthen it. Scarborough further suggested that portions of Mullins' argument did not properly harmonize certain texts of Scripture.[67] In his reply, Mullins argued that his understanding did harmonize the texts in question (Matt 3:11 and Acts 2:38).[68] In the course of the interchange between these two Baptist giants it is evident that both held to the full authority of Scripture and to the principle that Scripture should be used to interpret Scripture.[69]

Many argued from Mullins' *The Christian Religion in its Doctrinal Expression* that he sought to make religious experience the basis upon which a person determined what to believe. Did Mullins intend to elevate experience to so lofty a position? "The Christian religion has to do with two great groups of facts: the facts of experience and the facts of the historical revelation of God through Christ." Mullins argued that neither personal experience nor revelation should be viewed separate from the other.[70] It was precisely the historical revelation of God in Christ in the Scriptures which served as a safeguard against a purely subjective

66. Mullins, "What is the New Testament Teaching on the Relation of Baptism to the Remission of Sins and the New Birth?" *CI*, 3 May 1906, 2.

67. Scarborough to Mullins, 2 June 1906, E. Y. Mullins Collection, BCL.

68. Mullins to Scarborough, 15 June 1906, E. Y. Mullins Collection, BCL.

69. This should not be taken to mean, however, that either felt linguistic or historical studies were unnecessary, as subsequent letters delved deeply into the lexical understanding of terms as well as grammatical constructions.

70. Mullins, *The Christian Religion in its Doctrinal Expression*, 18.

religion.[71] For Mullins and the other members of the 1924 Committee the final determining issue was not religious experience but loyalty "to the facts of Christianity as revealed in the Scriptures."[72] For Mullins and his generation the clear teachings of the Bible stood as the certain, final arbiter and safeguard against a relativist or subjectivist faith rooted in experientialism.[73]

The Battle against Modernism

Though not impacted as directly as Baptists in the North, Baptists in the South faced the challenge of Modernism. They faced the problem in several ways.

The "Fraternal Letter"

In the beginning of the twentieth century, Baptists in the North and South faced a number of questions as a result of the rise of modernity. Evolution was gaining ground in many areas of investigation.[74] German higher criticism and liberal theology threatened institutions of higher education where ministers sought training.[75]

Baptists in the South held to their confessional heritage and set forth the "Fraternal Letter" as a document of accountability for missionaries.[76]

The "Fraternal Letter" generated its own controversy. Edward Pollard, of Crozier Seminary, came out against it in an article published in the

71. Ibid., 20, 41.

72. *Annual of the Southern Baptist Convention 1925*, 76.

73. Mullins presents the reader of his works with great difficulty at this point. His emphasis on personalism, individualism, and pragmatism can be used to build a theological method that subordinates Scripture to the individual's religious experience. As seen above, however, he often follows what the Puritans called the "rule of faith," letting Scripture interpret Scripture.

74. For an example of evolutionary influence in theology, see Strong, *Systematic Theology*, 391–97.

75. Extract from Minutes of Conference at Columbia, Missouri, 1923?, BCL. Developments at the University of Chicago and Colgate-Rochester Divinity School demonstrate that Northern Baptists found themselves more hard-pressed by the liberal threat than their Southern brethren. An attempt made by leaders in both denominations to forge a common confessional statement intended to stem the tide of liberalism, with E. Y. Mullins as co-chairman of the joint committee, failed.

76. The first document was the "Fraternal Letter" of 1920. It contained a short doctrinal summary which all Foreign Mission Board appointees were expected to sign. See McBeth, *A Sourcebook for Baptist Heritage*, 485.

RH. Pollard said, "Is this a step toward leading Baptists to a creedal basis of fellowship? Formerly their fraternalism was supposed to rest upon an experience basis." He also questioned whether a doctrinal formula could serve the purpose of uniting Baptists.[77] Clearly some feared that any confessional statement adopted by a Baptist body larger than the local association posed a serious infringement upon the principle of soul liberty. Such concerns existed, not only among the Northern Baptists, but also among some Southern Baptists.

The Baptist Faith and Message 1925

The "Fraternal Letter" proved insufficient to assuage the fears of many Southern Baptists concerning the encroachment of modernist thinking in Southern Baptist schools. In 1924 the Convention appointed a Committee on Baptist Faith and Message, and Mullins, as Convention President, chaired it. The Committee presented to the 1925 Convention in Memphis, Tennessee, the Baptist Faith and Message. This document, essentially a revision of the New Hampshire Confession of Faith, sought to affirm all the essentials, or fundamentals, of the Baptist faith, but failed to denounce evolution by name.

Certain conservative leaders in the Convention felt the statement should more directly confront the threat of evolutionary teaching. C. P. Stealey, of Oklahoma, introduced an amendment to replace the proposed article on "The Fall of Man" in which he affirmed the direct creation of man in the image of God and used language specifically designed to rule out evolution.[78]

Mullins anticipated the conservative reaction in his address before the Convention. Mullins stated, "It was said in the morningpaper [*sic*] that there was nothing about Evolution in this report, and that isn't true." He went on to say, "There is, in this report, a very definite reference to Evolution." He then read from the section on "Science and Religion" where the Committee placed the burden of proof squarely on the shoulders of the scientific community to prove their theory. The same quotation affirmed man as a direct creation of God.[79] Nevertheless, some did not think the language of the BFM 1925 or Mullins' speech strong enough

77. Pollard, "An Open Letter to Dr. Love," *RH*, 29 January 1920, 2.

78. *Annual of the SBC 1925*, 76.

79. Address by E. Y. Mullins to the Southern Baptist Convention, 1925, E. Y. Mullins Collection, BCL, 1.

to exclude evolution, and were quite vocal about it.[80] After lengthy debate Stealey's motion failed and the BFM was adopted as presented to the Convention.[81]

The McDaniel Statement, 1926

At the 1926 Convention the issue of evolution resurfaced. George W. Truett nominated and the Convention elected George W. McDaniel of Virginia, for president, of the Convention.[82] McDaniel, in his May 12 address to the Convention, concluded by stating

> This Convention accepts Genesis as teaching that man was the special creation of God, and rejects every theory, evolution or other, which teaches that man originated in, or came by way of, a lower animal ancestry.[83]

M. E. Dodd of Louisiana made the motion that the "McDaniel Statement" (as it came to be known) be accepted as the sentiment of the Convention. The motion passed unanimously.[84]

On 15 May S. E. Hull offered a resolution to the Convention recognizing the rejection of evolution on 12 May, and gratefully acknowledged Southwestern's acceptance of the Statement. His resolution further called on all Convention schools and agencies "to give like assurance to the Convention and to our Baptist Brotherhood in general, of a hearty and individual acceptance of the said action of the Convention" for the purpose of bringing an end to the question of evolutionary teaching among Southern Baptist funded entities.[85]

David William Downs, in his Th.M. thesis, saw the adoption of the McDaniel statement as an instance of encroaching creedalism in Southern Baptist life. He offered this assessment of confessions: "Baptists have traditionally interpreted their confessional statements as guides for faith and not as creeds requiring personal assent."[86] Downs argued that the

---

80. Autrey to Mullins, 15 July 1925, E. Y. Mullins Collection, BCL.

81. *Annual of the SBC 1925*, 76.

82. *Annual of the Southern Baptist Convention 1926*, 17.

83. Ibid., 18.

84. Ibid.

85. Ibid., 98.

86. Downs, "The McDaniel Statement: An Investigation of Creedalism in the Southern Baptist Convention," 1. See chap. 4 of this work for an evidentiary refutation of Downs' view of Baptist confessionalism.

McDaniel statement "later became a tool by which some in the Southern Baptist Convention sought to bring about theological uniformity."[87]

It is more likely the case that Southern Baptists, more familiar with the past history of confessional usage in the churches, held on to a practice of doctrinal accountability they inherited from their spiritual ancestors. Mullins teaching on soul competency required a reformulation of the legitimate uses of Baptist confessional statements in a manner consistent with the prevailing *Zeitgeist* of individualism.

In its 1925 report to the Convention, the Committee on Baptist Faith and Message included a supplementary statement on "Science and Religion" which they did not include as a formal part of the confession. After giving a lengthy affirmation of the supernatural elements of the Christian faith, the statement noted, "We believe that adherence to the above truths and facts is a necessary condition of service for teachers in our Baptist schools." "Teachers in our schools should be careful to free themselves from any suspicion of disloyalty on this point."[88]

Apparently, the vast majority of messengers present did not see such requirements from educators in Baptist schools as an infringement on liberty of conscience or any violation of the principle of soul competency, for the motion to adopt the BFM 1925 carried. This represents an admission of the possible use of confessions as documents of accountability which Baptists had followed in previous centuries.

Reinterpreting the Role of Baptist Confessions

Mullins received the primary task of editing the New Hampshire Confession of Faith to suit the contemporary needs of Southern Baptists in 1925. In so doing, he wrote an "Introduction" which did not make the final draft, although the Preamble contained the essential substance of it in a much shorter form. In his Introduction Mullins highlighted several potential dangers of a confessional statement. The first danger focused on the possibility that some would attempt to substitute a creedal formula for the Scriptures as authoritative. A second danger was that mere orthodoxy will be confused with saving faith. A third danger noted that the statement could be used like a whip to compel conformity. A fourth danger was that it might weaken the local churches' sense of autonomy in their

87. Ibid.

88. *Annual of the SBC, 1925,* 76.

responsibility to interpret Scripture. Lastly, he noted that the various bodies of the Convention did not exist primarily for doctrinal purposes, and so such a statement could, if misused, weaken the cooperative principle.[89]

As a check on these dangers, Mullins suggested certain limitations on the use of confessional statements generated by and for the denomination. First of all, such confessions should be viewed as "setting forth in brief outline" the beliefs held by the group at that time. They should never be viewed as legislative documents or as having any power to coerce the conscience of others. Confessions usually arise out of times of doctrinal confusion and serve the purpose of putting at ease those who are disturbed, and establishing doctrinal signposts for those who have difficulty in discerning truth from error. Any confession must be drawn, then, from the Scriptures and must answer to the religious needs of humanity.[90]

Secondly, confessions cannot limit themselves simply to prescribing the way of salvation. They cover a variety of doctrinal matters, but also do not exhaust the field of doctrinal inquiry or provide final answers to all questions. "Each statement is an attempt to express the meaning of the teachings of Scripture. The common basis of all is loyalty to the Scriptures." Where difference of interpretation arises regarding some article of the faith, the final test remains loyalty to the Bible as God's word. Mullins called the Bible "the common ground on which all should stand."[91]

In the final text of the BFM 1925 the Preamble listed five basic presuppositions which attend to the Baptist practice of circulating confessional statements. The first was the principle of consensus. Such documents form a consensus of the views held by those who adopt the confession and should serve only as guides. Acceptance of the confessional statement does not ensure salvation for anyone. Secondly, they were never regarded as complete systems of theology. They remain subject to revision by later generations. Thirdly, any group of Baptists had the right to write and distribute its own confessional statement. Fourthly, "That the sole authority for faith and practice among Baptists is the Scriptures of the Old and New Testaments." Fifthly, "they are statements of religious convictions, drawn from the Scriptures."[92] A number of Southern Baptists attempted to reject

89. Mullins, "Introduction" to Mullins' revision of the New Hampshire Declaration of Faith, 6 March 1925, E. Y. Mullins Collection, BCL, 2–3.

90. Ibid., 1–2.

91. Ibid., 2.

92. *Annual of the SBC 1925,* 71.

the confessional heritage of the Convention, or at least redefine it in terms which allowed greater latitude in matters of private interpretation.

The BFM 1925 and Anti-Confessionalism

Two controversies erupted around the BFM 1925. A conservative reaction sought a more open refutation of evolution described above. The other was an anti-confessional reaction. Not everyone got what they wanted from the new confession adopted by the Convention in 1925.

John H. White set forth the anti-confessional argument in the *RH* by reproducing the 1856 statement of Francis Wayland on creeds in Baptist life. Then he made the statement: "The question we will have to face in Memphis is whether the Southern Baptist Convention is authorized to take a step in the direction of abandonment of the Baptist position on creeds." He feared that the Convention would establish itself as an ecclesiastical authority over the local churches.[93] In another article Hilton Jackson attributed the weak leadership among Northern Baptists to the repeated attempts to adopt a confessional statement and feared that the mere introduction of such a document would weaken the role of leaders in the SBC.[94] In yet another article, W. O. Carver accused the leadership of the SBC of "Presbyterianizing" the Convention by pressing for the adoption of a confession.[95]

It appears that the Preamble to the BFM 1925, along with the fact that the Convention did not require any church to change its own confession or adopt the new one, provided a sufficient answer to the charges raised by the voices of anti-confessionalism. No record exists in the Convention *Annual* for 1925 of any debate about the propriety of the Committee's recommending a confession to the Convention. That the Convention did not require churches to subscribe to the new confession, however, did not mean that it could not require persons in denominational institutions to do so, as will be seen below.

93. White, "An Old and Strong Statement of the Baptist Position on Creeds," *RH* (Richmond), 2 April 1925, 3.

94. Jackson, "That Creedal Business," *RH* (Richmond), 16 April 1925, 3, 7.

95. Carver, "The Baptist, His Creed, and His Fellowship," *RH* (Richmond), 7 May 1925, 11.

The BFM 1925 and Fundamentalism

The adoption of the BFM 1925 came at a pivotal time, not just in the Convention's history, but in the history of Christianity in the United States. The battle raged between Liberalism and Fundamentalism. In the midst of this battle, what kind of document was the BFM 1925? The members of the Committee saw it as a document which sought to defend the fundamentals of the faith so that the SBC would not go down the path its Northern brethren had taken. This can be proven by looking at what the document affirmed and did not affirm.

Mullins and the Committee used great care, as seen above, to defend in the strongest possible language, the supernatural elements of the Christian faith. The Bible, not experience, remained the central test for doctrinal fidelity in the Preamble and in Article One, "The Scriptures." In Article Two the document speaks of man as a special creation of God as recorded in Genesis. Without specifically naming evolution, this statement excludes it. Article Four affirms the virgin birth of the Lord, and Article Sixteen affirms the bodily resurrection. Without falling into theological hairsplitting, the document carries a fundamentalist tone throughout. Mullins himself declared before the Convention that no modernists served on the Committee on the Baptist Faith and Message.[96] Inasmuch as the document was designed to refute the growing anti-supernaturalist tendencies that were at work in the nation, the BFM 1925 stood as a fundamentalist document. That is not to say that every self-avowed Fundamentalist preferred it. The record clearly shows that some did not like it. However, Mullins himself spoke of a brother at the convention, "one of the most conservative brethren in this convention" who said he could not see why any conservative Southern Baptist would reject the BFM 1925.[97]

In 1925 Baptist confessionalism, though modified somewhat from its original usage, survived. Trends set in motion by the writings of E. Y. Mullins himself, however, would make that more difficult in the days ahead. Mullins introduced Southern Baptists to a more subjective approach to Christian faith and doctrine. This approach, as seen above, shared affinities with the philosophical systems of James (individualism) and Bowne (personalism), and the theological approach of Schleiermacher

96. Mullins, Address, 2.
97. Ibid.

(experientialism). Furthermore, though Mullins continued to embrace the Baptist confessional heritage, he made significant modifications in it, possibly as a result of his experience with Baptists in the North, who rejected denominational confessionalism.

BAPTIST CONFESSIONALISM AND THE GROWTH OF INDIVIDUALISM

Mullins's *The Christian Religion in its Doctrinal Expression* replaced Boyce's *Abstract of Systematic Theology* as the standard textbook at SBTS during Mullins's time there as President and teacher. In this way Mullins's influence spread from Southern to other schools, where others further modified his new approach to Baptist doctrine. W. T. Conner stands as one of the Convention's leading voices in theology from the mid 1930s to the time of his death in the 1950s. His position at SWBTS enabled him to influence many pastors and potential denominational leaders. Four members of the 1963 Committee studied at Southwestern: W. Burman Timberlake held a Th.D., Nane Starnes held a Master's degree, Hugh R. Bumpass held a Master's degree, and James H. Landes held a Master's degree.[98] Conner's influence extended beyond the boundaries of Southwestern through the publication of his works on Christian doctrine.[99]

Tracing out further modifications to Mullins's theological approach and its impact on Southern Baptist life requires an examination of Conner's life and work.

W. T. Conner

Walter Thomas Conner was born 19 January 1877, to Philip Orlander Conner and Frances Jane Monk Conner, in Cleveland County, Arkansas. The family moved in 1892 to present day Tye, Texas, near Abilene. He came to faith in Christ in 1894, at a Methodist meeting, received baptism and united with the Harmony Baptist Church, Caps, Texas. He made his

---

98. Webb, BP, 19 July 1962.

99. Conner, *Revelation and God*; Conner, *The Gospel of Redemption*; Conner, *Christian Doctrine*. Conner published numerous other works, including a NT theology. *Christian Doctrine* is a condensed, single volume version of *Revelation and God* and *The Gospel of Redemption*.

first public acknowledgment of a call to the ministry in 1895, and assumed his first pastorate at Tuscola, Texas, in 1898.[100]

Conner's formal ministerial education began at Simmons College (now Hardin-Simmons University). He completed his B.A. at Baylor University, and also pursued his Th.B. at Southwestern Seminary under B. H. Carroll. He received his M.A. from Baylor University. He taught briefly at Baylor and, when offered a teaching position at Southwestern upon satisfaction of academic credentials, moved to Rochester Theological Seminary where he received his B.D. in 1910. He also studied briefly at the University of Chicago under George B. Foster. In 1914 he received a study leave and moved to Louisville, Kentucky, where he studied theology under Mullins and psychology of religion under Carver. He received the Th.D. in 1916 after writing his dissertation, "Pragmatism and Theology." He returned in 1920 for six weeks to the University of Chicago. Upon writing an additional thesis on "The Idea of the Incarnation in the Gospel of John" he received a Ph.D. from SBTS in 1931.[101]

Subordination of Scripture

Conner subordinated the Scriptures to other factors in his consideration of the doctrine of revelation. His understanding of persons as spiritual beings found its basis in the philosophy of personalism rather than biblical teaching. Garrett noted that "Conner clearly differentiated revelation and the Bible, which is the product and record of unique and historic divine revelation and a book of religion."[102] Bush and Nettles noted that Conner believed the Bible had "revelation value for us." Conner located the central problem in the area of hermeneutics. The biblical text's total context had to be taken into account when interpreting it. The interpreter had to "distinguish between form and substance" in the Bible. This served as Conner's method of preserving the "spiritual truth" of Scripture regardless of the prevailing knowledge of ascertainable scientific facts which might appear to contradict the biblical record.[103]

---

100. Garrett, "Walter Thomas Conner," in *Baptist Theologians*, ed. George and Dockery, 419–20.

101. Ibid., 422–23. At Rochester, Conner studied under Walter Rauschenbusch, A. H. Strong, William A. Stevens, and H C. Mabie.

102. Ibid., 425.

103. Bush and Nettles, *Baptists and the Bible*, 287–89.

Conner's theology of revelation and Scripture showed heavy influences from Strong and Mullins. For Conner the Bible focused on redemption, and Christ served as the interpretive key to its contents.[104] Conner, more than Mullins, focused on the religious experience of the believer. This led him to discount the debate over biblical inerrancy. He recognized the Bible as an inspired record which demanded proper interpretation, and he viewed its authority as final as the voice of Christ.[105]

Elevation of the Individual Over the Corporate

McNeil pointed out that Conner shared in the philosophical outlook of Mullins in emphasizing personalism and individualism. He viewed the church as a voluntary association of individuals constituted as a church by the Holy Spirit. The church as a Christian democracy flowed from Conner's concept of the individual indwelt by the Holy Spirit. Though Conner, at points, emphasized the corporate nature of the priesthood of believers, "By the middle of the twentieth-century, the individualistic interpretation given to the doctrine . . . was well entrenched in Southern Baptist thought."[106]

"Statement on Baptist Distinctives," 1946

In 1946 the SBC adopted a "Statement on Principles" in order to "define their meaning and mission in relation to the gospel and in relation to the world." According to this statement the distinctive Baptist contribution to Christian thought "is our Doctrine of Man in the personal order of life."[107]

In this statement four key distinctives about man appeared: (1) the infinite value God places on the individual; (2) personal competency from God enabling each person to deal with God and others; (3) individual rights and privileges given inalienably by God; and (4) "Man consequently has supreme and compelling responsibility under God for the full realization of his possibilities as a human being."[108]

104. Garrett, "Walter Thomas Conner," 425.

105. Bush and Nettles, *Baptists and the Bible*, 290; Garrett, "Walter Thomas Conner," 425.

106. McNeal, "The Priesthood of All Believers," in *Has Our Theology Changed?* ed. Basden, 216–17.

107. Fuller et al., "Statement of Principles," in *Annual of the Southern Baptist Convention, 1946*, 38.

108. Ibid.

From this the committee drew five Baptist convictions regarding religious experience: (1) regeneration and conversion stand as the first religious experience and as such must precede church membership; (2) the local church as a voluntary body of individual believers is accountable only to Christ and its form of governance is democratic; (3) the New Testament, "as the divinely inspired record and interpretation of the supreme revelation of God" given in Christ is the only authority for doctrine and practice; (4) church and state must serve the public welfare in their respective areas without intruding upon the other; and (5) all of these principles taken together necessitated complete religious freedom, which includes the freedom to evangelize and propagate religious views as a basic right given by God.[109]

In the "Statement of Principles" the influence of Mullins and Conner on Baptist thought stands out. The following items from the "Statement on Principles" are worthy of special notice. First, the emphasis on the individual person shows continuity with the preceding discussion of personalism, religious experience, and individualism highlighted in the treatment of Mullins and Conner. Secondly, the affirmation that the Bible, or more specifically, the New Testament, is the "record" of God's revelation demonstrates yet another confirmation of the shift in Baptist thought reflected first in the writings of Mullins, and then in Conner. Thirdly, the emphasis on the inalienable individual right to religious liberty rooted in soul competency rather than God's lordship over the conscience stands as a significant departure from previous centuries of Baptist writings on the subject as demonstrated in the previous chapter. The very foundations of Baptist ecclesiology and religious liberty were in the process of change. A new philosophical paradigm shift occurred which could result only in conflict as Baptist educators on the one hand sought to exercise liberty in the classroom and rank and file Baptists on the other expected doctrinal orthodoxy from those graduating from the Convention's schools.

Conflicting Views of Baptist Confessionalism in the Early 1960s

By the early 1960s Southern Baptists had developed a conflicted sense of identity in regard to the use of confessions of faith. As Mohler noted, "soul competency also serves as an acid dissolving religious authority, congre-

---

109. Ibid.

gationalism, confessionalism, and mutual accountability."[110] Hudson, too, noted that "The practical effect of the stress upon 'soul competency' as the cardinal doctrine of the Baptists was to make every man's hat his own church."[111] Baptist ambivalence towards confessions as instruments of accountability received further impetus from W. L. Lumpkin, with his *Baptist Confessions of Faith*, first published in 1959. In chapter 1 he wrote, "The Baptist Movement has traditionally been non-creedal in the sense that it has not erected authoritative confessions of faith as official bases of organization and tests of orthodoxy."[112]

"No creed but the Bible"

The Committee on Baptist Faith and Message found itself confronted on one had by those who advocated "no creed but the Bible." Advocates of this position wrote in the state papers and in personal letters to the Committee.

In the 14 June 1962 issue of the *AIB*, Macon commended Hobbs for his handling of the Convention in general, and specifically for the resolution to revisit the BFM 1925. The Committee would not make the statement "final" and so would prevent it from assuming the status of "creed." Macon clearly equated an unalterable doctrinal statement with a "creed" and commended Hobbs for avoiding creedalism of this type.[113]

Erwin L. McDonald, writing in the *AkB*, expressed dismay at attempts by freedom loving Baptists to judge the orthodoxy of another person. Writing of the concerns over Elliott and Moody which prompted the formation of the Committee on Baptist Faith and Message, McDonald said, "It was a strange order of business for a convention of Baptists, who have

---

110. Mohler, *Baptist Theology at the Crossroads*, 19.

111. Hudson, *Baptists in Transition: Individualism and Christian Responsibility*, 142. Hudson, in the paragraph prior to the quote cited, notes that the individualistic tendency in Baptist apologetics of the early twentieth century failed "to provide detailed guidance for questions of church order beyond such generalized corollary axioms as 'all believers have a right to interpret the Bible for themselves' and 'all believers have a right to equal privileges in the church'; but it also served to dissolve any real concept of the church, for it interpreted the faith as a one-to-one relationship between God and the individual."

112. Lumpkin, *Baptist Confessions of Faith*, 16. Numerous articles have appeared since 1963 in both *BHH* and *R&E* in an attempt to argue for and against the use of confessions in Baptist life as sources of accountability. See the bibliography for a listing of these articles.

113. Macon, "At the Convention," *AIB* (Birmingham), 14 June 1962.

prided themselves across the centuries for their religious liberty, to at-tempt to put a theological straight-jacket of conformity on everybody."[114]

Mrs. W. A. Breining, of Amarillo, Texas, wrote to Hobbs on 23 May 1962, and called on the Convention simply to "pledge allegiance to the Bible" like the Church of Christ.[115] This tendency to minimize confessions and just "believe the Bible" continued to grow from the mid-nineteenth century down to the early 1960s, yet it never completely dominated the SBC.

Calls for Confessional Accountability

Many Southern Baptists demonstrated alarm over the teachings of Moody and Elliott. They saw that confessional accountability served as a potential check on aberrant teachings in denominational schools. L. E. Barton, a ninety-three year old retired Southern Baptist pastor from Montgomery, Alabama, wrote to Hobbs on 29 June 1962. He accused Hobbs of affirm-ing that Baptists never had a confession of faith. He pointed out the long history of Baptist confessions while noting that they were never made "binding on others." He listed several key fundamentals of the faith and accused those who would teach contrary to such doctrines of not being genuine Baptists. Such teachers should be dismissed from teaching in Southern Baptist seminaries. He expressed deep concern over the tenacity with which east coast liberals fought for the right to teach heresy under the banner of academic freedom.[116] Hobbs responded to Barton that he understood that Baptists always had confessions of faith, but that there is a distinction between a confession and a creed. He said nothing in the letter about how he understood the distinction.[117]

Ted Moorhead Jr. of Central Baptist Church, Melbourne, Florida, wrote to Hobbs to caution him regarding the inherent authority a confes-sional statement coming from the Convention would carry. Only those doctrines upon which all find common agreement ought to be included, and Moorhead favored a complete rewrite over revising the 1925 BFM. He preferred a shorter statement covering only the most fundamental of doctrinal concerns as a way of securing denominational unity. On the

114. McDonald, "Who is to be papa?" *AkB* (Little Rock), 14 June 1962, 4.

115. Breining to Hobbs, 23 May May 1962, BFM file, folder 1, SBHLA.

116. Barton to Hobbs, 29 June 1962, BFM file, folder 1, SBHLA.

117. Hobbs to Barton, 10 July 1962, BFM file, folder 2, SBHLA.

whole Moorhead sought to encourage Hobbs and the Committee and commended them for their dedication and labor.[118]

THE CONFLICTED ROLE OF THE COMMITTEE

Preserve a Place for Individual Autonomy

In light of the trend toward individualism, personalism, and religious experience in the aftermath of E. Y. Mullins and W. T. Conner, the Committee on Baptist Faith and Message found themselves faced with the need to preserve a strong position for individual autonomy. The concept of the right to personal interpretation became deeply ingrained in Southern Baptist life. The Committee faced a careful balancing act in its need to reassure Southern Baptists that doctrinal standards would be maintained while at the same time not appearing to intrude upon the rights of the individual.

Preserve a Semblance of Confessional Orthodoxy

Southern Baptist pastors and lay members alike expressed alarm over the teachings and writings of Elliott and Moody. The Committee knew full well that any doctrinal statement must not appear to weaken Southern Baptist orthodoxy. Hobbs wrote reassuringly to David Anderson, of North Charleston, South Carolina: "I do not anticipate a great deal of change in the body of the statement."[119] This proved to be a repeated theme in a number of letters Hobbs wrote to concerned Southern Baptists between June of 1962 and March of 1963 when the final draft was released to the public via BP. As Hefley pointed out, the responsibility fell to Convention leaders to "hold down the right" and "reassure the people that 'all Southern Baptist teachers believe the Bible.'"[120]

CONCLUSION

Chapter 4 demonstrated that in Southern Baptist life prior to the twentieth century the concepts soul liberty and corporate accountability rested harmoniously on four supports: (1) the rights of the individual as a member of society; (2) a commonly shared view of the Bible along with a com-

---

118. Moorhead to Hobbs, 25 July 1962, BFM file, folder 3, SBHLA.

119. Hobbs to Anderson, 6 July 1962, BFM file, folder 1, SBHLA.

120. Hefley, *The Conservative Resurgence in the Southern Baptist Convention*, 28.

monly held principle of interpretation; (3) the individual as a Christian living in voluntary fellowship with other Christians in the church; and (4) the local church living in fellowship with other churches through voluntary associational ties.

Prior to the writing and teaching ministries of Mullins and Conner Baptists knew nothing of the concept of using Jesus Christ as an interpretive key (in the sense of a "corrective" key) to the Scriptures (as assumed by some in the BFM 1963).[121]

With *The Axioms of Religion* and *The Christian Religion in Its Doctrinal Expression* Mullins set Southern Baptists on a new trajectory in Baptist identity. This new direction undermined the role of confessions as instruments of accountability as it received further development at the hands of Conner, the Committee on Baptist Principles, and the emphasis on personal experience in the writings of Hobbs.

When the crises surrounding Moody and Elliott prompted the SBC to form a new Committee on Baptist Faith and Message the theological and philosophical makeup of the Convention had broadened considerably from that which the Mullins committee faced. In order for the Committee to apply the use of Baptist confessions in a manner consistent with the 1925 Preamble, changes would have to allow for this broadened constituency.[122] At the same time the Committee had to assure the conservative core of the Convention that received doctrinal norms would be upheld. In its final form the Preamble to the 1963 BFM preserved the accepted view of Baptist confessionalism handed down by Mullins in 1925 and further augmented it in the direction of the individual's experience of Jesus. How the Committee went about making changes in the confessional expression of Baptist doctrine is the subject matter of chapter 6.

---

121. Dunn seems to contest this in his article, but when Mullins is read in context the argument seems unconvincing. See Dunn, "Soul Comptetency," 63.

122. Both the 1925 and the 1963 Preamble states that "That [confessions] constitute a consensus of opinion of some Baptist body." Herschel H. Hobbs, et. al., "Report of the Committee on Baptist Faith and Message" in *Annual of the Southern Baptist Convention 1963*, 269.

6

The Work of the Committee
on Baptist Faith and Message

FORMATION OF THE COMMITTEE, SUBCOMMITTEE
AND INITIAL DRAFTS

I N LIGHT OF THE theological controversies surrounding Elliott and Moody, the leadership of the SBC took action to assure the grass-roots constituency of the theological soundness of the Convention's institutions.

Hobbs later noted that Elliott's book occasioned but did not cause the doctrinal controversy. In early 1962 Hobbs met with Porter Routh and Albert McClellan in his office to discuss the matter. Routh suggested a new Committee to make a fresh study of the BFM 1925. Hobbs and McClellan agreed. They determined that the state convention presidents would be closest to the people, and so they would make up the Committee. Hobbs said that the initial plan also included the presidents of the seminaries.[1]

At the recommendation of K. Owen White, the 1962 Convention approved a resolution affirming the Convention's belief in the Bible as God's written word. Hobbs, at the direction of the 1962 Convention, and acting as president, wrote the leaders of the seminaries and other SBC agencies, noting that the Convention "courteously requested that all of our agencies shall work out any problems within the framework of the freedom inherent in the structure of the agencies." The Convention "issued no mandates," and Hobbs wrote, "I know that all of us will be mindful of these actions as we make any adjustments that might be necessary."[2]

1. Hobbs, "The Baptist Faith and Message," in *The People Called Baptists and The Baptist Faith and Message*, 28.

2. Hobbs to McCall, 16 June 1962, BFM file, folder 1, SBHLA. Each seminary president received the same letter, and denominational agency heads received similar letters.

Hobbs and other leaders pursued a further remedy, also. At the 1962 Convention a recommendation passed authorizing the formation of a new Committee on Baptist Faith and Message to review the 1925 document with a view to revising it for the needs of the day.

> We recommend, therefore, that the president of this Convention be requested to call a meeting of the men now serving as presidents of the various state conventions, and who would qualify as a member of the Southern Baptist Convention committee under Article 18, along with one representative who shall be selected by each seminary to present to the Convention in Kansas City some similar statement which shall serve as information to the churches, but which may serve as guide lines to the various agencies of the Southern Baptist Convention.[3]

The following served on the Committee: Howard M. Reaves, Alabama; Ed. J. Packwood, Arizona; C. Z. Holland, Arkansas; W. Burman Timberlake, California; Malcom B. Knight, Florida; Dick H. Hall Jr., Georgia; Charles R. Walker, Illinois; Walter R. Davis, Indiana; Garth Pybas, Kansas; Verlin C. Kruschwitz, Kentucky; Luther B. Hall, Louisiana; Robert Woodward, Maryland; W. Douglas Hudgins, Mississippi; Paul Weber Jr., Missouri; R. A. Long, New Mexico; Nane Starnes, North Carolina; C. Hodge Hockensmith, Ohio; Hugh R. Bumpas, Oklahoma; David G. Anderson, South Carolina; E. Warren Rust, Tennessee; James H. Landes, Texas; R. P. Downey, Virginia; C. Vinton Koons, District of Columbia.[4]

Naylor wrote to Hobbs from Southwestern thanking him for the letter and assuring him that he had already sent a memo to every member of Southwestern's faculty informing them of the Convention's actions. Naylor to Hobbs, 18 June 1962, BFM file, folder 2, SBHLA.

3. Hobbs, "Memo on Baptist Faith and Message," BFM file, folder 1, SBHLA. The phrase "one representative who shall be selected from each seminary" was marked through and a possible change of wording was hand-written: "the presidents of the Seminaries and the executive secretary of the Sunday School Board." Neither of these phrases was included in the final proposal, and an attempt from the floor to include the seminaries in the formal project was rejected by the Convention. *Annual of the SBC* 1962. According to Hobbs the decision to leave out the seminary presidents came at the insistence of E. S. James, who said, "Whether or not it is right or wrong, the people regard the seminaries as a part of this problem." Hobbs, "Baptist Faith and Message," *Hobbs Lectureship*, 29.

4. Minutes of the Southern Baptist Committee "To Study the 1925 Statement of Baptist Faith and Message," 19–20 November 1962, BFM file, folder 4, SBHLA. In 2004 only three members of the Committee remained: Garth Pybas resided in Oklahoma; Walter Davis resided in Ohio; and Verlin Kruschwitz resided in Kentucky. Two of the Committee members were laymen. Twenty of the twenty-two preachers on the Committee were

Hobbs called the first meeting of the whole Committee to convene at the Sunday School Board, Nashville, Tennessee, on 12 July 1962 at 2:00 P.M. In advance of the meeting he sent each member a copy of the BFM 1925.[5] In a letter to Hall, Hobbs noted that he did not anticipate any significant changes in the BFM 1925. He did believe that some things might need to be added and that the introduction might need some work.[6] In this initial meeting the committee defined its task, chose W. Douglas Hudgins as vice-chairman and Dick H. Hall Jr. as secretary.[7] Hobbs chose a subcommittee of five to prepare an initial draft. He appointed to this subcommittee Landes, Starnes, Kruschwitz, Pybas, and Holland. Hobbs chaired the subcommittee, and Hall and Hudgins served as ex-officio members.[8]

The Subcommittee

Hobbs suggested August 9–15 at Ridgecrest, August 28–31 at Gulf Shores, Mississippi, and the day after the September Executive Committee meeting in Nashville as possible meeting dates for the subcommittee. Hobbs asked Hall to consider whether some items added to the New Hampshire Confession by the 1925 Committee should be retained, and whether some things could be combined. He also took notice that it might be necessary to add materials covering items not covered by the BFM 1925.[9] The first meeting of the subcommittee took place August 29–30 at Gulfport.[10] The only written record of action from the first meeting was the scheduling

---

seminary graduates, and six had received doctorates from Southern Baptist seminaries. Hobbs, "Baptist Faith and Message," *Hobbs Lectureship*, 30.

5. Hobbs to Bumpas, City, 20 June 1962, BFM file, folder 1, SBHLA. Each member of the Committee received a similar letter.

6. Hobbs to Hall, 10 July 1962, BFM file, folder 2, SBHLA. Reflecting later on the Committee's work, Hobbs noted that the Committee spent more time on the Preamble than any other single article in the statement. Hobbs, *My Faith and Message: An Autobiography*, 241.

7. Hobbs to Koons, 17 July 1962, BFM file, folder 2, SBHLA.

8. Hobbs to Landes, 16 July 1962, BFM file, folder 2, SBHLA. Each person who served on the subcommittee received a similar letter.

9. Hobbs to Hall, 16 July 1962, BFM file, folder 2, SBHLA.

10. Hobbs to Kruschwitz, 7 August 1962, BFM file, folder 3, SBHLA. Each member of the Committee received a similar letter. Gulf Shores Baptist Assembly is located at Gulfport, Mississippi.

of a second meeting for 20 September at Nashville.[11] Starnes wrote to Leo Garrett, who then taught at the SBTS, asking for a doctrinal statement which might serve as a guide for the Committee to use.[12] In his initial response Garrett suggested that Starnes contact Ray Summers, who had given a series of messages on the 1925 BFM at Ridgecrest.[13] Garrett took the time to compare the BFM 1925, another statement by E. A. McDowell which Starnes sent to him, and the doctrinal statement of Gambrell Street Baptist Church, Fort Worth, and constructed a fresh statement of faith using "the best content of the three" and sent that to Starnes on 22 August 1962.[14]

At Southern, McCall sent a memo to Ward, requesting that he make a copy of the original New Hampshire Confession, including the Preamble. His main concern focused on the doctrine of the church:

> What I am after is to put into the hands of Dick Hall, as secretary of the committee of the Southern Baptist Convention appointed to study the 1925 Statement of Faith, the evidence that the framers of the New Hampshire Confession of Faith did not object to the concept of "the church" though the body of the document does not refer to the church.[15]

A preliminary draft came out of the second meeting. Hall sent a copy to Ward, who had traveled to Cleveland, Tennessee, to preach revival services. This document is the first extant draft of the BFM 1963 known to exist.[16] Ward made numerous notes on this draft and wrote Hall a letter with suggestions for improvement. A comparison of the draft later sent to Mercer University shows that the subcommittee took Ward's suggestions seriously.[17]

---

11. Hobbs to Landes, 7 September 1962, BFM file, folder 3, SBHLA.

12. Starnes to Garrett, 19 July 1962, private collection.

13. Garrett to Starnes 2 August 1962, private collection. Garrett was preparing to leave for Arlington, Virginia, for his sabbatical leave and promised to send materials as soon as possible.

14. Garrett to Starnes, 22 August 1962, private collection. See Appendix 4 for "A Declaration of Basic Beliefs," by James Leo Garrett, private collection.

15. McCall to Ward, 20 July 1962, WWC.

16. Ward to Hall, 20 October 1962, BFM file, folder 4, SBHLA.

17. See Appendix 3, BFM file, folder 4, SBHLA, and WWC.

The Ward Draft

Structurally, what is here called The Ward Draft,[18] follows these divisions: Preamble; I. The Scriptures; II. God; III. Jesus Christ; IV. The Holy Spirit; V. Man; VI. Salvation; VII. God's Purpose of Grace; VIII. A New Testament Church; IX. Baptism and the Lord's Supper; X. The Lord's Day; XI. The Kingdom; XII. Religious Liberty; XIII. Peace and War; XIV. Education; XV. Social Service; XVI. Co-Operation; XVII. Evangelism and Missions; XVIII. Stewardship; XVIX. Last Things.[19]

Several characteristics of this draft stand out. First, the Preamble of this initial draft underwent a great deal of revision. It did not contain any of the materials from the 1925 Preamble. It contained five brief paragraphs, whereas the final Preamble contained twelve paragraphs, including the materials from the 1925 Preamble.

With regard to the doctrine of Scripture, the only substantive change from the 1925 document was the insertion of a sentence which said: "The criterion by which the Bible is to be interpreted is the person, work and teachings of Jesus Christ." According to Ward, he suggested this wording in a conversation with Hobbs over how to resolve the differences between certain aspects of Old Testament law and New Testament practice.[20] Garrett suggested a similar wording in the confession he wrote and sent to Starnes, though the location of the sentence fell in the middle of the article rather than at the end.[21]

While the treatment of God proper received no substantive change, the article on Jesus Christ met with an unsatisfactory review from Ward.[22] The subcommittee clearly meant to safeguard an orthodox Christology but lacked the precision of thought and expression to achieve this goal

18. See Appendix 1, for the An notated Ward Draft, BFM file, folder 4, SBHLA and WWC.

19. Comparisons to the 1925 BFM are based on the text as it appears in the 1925 *Annual of the Southern Baptist Convention*, 71–76.

20. Interview by author, Louisville, Kentucky, 17 April 2002.

21. See Appendix 4, Article I "Revelation and the Scriptures." Garrett wrote: "Written by men who were inspired by the Holy Spirit, the Bible is to be interpreted through careful exegesis under the guidance of the Holy Spirit [and] the criterion of the person, work, and teaching of Jesus Christ, who has fulfilled the law and the prophets and is the Way, the Truth, and the Life."

22. See below.

in the first draft.[23] The article on the Holy Spirit outlined the person and work of the Spirit in relation to revelation, Scripture, interpretation, and the life of the believer. The subcommittee remained silent on the up and coming charismatic question.

With regard to Man, Article V affirms man's created uniqueness in the same language as the 1925 document. The subcommittee replaced the concept of original holiness with original innocence. Man's fall into sin lacked any discussion of the role of the Tempter.[24] In affirming the dignity of each individual as created in the image of God this draft noted, "As such he possesses dignity and is worthy of respect and Christian love, regardless of race or class." At a time when the Civil Rights Movement created unrest for many, this stood as a bold assertion which failed to make the final draft.

Article VI, Salvation, combined what had been Articles IV–VIII and X in the 1925 document. This article, which remained largely unchanged in the final draft, dealt with salvation in terms of regeneration, sanctification, and glorification. Holding to a traditionally Calvinistic understanding of salvation, regeneration "is a change of heart wrought by the Holy Spirit through conviction of sin, to which the sinner responds in repentance toward God and faith in the Lord Jesus Christ."[25] Justification fell under the heading of regeneration as a result of faith in Christ and involves "God's gracious and full acquittal . . . of all sinners who repent and believe in Christ."[26] The article defined sanctification in terms which were both punctiliar and progressive. A single sentence described glorification as the final state of the redeemed.

On the heels of the Apostasy Controversy, the subcommittee combined the paragraph on Perseverance (1925 Article XI) into Article VII, God's Purpose of Grace. They enlarged this paragraph to deal with the issue of eternal security, backsliding, and the operation of the Spirit of

---

23. Ward commented in his letter to Hall of 20 October 1962, "The writing of a Statement of Faith is the most demanding assignment ever undertaken by a group of Christians. It requires more knowledge of sound biblical exegesis, more thorough understanding of the doctrinal debates of church history, and more awareness of the current theological scene than any other Christian task."

24. See Ward's comments below.

25. See Appendix 1, Article IV, 1. See also chapter 7 for a fuller discussion of the doctrine of salvation in the BFM 1963.

26. Ibid.

God in restoring to repentance all who are truly born again. The subcommittee made it clear that Southern Baptists affirm the eternal security of true believers in terms that could not be denied or misconstrued. Minor changes in wording also took place in the first paragraph.

Article VIII, A New Testament Church, reflected more fully the Baptist emphasis on local church autonomy with a new paragraph affirming the headship of Christ over each congregation and the equality of every member. A single sentence stood out as quite significant: "The New Testament speaks of the church as the body of Christ which includes all of the redeemed."[27] This stood as a radical departure from the dominant Landmarkist ideology prevalent in certain portions of the Convention.

Article IX, Baptism and the Lord's Supper, received only one change of wording reflecting a change of practice. Whereas the 1925 Statement said the elements were "bread and wine," this draft stated that they were "bread and the fruit of the vine." This change reflected the effects of Prohibition on Baptist practice in regard to the Lord's Supper.[28] Also, where the 1925 Statement had only one paragraph treating both ordinances, this early draft divided the material into two paragraphs.

Where the 1925 Statement contained three separate articles related to eschatology immediately following the article on The Lord's Day,[29] the 1963 subcommittee dropped these, wrote a new, single paragraph on eschatology and placed it at the end of the document in the Ward Draft.

In evaluating the article on The Kingdom in the 1925 Statement, the subcommittee chose to replace it completely with portions of Garrett's Article IX, Last Things.[30] The subcommittee chose to omit Garrett's comments about God's election of Israel in the Old Testament as well as the purely eschatological materials due to the treatment of eschatology under a separate heading.

After receiving Ward's comments on this initial draft, the subcommittee prepared a second draft. This second draft, reflecting many of the

27. Ibid., Article VIII.

28. See Dobbins, *Baptist Churches in Action*, 157, for an early statement allowing the use of grape juice instead of wine in the Lord's supper.

29. The following articles underwent no substantial changes except, perhaps, in order of arrangement: The Lord's Day, Religious Liberty, Peace and War, Social Service, Co-Operation, and Stewardship.

30. See Appendix 4, Article IX.

changes suggested by Ward,[31] Hall sent to the Department of Christianity at Mercer University.[32]

The Mercer Draft

By looking at the Mercer Draft it can be determined how much Ward influenced the Committee's work at this stage.[33] The Preamble to the Mercer Draft reflected some stylistic changes and one substantive change suggested by Ward.

Structurally, Ward suggested placing the articles on Evangelism and Missions, Education, Stewardship, Co-Operation, The Christian and the Social Order, and Religious Liberty, after the article on Baptism and the Lord's Supper and before the article on the Lord's Day. He also suggested placing the article on Peace and War before the article on The Kingdom. The Mercer Draft follows these structural suggestions exactly.

Without getting into the details of Ward's suggestions, it is sufficient to say at this point that the Mercer Draft reflected his comments. The details of the suggestions made by the Mercer Faculty will be discussed below. From these two early drafts and the suggestions received from Ward and Mercer, the Committee prepared a third draft which they voted to send to the six seminaries and the Sunday School Board for review and comment. Routh's office prepared the copies and distributed them. The Committee also appointed six subcommittees of two members each to meet with representatives from the seminaries.[34]

ENLISTMENT OF OUTSIDE ASSISTANCE

From the very beginning of the process Hobbs sought outside assistance.[35] He demonstrated an acute awareness of the growing diversity within the Convention and planned to produce a document that all could accept

31. The details of Ward's suggestions will be discussed below.

32. Hall to Hobbs, 13 December 1962, BFM file, folder 5, SBHLA. In this letter Hall informs Hobbs that he has sent copies of the Statement to Mercer and planned to meet with John Hurt when the faculty had completed reviewing the document.

33. For the text of the Annotated Mercer Draft see Appendix 2, BFM file, folder 5, SBHLA.

34. Minutes of the Southern Baptist Committee to Study the 1925 Statement of Baptist Faith and Message, 19–20 November 1962. Hall to Ward, 23 November 1962, BFM file, folder 4, SBHLA.

35. Hobbs to Koons, 17 July 1962, BFM file, folder 2, SBHLA.

without sacrificing the conservative doctrinal base of the Convention.[36] Although the plans to include the seminaries as a formal part of the Committee never materialized, Starnes suggested and the Committee agreed to the necessity of working with the seminaries.[37]

Seminary subcommittees

The following subcommittees met with faculty committees from each of the six seminaries: Golden Gate, Doug Hudgins and Jimmy Landes; Midwestern, C. Z. Holland and Robert Woodward; New Orleans, Howard Reaves and David G. Anderson; Southwestern, Warren Rust and Paul Weber Jr.; Southern, Verlin Kruschwitz and R. P. Downey; Southeastern, Dick Hall Jr. and Nane Starnes.[38] No extant records of the meetings with any of the seminaries have been found to date except at Southern Seminary, and these are inaccessible.[39]

All of the seminaries agreed to participate in the review of the document, and the full Committee met again on 6 February 1963 with plans

36. Hobbs to Moorhead, 10 August 1962, BFM file, folder 3, SBHLA. Moorhead to Hobbs, n.d., BFM file, folder 3, SBHLA. Hobbs to Lewter, 5 October 1962, BFM file, folder 3, SBHLA.

37. Starnes to Hobbs, 27 July 1962, BFM file, folder 1, SBHLA.

38. Hobbs, Oklahoma City, to Members of the Seminary Subcommittees, 10 January 1963, courtesy of SBHLA.

39. The only records available related to Southern Seminary are those which have been graciously shared by Wayne Ward and James Leo Garrett, and what is contained in the Dale Moody Collection at the James P. Boyce Centennial Library. According to the President's Office, the records related to these events are legally sealed or are of too sensitive a nature to be made public at this time. In a letter dated 2 July 2002, Paige Patterson wrote that "we have no records that we have been able to find concerning the 1963 *Baptist Faith and Message*." He further noted that "a number of the records from the library disappeared at the time of the coming of my predecessor to be President at the Seminary. If there were records of the involvement of Southeastern and the 1963 *Baptist Faith and Message* my guess is that they left with the records that were taken." From Midwestern Craig Kubic, the librarian, wrote on 25 September 2002, that "our Library does not contain any records related to Faculty discussion on this matter." A personal, thorough search of the Berquist Files failed to find any such records. Michael Pullin, librarian at Southwestern wrote on 5 July 2002, "I searched through the records of Dr. Robert E. Naylor . . . and found nothing on discussions concerning the 1963 Baptist Faith and Message." In an undated, handwritten response, J. Michael Garrett, wrote from New Orleans, "I have been unable to locate any materials here at NOBTS that relate to the 1963 statement." No response to requests for information has been received from Golden Gate Seminary.

to work through 8 February preparing the final draft.[40] H. Leo Eddleman, president of NOBTS wrote to Hobbs expressing his school's readiness to work with Committee.[41] Likewise, Robert Naylor, of Southwestern expressed a ready willingness to assist the Committee.[42]

At Southeastern the response was positive but guarded. Hall wrote to President Stealey in November 1962 requesting a meeting with a faculty committee.[43] Hobbs also wrote to Stealey, "We want our seminaries to share with us their wisdom in these matters so that it may be reflected in the report itself. We need the counsel of all of you."[44] In responding to this Stealey wrote to Hobbs the following:

> I am just wondering if it is understood that what suggestions we make will not be taken as fully sanctioning the whole statement. I do not intend to open a discussion here as to whether or not we should adopt such a statement or this statement in particular. I intend just to ask for better ways of saying whatever is said or for possible changes where some slight changes might be of benefit. The main point is, that I would not like it to be interpreted that the seminary either condemns or approves the statement as a whole.[45]

Hobbs responded that the cooperation of the school would not be interpreted as the school's having sanctioned the document in whole or part. The Committee only desired to have the added input and wisdom of the seminaries.[46] Hall also wrote to Stealey to assure him that "It is not my understanding that we will quote any one or commit any one from these discussions." Hall proposed four possible meeting dates in January of 1963.[47] Pope Duncan and James Tull served as the faculty committee, with Stewart Newman as an alternate.[48]

Perhaps because Hobbs had strong ties to Southern, faculty members from it had been involved with the Committee from a very early point,

40. Hall to Hobbs, 3 December 1962, BFM file, folder 5, SBHLA. Hobbs to Members of the Subcommittee, 10 January 1963, BFM file, folders 5 and 7, SBHLA.

41. Eddleman to Hobbs, 19 December 1962, BFM file, folder 5, SBHLA.

42. Naylor to Hobbs, 29 November 1962, BFM file, folder 4, SBHLA.

43. Hall to Stealey, 21 November 1962, BFM file, folder 4, SBHLA.

44. Hobbs to Stealey, 27 November 1962, BFM file, folder 4, SBHLA.

45. Stealey to Hobbs, 1 December 1962, BFM file, folder 5, SBHLA.

46. Hobbs to Stealey, 11 December 1962, BFM file, folder 5, SBHLA.

47. Hall to Stealey, 13 December 1962, BFM file, folder 5, SBHLA.

48. Stealey to Hall, 14 December 1962, BFM file, folder 5, SBHLA.

as has already been noted. Starnes wrote to Ward in November asking that he "try your hand at writing on 'Jesus Christ'—and on 'Man,'" two articles Ward criticized strongly in the original draft.[49] Hall wrote to Ward suggesting a faculty committee of three to meet with the subcommittee.[50] Hobbs wrote to McCall informing him of the Committee members who would be coming to Southern and asking that he and Downey set the time for the meeting. He also expressed his great appreciation for the help the Southern faculty had given.[51] Kruschwitz received a letter from Downey informing him that he and Downey would meet with McCall and the Southern faculty committee on 18 January 1963.[52] The faculty committee consisted of Wayne Ward and Ray Brown, each of whom had instructions to speak for himself and "reflect . . . as much of the insight of the Southern Seminary faculty as they can."[53]

Input from Southern's Faculty

Based on the available documentation the greatest influence on the Committee's final draft came from members of the faculty of Southern Seminary. Documents indicate that the greatest single influence came from Ward, though Moody's thoughts on Scripture show up in the final draft of the BFM 1963. Garrett also played a part, as previously noted, in some aspects of the work.

Ward

On 20 October 1962 Ward wrote to Hall expressing his appreciation for the Committee's work and the opportunity to evaluate what they had produced. He expressed overall approval with the Committee's work, though he had some concerns. Ward believed the article on "Salvation" improved upon the 1925 document. The editorial work of combining several articles served to improve the overall readability of the document. Ward especially commended the threefold treatment of salvation as instantaneous, ongoing, and future as very helpful.[54]

---

49. Starnes to Ward, 9 November 1962, WWC.
50. Hall to Ward, 23 November 1962, WWC.
51. Hobbs to McCall, 10 December 1962, BFM file, folder 2, SBHLA.
52. Kruschwitz to Hobbs, 21 December 1962, BFM file, folder 5, SBHLA.
53. McCall to Kruschwitz and R. P. Downey, 1 January 1963, WWC.
54. Ward to Hall, 20 October 1962.

Ward's greatest concerns revolved around the treatment of the incarnation of Jesus Christ. He considered the wording "ambiguous" and liable to imply Christological heresies the Committee did not intend. He found the distinction between Jesus' humanity and deity especially reminiscent of Nestorianism. In his final evaluation of the article he said, "This one [article] desperately needs complete re-writing."[55]

Ward also criticized the wording of the article on Man with regard to the origin of sin. He commended the wording on the image of God and the handling of racial issues. He wrote, however, "The source of sin lies ultimately with the Tempter *and not in man*; otherwise man would be irredeemable." He noted that the article said nothing of the role of the Tempter in the fall and commented that this tended to undercut the atonement as presented in the New Testament.[56]

Ward anticipated the day when all faculty members at the seminaries might be required to subscribe to the BFM, and in the form in which he received it, he could not sign it "because it is too unorthodox and misleading in some of its wording." He found traces of Unitarianism because the statement did not sufficiently qualify the unique sinlessness of Jesus.[57] On the basis of these comments Starnes asked Ward to draft new articles on Jesus Christ and Man in the above mentioned letter.

Ward's hand-written comments appear throughout the document, and a careful examination of the draft sent to Mercer shows that the Committee generally followed his recommendations.[58] Many of his notes involved clarification of wording and style, but some, such as the comments above focused on the substance of the articles.

In Article I, The Scriptures, Ward suggested stating that "The Holy Bible is the record of God's revelation of Himself to man." The statement regarding the criterion for interpretation has already been discussed and attributed to him.[59] Related to the production of the Bible, Ward suggested stating that the Holy Spirit "inspired holy men to write the Scriptures."[60]

---

55. Ibid.

56. Ward to Hall, 20 October 1962, emphasis his.

57. Ibid.

58. See Appendix 3.

59. See Appendix 1, Ward Draft, Article I.

60. See Appendix 1, Ward Draft, Article IV.

In Article V, Man, Ward suggested dropping the last clause of the article: "regardless of race or class."[61] Commenting on Article VI, 1., Ward added "It [justification] bring us into a state of peace and favor with God." He also added clarity to the wording on sanctification. In Article VII, God's Purpose of Grace, Ward suggested replacing "saves" with "glorifies."

Ward offered only minor suggestions to Article VIII. A New Testament Church, mostly in the area of more contemporary language or points of clarity. His comments on the ordinances of baptism and the Lord's Supper are of a similar nature.

In Article XV, Social Service, Ward offered an important note of clarity regarding the relationship of the gospel to social ministry. He added that social ministry only has lasting effects when rooted in the conversion of the individual by grace.[62]

In Article XIX Ward inserted "personally and visibly" to denote the nature of the second coming of Christ to the earth.

Evidence indicates that of all the outside influences on the Committee, Ward occupied the greatest level of trust and involvement. It could be argued that the document reflected his theology almost as much as that of Hobbs.

Moody

On 7 January 1963 Moody wrote to McCall with his suggestions for the BFM. He commented extensively on Articles I, II, VI, VII, VIII, IX, XVI, and XIX. With regard to The Scriptures Moody commented that "without any mixture of error" in the New Hampshire Confession referred only to what the Abstract of Principles termed "saving knowledge, faith and obedience." The phrase, he complained, "has been used since to oppose scientific knowledge and the historical-critical study of the Bible." He further suggested that "the teachings of Jesus Christ" be struck from the statement on criterion of interpretation, noting that

> it is already being used by fundamentalists to prove that Moses wrote all five books of the Pentateuch (as they interpret John 5:46f.), the unity of the book of Isaiah (as they interpret Matt 12:17), and the Exile date for Daniel (as they interpret Matt 24:15). This well intended phrase could, under the shadow of the Elliott

61. See Appendix 1, Ward Draft, Article V.

62. This is a paraphrase. For the exact wording see Appendix 1, Ward Draft, Article XV.

controversy, set off a heresy hunt against most of the men who teach Old Testament in the six seminaries.[63]

Moody proposed replacing "He is revealed" with "His eternal reality is revealed" in Article II, God, because he feared the proposed wording could lead to Sabellianism.[64]

He opposed, in Article VI, Salvation, language that reflected Kantian idealism and what he called "faculty psychology" in favor of wording that reflected a more Scriptural expression such as "in the disposition of man."[65]

With regard to Article VII, God's Purpose of Grace, Moody believed that the phrase "real believers" needed defining and suggested retaining from the 1925 Statement "Their continuance in well-doing is the mark which distinguishes them from mere professors." He also noted that excluding the phrase "effectually called" created a "vagueness" of meaning, and he commented on the two schools of thought regarding sanctification (punctiliar versus progressive) and viewed the proposed statement as a shift in Baptist thinking more toward progressive sanctification. He also criticized the statement for failing to harmonize eternal security with Galatians 5:4.[66]

Moody viewed Article VIII as too focused on the local congregation as the expression of the church. "Not even the last sentence recognizes the teaching of the New Testament on the one body of Christ on earth, here and now." He suggested a completely new article based on the Scriptures or the use of the statement in the Abstract of Principles. He also disagreed with the use of "pastor" as the title of an officer. He viewed the term as descriptive of a function and preferred the title "elder" which appeared in previous Baptist confessions.[67]

Moody argued against changing "wine" to "fruit of the vine." He said, "I think the arguments against wine being used in the New Testament celebration of the Lord's Supper, as expressed in an article by Dr. H. H. Hobbs in the Oklahoma *Baptist Messenger*, are untenable." Nevertheless, if

63. Moody to McCall, 7 January 1963, Dale Moody Collection, BCL.

64. Ibid.

65. Ibid.

66. Ibid.

67. Ibid.

the term wine must be dropped Moody proposed the wording "the bread and the cup" as less awkward.[68]

With regard to Articles X–XV, Moody simply questioned why they should even be included in a doctrinal statement.[69]

Some of Moody's comments are hard to pin-point in the document. He objected to the final sentence in Article XVIII and proposed "the full consummation of the ages in the kingdom awaits the return of Jesus Christ" as more fully in line with New Testament teaching. He also suggested replacing Article XIX with Articles XIX and XX from the Abstract of Principles because the proposed article did not deal with the intermediate state of the dead.[70]

Of all of Moody's comments, only the sentence on the criterion for interpreting Scripture appears to have found its way into the final draft. In notes on a copy of the BFM received by the faculty bearing Calloway's name this sentence contained notations similar to Moody's.[71] In a letter Kruschwitz denied that input from the faculty had any bearing at all on the final wording of Article I:

> my recollection is that the full BF&M committee, believing the shorter sentence about "the criterion" in the final draft said everything the longer sentence in the early draft said, unamiously [sic] agreed . . . to go with the shorter sentence. The visit of two members of the committee with the faculty at Southern had absolutely nothing to do with the choice of the shorter sentence.[72]

Garrett

The principle contribution of Garrett has been noted. From his confession the Committee lifted and slightly modified the following for the new article on The Kingdom:

> The Kingdom of God, or God's rule or reign, includes both His general sovereignty over the universe and His particular kingship over men who wilfully acknowledge Him as King. The Kingdom is

68. Ibid. See Hobbs, *The Baptist Faith and Message*, 88.

69. Moody to McCall, 7 January 1963.

70. Ibid.

71. "The Baptist Faith and Message" 1925 and 1962 in parallel columns used by the faculty of the Southern Baptist Theological Seminary, courtesy of WWC.

72. Kruschwits to Smith, 22 May 2003, in the author's possession.

the realm of salvation into which men enter by trustful, childlike commitment to Jesus Christ. Christians ought to pray and labor that the Kingdom may come and God's will be done on earth. Yet the full consummation of the Kingdom awaits the return of Jesus Christ and the end of this age.[73]

This material was taken out of the final article entitled "Last Things." The complete article as submitted by Garrett traced the Kingdom through its historical roots in the election of Israel as the unique people of Yahweh living under his rule. The reign of God, according to Garrett, "was brought near to men with the advent of Jesus and actualized by the reign of God over the subjects of Christ."[74] Garrett further affirmed the Christian hope and expectation of the bodily resurrection of the dead, the final judgment and eternal bliss for God's people and eternal punishment for the wicked.[75]

While the Committee did not use this additional material from Garrett in the BFM treatment of Last Things, the substance of the eschatological hope remained consistent with that he expressed.

Input from Mercer's Faculty

Mercer University's Department of Christianity examined the second draft of the proposed document and returned it with two pages of commentary.[76] First they noted that "the introductory sentence of the draft statement omits the object of our faith: Jesus Christ."[77]

They further critiqued the Preamble, noting that "a growing understanding of truth" reflected nineteenth century liberalism's and twentieth century modernism's infatuation with "progressive revelation." Commenting on addressing the needs of the new generation, they stated

73. See above and Appendix 4, Article IX.

74. Ibid.

75. Ibid.

76. See Appendix 2, Mercer Draft. Mercer's Department of Christianity faculty was composed of the following persons: Henry Lewis Batts, Ph.D., Hartford Seminary, Park Harris Anderson Jr., Th.D., NOBTS, Charles Ray Brewster, S.T.M. Union Theological Seminary, Joseph Millard Hendricks, B.D., SBTS, Thomas Joseph Holmes, B.D., SEBTS, Thomas Young Holloway, Ph.D., Yale University, Hansford Duncan Johnson, LL.D., Newton Theological Institution, Edwin Dargan Johnston, Ph.D., University of Manchester, and Harold Lynn McManus, Ph. D., Yale University; source: "College of Liberal Arts, 1962–1963," *Mercer University Bulletin* 49 (March 1962), no. 2: 11–15.

77. See Appendix 2.

that "this is a concern of humanism and not of Scripture. The gospel witnesses to individuals, and discloses to them the true nature of their 'needs.'" They also recommended excluding "nor as binding upon the consciences" as tacitly condoning false witness. Affirming the historic succession of Baptist confessions appeared to the faculty to put tradition on par with Christ in authority.[78]

Mercer's faculty rejected the phrase "and especially in the New Testament" as a denial that all of Scripture gives uniform testimony to Christ (John 5:39). The entire paragraph on soul competency was marked out, and the note said,

> A. This paragraph ignores that for Baptists, the object of "the individual soul's competency," "freedom in religion" and "the priesthood of the believer" is God, and not "soul" itself, "freedom" itself, the "believer" himself.
>
> B. This draft "statement of faith" ignores in its main body the "great emphasis" of "the individual soul's competency" and "the priesthood of the believer."
>
> C. The paragraph tends to undermine Article I, the Scriptures, by assuming that man is free to select those "certain definite doctrines" which he "holds dear."[79]

All in all, the original Preamble did not fair well with Mercer. The final sentence they rejected entirely as both repetitive and inaccurate in expressing the Scripture's concern, which they noted was "with God's grace and man's rebellion, and not with 'principles' *about* God or man.[80]

In the same way the faculty rejected the expression "principles by which" in Article I, favoring to word the sentence, "It reveals the way God will judge us." The statement regarding the criterion for interpretation met with a similar reception. Mercer recommended: "Scripture is the history of the covenant between God and man revealed in Jesus Christ, and must be read, heard, and interpreted in His light." The proposed criterion statement appeared redundant in light of Article III in their estimation. They further criticized the use of the term "criterion" as connoting "the

---

78. Ibid.
79. Ibid.
80. Ibid., emphasis theirs.

existence of a yardstick by which man can measure or judge Scripture, rather than Scripture measuring and judging man."[81]

According to the Mercer faculty Christ is the locus of trinitarian revelation. In notes in the text on Article II, the faculty amended the sentence to read "He is revealed *by Christ* as Father, Son, and Holy Spirit."[82]

Turning to Article III, they faulted the subcommittee for not affirming the virgin birth and specifying Jesus' bodily appearance before his disciples after his resurrection.[83] The sentence beginning with "He ascended " they considered too content laden for one sentence but could not devise a better replacement on short notice.[84]

With regard to the Holy Spirit, the Mercer faculty considered portions of the text redundant in light of the affirmations about Scripture in Article I.[85]

In the treatment of salvation the faculty found logical inconsistency in stating that sinners are "justified by faith alone," and then asserting what they termed a Pelagian notion: "nothing . . . except man's failure." They further rejected the three-stage approach to explaining salvation as contradicting Paul's teaching. The statement regarding becoming "partakers of the divine nature" through the new birth they likewise rejected as contradicting Paul's teaching in Galatians 2:20ff and 2 Corinthians 5:17ff. They suggested changing "upon principles of His righteousness" to read "on the basis of his righteousness."[86]

Sanctification, as spelled out in this draft, came under intense criticism as tending towards the Holiness movement, in falling into the Enlightenment idea of progress, and the phrase "moral and spiritual perfection" sounded like echoes of humanism.[87]

Without reference to either the state of the redeemed dead or a bodily resurrection, the Mercer faculty found the sentence on glorification empty of any useful or helpful content.[88]

---

81. Ibid.
82. Appendix 2, italicized words denotes their insertion.
83. Ibid.
84. Mercer faculty notes.
85. Ibid.
86. Ibid.
87. Ibid.
88. Ibid.

Mercer's faculty, though lacking in time by their own admission to make a thorough study of the draft, found much in it that needed more work.

CONCLUSION

While Hobbs served as chairman of the Committee and took great pains to involve himself in its revision from beginning to end, the BFM in its 1963 form owed much to many thoughtful contributors. In spite of the fact that Hobbs did not anticipate any significant changes,[89] the document underwent significant changes in several key areas. Exploring those changes will be the focus of chapter 7.

89. Hobbs to Callendar, 10 July 1962, BFM file, folder 2, SBHLA.

7

Substantive Changes in the Baptist Faith and Message

"One of the most drastic revisions of Baptist statements of faith
was in 1963."[1]

HOBBS'S INTENTION AND THE FINAL OUTCOME

H OBBS FACED TWO COMPETING and compelling needs. On the one
hand he expressed a reluctance to alter the content of the BFM 1925
in any substantive way.[2] On the other hand, he expressed a desire to have
a document with which a broad theological base could live.[3] At the outset
Hobbs believed the Committee had three possible choices: (1) recommend a reaffirmation of the 1925 Statement; (2) write a completely new
statement; or (3) revise the 1925 BFM to address the pressing needs of the
Convention. The Committee chose the third option, and in revising the
document the Committee took great pains to protect the conscience of
the individual. In the end Hobbs asserted, "In no sense did it delete from
or add to the basic meaning of the 1925 statement."[4] The evidence shows
that the 1963 BFM reflected changes in Baptist doctrine and practice in-

---

1. Moody, *Who are Sinners?*, audio recording of lecture CA 6089, the Southern Baptist
Theological Seminary Audiovisual Library, 14 May 1984.

2. Hobbs to Callendar, 10 July 1962, BFM file, folder 2, SBHLA.

3. Hobbs to Moorhead , 10 August 1962, BFM file, folder 3, SBHLA.

4. Hobbs, "The Baptist Faith and Message," in *The People Called Baptists and The Baptist
Faith and Message*, 30. Compare with Hobbs, "Southern Baptists and Confessionalism:
A Comparison of the Origins and Contents of the 1925 and 1963 Confesssions," *R&E*
(Winter 1979): 55: "a comparative study of the texts of the documents ... will note in detail
changes, additions, and omissions in the 1963 Confession from the 1925 confession."

dicative of a widening theological base very different from that of the Convention founders, or even Mullins and the 1925 Committee.[5]

In this chapter four key areas of faith and practice will be examined. In each case the reader will see wording reflective of divergent theological perspectives within the document expressive of differing theological viewpoints within the Convention. Changes relative to the arrangement of materials will be considered only as they apply to doctrinal content.

FOUR KEY AREAS OF DOCTRINAL CHANGE

Hobbs acknowledged that the Committee spent more time on the Preamble than on any other single article in the BFM.[6] As the frontispiece the Preamble defined the purpose and potential uses as well as limitations of the document. Chapters 4 and 5 briefly noted Jeff Pool's assessment of the Preamble as the preeminent article of faith for Baptists. The emphasis in the Preamble on the rights of the individual and the limits on the confession to hold accountable professing Southern Baptists in churches and institutions must, in Pool's estimation, remain inviolate. Hobbs believed that without the Preamble neither the 1925 nor 1963 versions would have been approved by the SBC.[7]

While a close examination of the Preamble might prove profitable for understanding the Committee's concern with the right of private interpretation, and while other articles within the document dealing with peripheral issues need examination, this chapter will limit itself to the areas of Scripture, anthropology, soteriology, and ecclesiology. These four

5. Hobbs, "Southern Baptists and Confessionalism," 61–67. Among the changes that Hobbs noted were stylistic revisions to increase readability, content revisions to clarify and give more detail (especially on the doctrines of God and salvation). There was a structural reorganization that reduced the total number of articles from twenty-four to seventeen. Hobbs noted that the Committee utilized the 1962 Convention motion creating the Committee and the "five introductory points" of the 1925 BFM in combination with the Committee's own thoughts to create Preamble. In this article Hobbs recounted the nature and content of the Committee's handling of the articles on Scripture, God, Man, Salvation, God's Purpose of Grace, the Church, Baptism and the Lord's Supper, the Lord's Day, the Kingdom, Last Things, Evangelism and Missions, Education, Stewardship, Cooperation, the Christian and the Social Order, Peace and War, and Religious Liberty. He noted which of these articles underwent change, the kind of change and what it meant for Baptist doctrine.

6. Hobbs, *My Faith and Message*, 241. Hobbs comments: "Our concern was to protect the individual conscience and to guard against a creedal faith."

7. Ibid.

areas are foundational doctrines which underwent significant revision and so deserve the closest scrutiny.[8] Hobbs doctrinal expositions prior to the Committee's work in book form will be examined to reflect the extent that the document expressed Hobbs's own theological outlook. Comparisons with the comments from various outside sources will note the influence others had on the final outcome of the document.

The Scriptures

Elliott's book *The Message of Genesis* catapulted suspicions of theological heterodoxy onto the center stage of Convention life, according to Hobbs.[9] Elliott's book showed Southern Baptists that not everyone in the Convention viewed the inspiration and accuracy of the Bible in the same way. Following a long line of Baptist confessions, the BFM set the treatment of the Scriptures as the first article. In revising the 1925 Statement, the Committee reflected a subtle change in Baptist thinking regarding Scripture. The Committee also set forth parameters for interpretation, something which had not appeared in a Baptist confession since the Second London was published in 1689.[10]

When the Committee inserted the words "the record of God's revelation of Himself to man" they expressed an idea which became current in theological circles in the late nineteenth and early twentieth centuries.[11] The 1925 Statement asserted its divine inspiration and its content of "heavenly instruction."[12] While the expression "record of revelation" did not occur in the first draft, Hobbs used it in print as early as 1960: "[The Bible] is the written record of God's will for man."[13] Ward suggested the insertion of this phrase in his comments on the first draft.[14] Calling the

---

8. For purposes of comparison the "Statement on Baptist Faith and Message" as published in the *Annual of the Southern Baptist Convention*, 1925, and the "Baptist Faith and Message: A Statement Adopted by the Southern Baptist Convention" are the texts used.

9. Ibid., 28.

10. See the Second London Confession, Chapter I, 9: "The infallible rule of interpretation of Scripture is the Scripture it self." Texts that speak more clearly to a subject, in the minds of these Baptists, served as the basis for interpreting more difficult passages.

11. See chapter 5.

12. 1925 BFM Article 1.

13. Hobbs, *Fundamentals of Our Faith*, 7.

14. See Appendix 1, Article I.

Bible the "record" of revelation moved the text one step away from revelation itself.

At the turn of the twentieth century, evangelical liberals spoke of the Bible as the "record" of revelation. Longfield noted that Henry Sloane Coffin, a prominent liberal Presbyterian, considered the Bible "the record of the progressive religious experience of Israel culminating in Jesus Christ." This view of the Bible, coupled with an emphasis on experience as the source of certainty, reduced the Bible to "*a standard of religious experience.*"[15]

That some in Baptist life could push the division between revelation and the record of it beyond the scope intended by the Committee can be demonstrated by Torbet's assertion, "[Christ] alone is the final norm for truth. In this sense our ultimate authority is *not a book*, nor an institution, nor a creed, but a living Person, the incarnate Son of God."[16]

Conner wrote of the "revelation value" of Scripture as the record of God's dealings with men in which he revealed himself to them, and they, in turn, wrote down their reflections on their experiences with God:

> It was rather that these men, as they lived their lives, wrestled with their problems, received in different ways thoughts about God, had experiences with God. These thoughts and experiences they wrote down. These records, in God's good providence, have been passed down to us."[17]

Conner then said,

> To have revelation value for us, then, they must be the record of a revelation to the people there. The record may have revelation value for us because the events and experiences therein recorded were a means of revelation to the people there concerned.[18]

For Conner it was *possible* for the Bible to have revelation value. While he connected Scripture and revelation closely, he did not see the

---

15. Longfield, *The Presbyterian Controversy*, 90, emphasis his. Hobbs based his argument for the inspiration of the Bible on personal experience, see "Fundamentals of Our Faith," 12.

16. Torbet, "Baptists and Biblical Authority," *AkB* (Little Rock), 24 May 1962, 14, emphasis mine.

17. Conner, *Revelation and God*, 78.

18. Ibid., 79. For a fuller discussion of Conner's view of Scripture and revelation see Bush and Nettles, *Baptists and the Bible*, 286–91.

Bible as revelation but as the product of revelation which may yet communicate revelation to people today.

Conner and Torbet reflected the influence of liberal evangelicals such as Coffin, at the turn of the twentieth century, who found a linkage between the language of the Bible as "record" and establishing a subjective standard of interpretation based on the perceived person of Jesus: "Because the Bible was not the inerrant Word of God but an historically limited record of the ever-evolving religious experience of the Hebrew people, the less well developed portions of Scripture had to be interpreted in terms of the climax of the 'faith of Jesus.'"[19]

Hobbs defined revelation as "the process by which God unveils himself and his will." Inspiration expresses how God enabled the human recipient of revelation "to deliver or record God's revealed message."[20] In Hobbs understanding, to say that the Bible was the record of revelation and to say that it was the inspired word of God went hand in hand: "It is divine in that it is the inspired Word of God. It is human in that God chose to record his revelation through men divinely inspired, who were guided in their work and were guarded against error in it."[21] Hobbs' understanding of the Bible as the "Word of God" coincided with previous generations of Bible-believing Baptists, even if he did express it in terms unfamiliar to them.[22] But as the above comments from Torbet and Conner show, this change of wording reflected a gradual shift in how some Southern Baptists might understand the Bible and its authoritative role in the life of the believer.[23]

When the Committee agreed to follow a shortened form of the "criterion" sentence they played into the hands of men such as Moody. To say that "the criterion by which the Bible is to be interpreted is Jesus Christ"[24] without qualification raised a host of questions. Marvin Tate,

19. Longfield, *Presbyterian Controversy*, 90.

20. Hobbs, *The Baptist Faith and Message*, 21.

21. Ibid., 25.

22. For a thorough survey of Baptist views of the Bible, see Bush and Nettles, *Baptists and the Bible*.

23. Note the assertion of Anthony Sizemore at the 2000 SBC, "The Bible is still just a book." Miller, "Southern Baptists Overwhelmingly adopt revised Baptist Faith and Message," Baptist Press [on-line]: accessed 15 June 2000; available from http://www.sbcannualmeeting.org/sbc00/news.asp?ID=1927611432&page=2&num=5; Internet.

24. 1963 BFM Article I.

who taught Old Testament at Southern from the early 1960s until his retirement, commented: "Back in 1963 I asked, 'What does that mean?' It doesn't mean anything."[25]

According to Garth Pybass, for the Committee the statement conveyed "biblical infallibility based on Christ's testimony of it in the gospels."[26] Hobbs noted:

> The center of the problem concerning *The Message of Genesis* was the treatment of Melchizedek as probably being a priest of Baal. Those objecting to this saw it as a reflection upon/against the priesthood of Jesus Christ. The committee, therefore, added the sentence "The criterion by which the Bible is to be interpreted is Jesus Christ." Of course, the purpose of this "criterion" extends far beyond the above instance. He is the full and final revelation of God to man.[27]

For Moody the exclusion of the original qualifiers meant the ability to deny Mosaic authorship of the Pentateuch, the unity of Isaiah, and an exilic date for Daniel.[28] Tate characterized the sentence well, for it allows too broad a scope of interpretation.[29]

Making "Jesus Christ" the interpretive key to Scripture expressed a move in the thinking of some in the SBC away from the longstanding practice expressed in the Second London Confession of using Scripture to interpret Scripture (see chapters 4 and 5). Failure to recognize the long contribution of previous centuries of Baptist voices, and fixating on the theological paradigm shift brought in by Mullins let this change in Baptist hermeneutics open the flood gates for doctrinal innovation and undermined the ultimate authority of the Bible.

---

25. Personal conversation with Marvin Tate, 5 August 2004, quoted with permission. Tate posed this question to other members of the faculty at Southern and says he often repeated it to students.

26. Pierce, "Elder Baptist says '63 BF&M intended to clarify Bible belief," BP, 8 January 2002.

27. Hobbs, "Southern Baptists and Confessionalism," 62.

28. Moody to McCall, 7 January 1963, Dale Moody Collection, BCL. A copy of the draft sent to Southern Seminary, and bearing Calloway's name, has the qualifiers marked with the comments, "This can be used, Matt 12:17: John 5:46; Matt 24:15." WWC.

29. When the 2000 revision was proposed without this sentence, it became a major source of controversy for moderates attending the Convention. See the above cited BP article by Norman Miller.

Anthropology

In the Committee's treatment of Man and the fall five changes occurred. First, the Committee chose to omit the direct quotations from Genesis 1:27 and 2:7.[30] Instead, they affirmed that God created man by a special act in his own image and that man "is the crowning work of His creation."[31] If anyone wanted to question Hobbs's position on evolution he need look no further than *Fundamentals of Our Faith* to find that Hobbs rejected it: "There is not one bit of fact to substantiate the theory of evolution; it has long since been discarded by men of true science."[32]

Baptists for hundreds of years affirmed that part of what it meant originally to be in the image of God was to be endowed with original righteousness and holiness.[33] The 1925 Statement affirmed this: "He was created in a state of holiness under the law of his maker, ... and fell from his original holiness and righteousness."[34] The Committee chose, in the 1963 BFM, to replace original righteousness and holiness with original innocence: "In the beginning man was innocent of sin."[35] In his commentary on the BFM Hobbs was explicit: "Created in a state of innocence, man was neither righteous nor sinful. Before becoming either he must exercise the right of choice."[36] In the *R&E* Hobbs said the Committee believed this wording conformed more readily with Scripture: "in a state of innocence man could not be *righteous* until by his free choice he chose *righteousness* instead of *unrighteousness*."[37] The question remains, however, whether this change reflects the biblical evidence or a philosophical presupposition about the nature and workings of the will in man prior to the fall.

---

30. Hobbs notes that the Committee chose to affirm the content of these passages without quoting them. See Hobbs, "Southern Baptists and Confessionalism," 63.

31. BFM 1963, Article III.

32. Hobbs, *Fundamentals of Our Faith*, 23.

33. See the Second London Confession, Chapter IV, 2; Keach's Catechism, Question 13; the Abstract of Principles, Article IV for examples.

34. BFM 1925, Article 3.

35. BFM 1963, Article III.

36. Hobbs, *Baptist Faith and Message*, 51–52.

37. Hobbs, "Southern Baptists and Confessionalism," 63. This concept of original innocence may be inferred from Mullins: "We should not here confound perfection in the sense of character achieved through long periods of trial and conflict with the sinlessness of man's original nature." "Man was created without sin, and as thus endowed he was capable of sin and a fall." Mullins, *The Christian Religion in Its Doctrinal Expression*, 259.

Those who argue for original holiness and righteousness do so on the basis of Scriptural affirmations. Boyce serves as an example of such biblical reasoning:

> (5.) This moral nature as originally existent must have been (a.) Not only without taint of sin, and (b.) without tendencies to sin, and (c.) not merely in a condition of such equipoise between sin and holiness as would make the soul indifferent towards the one or the other, but (d.) must have been entirely inclined towards the right, with a holy taste for the holiness of God, having capacity to discern its beauty, and inclination to love him as its possessor, accompanied by readiness to obey the law of God, and perception of man's duty to serve him.
>
> That such was the original condition of man's moral nature is evident from Eph. 4:24: "And put on the new man with after God hath been created in righteousness and holiness of truth." These elements, which belonged to the image of God in which man was created, have been lost. They are restored again in the renewing of man when created anew in Christ Jesus.[38]

In the 1963 BFM the concept of free will in relation to the fall took on a greater place of prominence. The treatment of free will, as far as it went, conformed to the Second London Confession's statement about man's original power of choice. The Second London affirmed man's power of choice prior to the fall: "Man in his state of innocency, had freedom, and power, to will to do that which was good, and well-pleasing to God; but yet was mutable, so that he might fall from it."[39] The 1963 BFM asserted that "In the beginning man was . . . endowed by his Creator with freedom of choice."[40]

Yet another significant change involved the language describing man's condition in the aftermath of the fall. The BFM 1925 followed the pattern of Baptist confessions back to the seventeenth century in describ-

---

38. Boyce, *Abstract of Systematic Theology*, 214.

39. "The Second London Confession, Chapter IX. 2," in *Baptist Confessions of Faith*, ed. W. L. Lumpkin, 263–64. Lest the reader think that by "state of innocency" the Second London refers to the same original state as the 1963 BFM, note that the former also states that "God . . . Created man, . . . after the image of God, in knowledge, righteousness, and true holyness; having the law of God written in their hearts, and power to fulfill it." Chapter IV. 2, Lumpkin, *Baptist Confessions of Faith*, 255–56.

40. 1963 BFM, Article III.

ing humanity as in bondage to sin and having a corrupt nature.[41] This left everyone from birth in a state of condemnation (note the word order here: "he . . . fell from his original holiness and righteousness; whereby his posterity inherit a nature corrupt and in bondage to sin, are under condemnation, and as soon as they are capable of moral action, become actual transgressors"). Condemnation comes from the inherited corruption of Adam's sin according to the 1925 BFM. In 1962 Leon Macon referred to this understanding of man's fallen state as "An Overlooked Truth" in an editorial in the *AIB*.[42]

In the 1963 BFM bondage to sin gave way to a "nature and an environment inclined toward sin, and as soon as they are capable of moral action become actual transgressors and are under condemnation."[43] Hobbs wrote at great length about the fall of Adam and Eve, but in regard to the effects of the fall on humanity he said little beyond quoting the above material from the BFM 1963.[44] In *Fundamentals of Our Faith* Hobbs defined total depravity to mean "that all men are sinners in that they have transgressed the will of God."[45] There was no discussion of the corruption of human nature or bondage to sin.

Hobbs explained this change of wording in article in *R&E*. In the 1963 BFM "'condemnation' comes upon individuals following transgression 'as soon as they are capable of moral action.' This, of course, agrees with the position generally held by Baptists concerning God's grace in cases of those under the age of accountability and the mentally incompetent."[46]

As explained by Hobbs the BFM 1963 should be interpreted at this point to support the teaching that persons are born innocent and do not come under condemnation until actual, wilful sin is committed. This perspective comports with the semi-Pelagianism of what A. H. Strong called the "New School," which stated that "all sin consists in sinning." According

41. BFM 1925, Article 3

42. Macon, "An Overlooked Truth," *AIB* (Birmingham), 19 July 1962, 3.

43. BFM 1963, Article III. The draft sent to the seminaries retained the word order of the 1925 BFM. No notation exists in Calloway's copy concerning discussion of the wording at this point, and no copies have been retrieved from other seminaries, so it is not possible to determine whether input from seminary faculty had any bearing on the final wording.

44. Hobbs, *Baptist Faith and Message*, 51–54.

45. Hobbs, *Fundamentals of Our Faith*, 71.

46. Hobbs, "Southern Baptists and Confessionalism," 63.

to this view, Strong said, sin is only and always an act and not a disposition. Strong refuted this notion and supported, in his own way, the historic Baptist concept of total depravity as expressed in the confessions of previous generations.[47] Strong wrote in opposition to the New Haven Theology espoused by Nathaniel Taylor. The 1963 BFM, on the other hand, reflected the influence of the New Haven Theology on sin and the fall, as well as the influence of Charles Finney.

Taylor, in "Advice to the Clergy," rejected the concept of a disposition or tendency to sin as the cause of sinning. He sought to disprove it by means of arguing from *reductio ad absurdum*. Moral depravity, according to Taylor, "*is man's own act, consisting in a free choice of some object rather than God, as his chief good;—or a free preference of the world and of worldly good, to the will and glory of God.*"[48]

Similarly, Finney argued that moral depravity consisted only in the act of sinning and could not be an attribute of human nature or constitution. "Moral depravity, as I use the term, does not consist in, nor imply a sinful nature, in the sense that the substance of the human soul is sinful in itself." Finney rejected culpability for those who were in infancy or a state of mental incapacity.[49]

Pelagius asserted that sin was learned rather than inherited. Sin consisted in doing evil rather than in inheriting a nature in bondage to evil. The habit of sinning began in childhood because of the problem of a corrupted environment and bad examples. "Doing good has become difficult for us only because of the long custom of sinning, which begins to infect us even in our childhood."[50]

Certainly the BFM 1963 did not move as far from the historic doctrine of total depravity as Pelagius did, but by embracing elements reminiscent of the New Haven Theology, its change of wording to "a nature and an environment inclined toward sin" did not express the severity of man's depraved nature so strongly as did the 1925 BFM. It certainly represented a shift toward a softer tone regarding the doctrine of total depravity.

Little attention has been given to the influence of New Haven Theology on Southern Baptist views of sin and the fall. Wills dealt with

47. Strong, *Systematic Theology*, 595.

48. Taylor, "Advice to the Clergy," in *Issues in American Protestantism*, 138–40. Emphasis his.

49. Finney, *Finney's Systematic Theology*, 244–46.

50. Pelagius, "Letter to Demetrias," in *Theological Anthropology*, ed. J. Patout Burns, 50.

the influence of New Haven Theology on Baptist preaching on the atonement in the 1800s.[51] Mark Coppenger did a study on the condition of fallen man in Southern Baptist preaching that deals with the issue from the perspective of the pulpit. Coppenger insightfully asked the questions and supplied the answer:

> Could it be that the perception of lost mankind's character and capability are improving in our preaching, much as they have in our doctrinal statements? Could it be that the unregenerate are being progressively perceived as less depraved? The evidence indicates that there has been an ascent of lost man in the thinking of Southern Baptists over the course of their history.[52]

Coppenger noted that Antebellum preaching focused on the sovereignty of God and the sinfulness of humanity.[53] After the Civil War, however, more preachers paid greater attention to human freedom, and a subtle shift towards God's "aid" in salvation replaces language of God's "power."[54] By the beginning of the twentieth century C. B. Williams began arguing for humanity's moral and spiritual worth as the chief glory of mankind. At the same time L. R. Scarborough used Revelation 3:20 to emphasize human freedom in the lost person as an evangelistic tool.[55] By the 1950s Roy McClain could preach on the "Baptist Hour" against the doctrine of election, leaving Coppenger to conclude: "This God has done what he can, and now he waits hopefully for us to pick up his cues."[56]

Adding more new material to the BFM, the 1963 revision asserted that "Only the grace of God can bring man into His holy fellowship and enable man to fulfill the creative purpose of God."[57] Here the Committee inserted the absolute necessity of God's grace for salvation.

51. George et al., "The *SBJT* Forum: Overlooked Shapers of Evangelicalism," *SBJT* 3 (Spring 1999): 87–91.

52. Coppenger, "The Ascent of Lost Man in Southern Baptist Preaching," *FJ* 25 (Summer 1996): 5.

53. Ibid., 6.

54. Ibid., 9–10.

55. Ibid., 11.

56. Ibid., 15. How did this influence come to pervade Southern Baptist life and thought? One possibility could be the general *Zeitgeist* of evangelicalism in the aftermath of the Second Great Awakening. Finney's "New Measures" had taken root and influenced a new generation of revival preachers and pastors. See Hardman, *Seasons of Refreshing: Evangelism and Revivals in America*, chaps. 7–10.

57. BFM 1963, Article III.

Because the Committee understood the difficulties attending the Civil Rights Movement they added to the BFM an affirmation of the dignity and sacredness of every human person as created in the image of God. This statement would have been stronger had it not been edited from its original draft, which included the words "regardless of race or class."[58]

In the end, Article III moved from being a tightly worded expression of the Calvinistic view of man's sinfulness to an article open to widely divergent theological interpretation. One can read it through either a Calvinist or New Haven lens on depravity and find it acceptable.

Soteriology

Structurally the 1963 BFM compressed six articles into one. The Committee accomplished this, in part, by treating Christ's saving work under Article II. B. The Committee omitted Article 6, The Freeness of Salvation, of the 1925 BFM completely, and it abridged Article 5 and incorporated it into the treatment of Regeneration, along with portions of Article 8, Repentance and Faith. The Committee treated salvation in a threefold scheme of regeneration, sanctification, and glorification.[59] Perseverance found a new home as a second paragraph in Article V. God's Purpose of Grace, whereas in the BFM 1925 it followed Article 10, Sanctification.

In the opening paragraph of Article IV the faculty of Mercer accused the Committee of allowing Pelagianism into the confession with the insertion of the statement, "Nothing prevents the salvation of a sinner except his failure to accept Jesus Christ as Saviour and Lord."[60]

In terms of content, the Committee made numerous substantial changes to the BFM. The most significant changes occurred in the treatment of regeneration, repentance, faith, justification, and sanctification. With regard to regeneration the Committee again focused on wording which could find acceptance among either Calvinists or Arminians. On the one hand, the 1963 BFM affirmed that when the Spirit regenerated a sinner, he or she "responds in repentance toward God and faith in the

---

58. See Appendix 3, Article III. See also Hobbs, "Southern Baptists and Confessionalism," 63.

59. Mercer's faculty found this framework entirely inadequate. See Appendix 2, n. 36.

60. See Appendix 2, n. 34.

Lord Jesus Christ."[61] This wording clearly made repentance and faith the fruit and effect of the Spirit's regenerating work. On the other hand, the same article said "regeneration, . . . is a work of God's grace whereby believers become new creatures in Christ Jesus."[62] This at least implied that faith preceded regeneration as a necessary condition (something the 1925 BFM positively affirmed).[63]

Hobbs, in treating the subject of regeneration in *Fundamentals of Our Faith* affirmed that regeneration resulted from conviction of sin, repentance and faith in Christ.[64] Again, in his commentary on the BFM, Hobbs affirmed that the new birth was the result of faith in Christ: "It is an instantaneous work of God's grace wrought by the Holy Spirit through faith in Jesus Christ."[65] This stands in stark contrast to the New Hampshire Confession, which stated that regeneration "is effected in a manner above our comprehension or calculation, by the power of the Holy Spirit, [in connection with divine truth,] so as to secure our voluntary obedience to the Gospel."[66]

In keeping with the Committee's treatment of sin, it significantly altered the content of the treatment of repentance. Whereas the 1925 BFM spoke of repentance in language similar to that found in The Abstract of Principles of Southern Seminary, the 1963 BFM shortened the description of repentance considerably. No discussion of "being deeply convinced of our guilt, danger, and helplessness" or of "unfeigned contrition, confession, and supplication for mercy"[67] can be found in the 1963 BFM discussion of repentance. The 1963 BFM described repentance simply as an experience of grace and "a genuine turning from sin toward God."[68]

Faith, in the 1925 BFM, meant "heartily receiving the Lord Jesus Christ as our Prophet, Priest, and King, and relying on him alone as the

61. 1963 BFM, Article IV. A.

62. Ibid.

63. 1925 BFM Article 7: "It is a work of God's free grace conditioned upon faith in Christ."

64. Hobbs, *Fundamentals of Our Faith*, 105.

65. Hobbs, *Baptist Faith and Message*, 60.

66. "New Hampshire Declaration of Faith," in McGlothlin, *Baptist Confessions of Faith*, 304. Hobbs comments on the Article IV in *R&E* are of a general nature, see Hobbs, "Southern Baptists and Confessionalism," 64.

67. 1925 BFM Article 8.

68. 1963 BFM Article IV. A.

only and all-sufficient Saviour.[69] The 1963 Committee redefined faith as "the acceptance of Jesus Christ and commitment of the entire personality to Him as Lord and Saviour."[70] Hobbs explained saving faith as "an act of the will whereby one trusts in Christ and commits himself to him, to his will and way."[71] While the wording and tone in the 1963 BFM differed from the1925 BFM, the essential meaning remained unchanged and comported with the definition of saving faith in The Abstract of Principles of Southern Seminary:

> Saving faith is the belief, on God's authority, of whatsoever is revealed in His Word concerning Christ; accepting and resting upon Him alone for justification and eternal life. It is wrought in the heart by the Holy Spirit, and is accompanied by all other saving graces, and leads to a life of holiness.[72]

A major shift took place in the treatment of sanctification in the 1963 BFM. In the 1925 BFM sanctification was presented as purely progressive and absolutely certain. The Committee changed sanctification to incorporate both punctiliar and progressive aspects, but also rendered it conditional.[73] Sanctification first meant that the believer "is set apart to God's purposes."[74] Sanctification happened at a specific point in time. Secondly, the believer "is enabled to progress toward moral and spiritual perfection." Sanctification involved an ongoing process for which the believer was enabled by the Spirit living within. This progress toward spiritual perfection "should continue throughout . . . life." Here the confession sounded strikingly conditional. Sanctification "should" continue, but is there any certainty here that it will? The 1925 BFM spoke with certainty, affirming that "It continues throughout the earthly life, and is accomplished by the use of all the ordinary means of grace."[75] In commenting on sanctification, Hobbs stated: "The glory of the gospel is that souls are regenerated.

---

69. 1925 BFM Article 8.

70. 1963 BFM Article IV. A.

71. Hobbs, *Baptist Faith and Message*, 61.

72. The Abstract of Principles, Article X. Faith.

73. Calloway wrote in his copy, "optional?" WWC.

74. 1963 BFM Article IV. B.

75. 1925 BFM Article 10.

But the tragedy is that so many Christian lives are lost to God's service through an incomplete understanding of sanctification."[76]

For Hobbs the emphasis in sanctification lay in its being an "instantaneous experience" rather than a progressive process. He noted that the 1963 BFM highlighted the difference "between growing *into* or growing *in* the state of sanctification."[77]

In the 1963 BFM the Committee separated the treatment of perseverance from sanctification and attached it to the treatment of election in Article V. In the face of the Apostasy Controversy the Committee took great pains to affirm the full security in Christ of true believers, while at the same time accounting for the lapses of believers during the course of their lives. The language of this paragraph shows a marked dependence on the Second London Confession, which stated,

> And though they may, through the temptation of Satan and of the world, the prevalency of corruption remaining in them, and the neglect of the means of their preservation fall into grievous sins, and for a time continue therein; whereby they incur Gods displeasure, and grieve his holy Spirit, come to have their graces and comforts impaired have their hearts hardened, and their Consciences wounded, hurt and scandalize others, and bring temporal judgements upon themselves: yet they shall renew their repentance and be preserved through faith in Christ Jesus to the end.[78]

Glorification completes the salvation experience, and so the Committee inserted a short paragraph expressing this biblical teaching as a new feature of the BFM treatment of salvation.[79]

Throughout the entire treatment of salvation in the 1963 BFM both its punctiliar and progressive aspects were emphasized. Salvation began in regeneration but did not end there. It progressed throughout life and would culminate in the glorified state. In his 1960 publication, Hobbs treated salvation in just this fashion. He divided salvation into three

---

76. Hobbs, *Baptist Faith and Message*, 62. Could Hobbs and the Committee have been attempting to account for a growing disparity between membership rolls and committed attendance in Southern Baptist Churches?

77. Hobbs, "Southern Baptists and Confessionalism," 64.

78. Second London Confession, Chapter XVII. 3. Lumpkin, *Baptist Confessions of Faith*, 273–74.

79. Mercer's faculty considered this sentence devoid of useful content, see Appendix 2, n. 41.

concepts: (1) instantaneous salvation; (2) continuing salvation; and (3) ultimate salvation.[80]

Again, as in the previous doctrines considered, the Committee left the Convention a document significantly altered (with the exception of the discussion of justification, which they altered more in tone than content). Key concepts were either re-defined in terms acceptable to widening evangelical perspectives (regeneration), or reduced to minimal definitions (repentance and faith), or expanded and augmented (sanctification).

Ecclesiology

Four major changes occurred in the treatment of the church and church ordinances. The first major change simply asserted what, for Baptists, had been a matter of practice since they came out of the Independent and Separatist movements in England.[81] The Committee inserted a new paragraph affirming both local church autonomy and the equality of every member as demonstrated in the democratic process of congregational self-rule under the Lordship of Christ.[82]

A more controversial change involved the addition of a paragraph affirming that the New Testament spoke of the "church as the body of Christ which includes all of the redeemed of all the ages." This new paragraph stood in marked contrast to the Landmarkist ideology which prevailed in portions of the South. Wendell Rone of Kentucky moved to have this paragraph struck from the document.[83]

Dockery pointed out that Hobbs understood the challenge of altering the statement on the church to include anything other than the local church. He also understood that the New Testament used "church" to denote "either a local body of baptized believers or . . . all the redeemed through the ages." The 1963 BFM added this universal concept to its statement on the nature of the church. Hobbs expected this to be challenged

---

80. Hobbs, *Fundamentals of Our Faith*, 102–03.

81. For an extended treatment of Baptist origins see Torbet, *A History of the Baptists*, McBeth, *The Baptist Heritage*, and Whitsitt, *A Question in Baptist History*.

82. 1963 BFM Article VI. Hobbs notes that "autonomy" as a word had been abused, and so the BFM affirms that the church's autonomy exists only under the Lordship of Christ." "Southern Baptists and Confessionalism," 65.

83. *Annual of the Southern Baptist Convention*, 1963, 63.

from the floor and had in hand a quote from J. M. Pendleton's *Church Manual* to support the new wording.[84]

Hobbs noted that a small debate occurred regarding the statement: "The New Testament speaks also of the church as the body of Christ which includes all of the redeemed of all ages." The statement passed overwhelmingly without any alterations.[85] This sentence, too, reflected Hobbs thinking. Hobbs noted in 1960 that the New Testament used the term "church" in two ways. One, he said, included "all believers in Christ in all ages."[86] While this sentence did not meet with Moody's approval,[87] it did embrace the Second London Confession's understanding of the universal church.[88]

A fuller treatment of baptism occurred in the BFM 1963. The Committee emphasized the fact that Christ commanded it as an act of obedience. The Committee also expanded the explanation of the symbolic meaning of baptism (Article VII).

A change involving the Lord's Supper centered upon a change of practice in the aftermath of Prohibition.[89] The Committee chose to replace the word "wine" with "fruit of the vine." Moody found this unacceptable for two reasons: (1) he found the wording awkward; (2) he objected to Hobbs explanation of the use of grape juice in the Lord's Supper. Moody preferred, if wine must be dropped, to use the word "cup" because it made

84. Dockery, "Herschel H. Hobbs," in *Theologians of the Baptist Tradition*, 228. Pendleton was one of the key leaders of the Landmarkist movement in the mid-nineteenth century. On the issue of the ordinances Baptists, on the whole remained committed in opposition to "alien immersion" and continued to practice "fencing" the Lord's Table, as can be seen in the wording of the 1963 BF&M. The only significant change on the ordinances came with replacing "wine" with "fruit of the vine." This reflected practical changes in Baptist practice in the wake of Prohibition. See Dobbins, *Baptists in Action*, 157. Virginia Baptists tended to be the exception to the rule on open communion, alien immersion and support for the ecumenical movement, see Alley, "Guard Well the Seminaries," *RH* (Richmond), 28 September 1961, 11.

85. Hobbs, "The Baptist Faith and Message," 33.

86. Hobbs, *Fundamentals of Our Faith*, 127.

87. Moody, to McCall, 7 January 1963, courtesy of BCL. Moody had embraced the ecumenical movement to a much greater degree than had most Southern Baptists, as is reflected in his comments in this letter. Moody felt the confession should express a recognition of a visible, universal church on earth, not just some as yet unseen spiritual church to be revealed at the eschaton.

88. Second London Confession, Chapter XXVI, Section 1.

89. Dobbins, *Baptist Churches in Action*, 157.

the sentence flow more smoothly.[90] In defense of grape juice Hobbs wrote in his commentary,

> The elements used in the Supper were unleavened bread and "the fruit of the vine." The word "wine" is not used. Some interpret "fruit of the vine" as wine. However, as the bread was unleavened, free of bacteria, was the cup also not grape juice? Wine is the product of the juice plus fermentation caused by bacteria. Since both elements represented the pure body and blood of Jesus, there is reason to ponder. The writer sees "fruit of the vine" as pure grape juice untainted by fermentation.[91]

Hobbs's argument went much further in defending the use of grape juice over wine than did Dobbins, some thirty-four years before. Dobbins wrote, "Every requirement of Scripture seems to be met in the use of grape juice instead of fermented wine."[92] Where Dobbins allowed for the substitution of grape juice Hobbs positively rejected the use of wine. Yet the wording of the 1963 BFM left the matter open to interpretation, as the phrase "fruit of the vine" could be applied to either substance. Here, again, Hobbs and the Committee found a way to word the document broadly and satisfy an increasingly diverse Southern Baptist Convention.

CONCLUSION

This chapter examined four areas of doctrinal formulation. The 1963 BFM reflected changing trends in Southern Baptist thought in each of these areas. In at least one area the change came more in the tone of expression than the meaning of the content (justification). The doctrine of Scripture in the 1963 BFM allowed a broader hermeneutical principle than Baptists of previous generations accepted. The articles on Man and Salvation were worded in such a way as to allow for a broadening evangelical interpretation, though not without some logical inconsistencies, especially in the treatment of regeneration. The doctrine of the Church gave renewed emphasis to the lordship of Christ in relation to local church autonomy while at the same time expressing a belief in a larger, universal church of all the redeemed. Considered under church practice were changes related to expression of the meaning of baptism and the proper elements of the

90. Moody to McCall, 7 January 1963.

91. Hobbs, *Baptist Faith and Message*, 88.

92. Dobbins, *Baptist Churches in Action*, 157.

Lord's Supper. Inasmuch as Hobbs's intention was for the confession to be an expression of what Southern Baptists in 1963 believed, the BFM reflected shifts in Baptist thinking and practice during the first half of the twentieth century.[93]

93. See the 1963 BFM Preamble, (1).

8

Conclusion

DOCTRINAL CRISES IN THE Southern Baptist Convention in the early 1960s propelled the Convention leadership into proposing the formation of a Committee to study the Statement on Baptist Faith and Message approved at the Southern Baptist Convention in 1925. That original document came out of the controversy over liberalism and modernism in American Christianity in general. The crises of the early 1960s focused on Southern Baptist educators, primarily Dale Moody and Ralph Elliott. As president of the Convention, Herschel H. Hobbs chaired the Committee. This work has brought forth evidence of the following: (1) The Committee, under Hobbs's leadership, reformulated certain key historic Baptist doctrines, and (2) it rendered some of these sufficiently vague to allow for a widening diversity of theological viewpoints within the Convention and its agencies. The available documents demonstrate no intention to correct any doctrinal error, although as shown in chapter 7, the Committee understood Article I in one sense and some seminary faculty understood it in an entirely different sense.

Other issues faced Southern Baptists in the 1960s. The Convention's presence spread beyond the traditional borders of the South through Southerners moving into western states and planting churches. This eventually brought new influences to bear on Southern Baptist life. The rise of the Civil Rights Movement created a crisis of conscience and awakened reactionary voices within the Convention. Along with most Americans, Southern Baptists lived in fear of the threat of Communism abroad and encroaching Socialism at home. Rising prosperity prompted concerns about materialism and self-indulgent spiritual laxness. Religious liberty and the relationship of the church to the state took on renewed interest with the election of John F. Kennedy, the United States' first Roman Catholic president. Catholic leaders in the United States began pushing for federal funding of parochial schools, expecting Kennedy's support for their efforts. The Ecumenical Movement threatened to undermine denominational distinctives in favor of a broad, latitudinarian move to reunite all churches under one common banner. Along with the doctrinal crisis precipitated by Elliott's *The Message of Genesis*, the Committee found itself confronted by these ancillary concerns.

Along the way the question of the role of Baptist confessions in relation to soul liberty and soul competency took on renewed importance. The Committee's (and especially Hobbs's) understanding of the role of Baptist confessions of faith as instruments of accountability required that this work explore the relevant data as far back as Baptist beginnings in England in the seventeenth century. Evidence of how Baptist confessions functioned prior to the twentieth century indicated that churches and associations held them in high regard as instruments of accountability. This enabled churches and associations to check deviant theology, whether it came from a single pastor or an entire congregation.

E. Y. Mullins brought to prominence in Southern Baptist life new philosophical influences borrowed from the Enlightenment, and a modified theological methodology from Bowne, James, and Schleiermacher. He introduced Southern Baptists to the concept of soul competency, and in the process redefined how sources of religious authority and accountability functioned in Baptist life. In the aftermath the balance shifted from congregational or corporate accountability to the rights of the individual, making confessional checks harder to enforce in denominational schools.

Chapter 6 examined how the Committee came into being and defined its task. Hobbs understood the need of the Convention for a doctrinal statement all could accept, and he also understood the human limitations of the Committee. He and other leading members of the Committee solicited outside help from the beginning of the process. Based on the available evidence, Wayne Ward's theological perspective dominated the document as much as did that of Hobbs. Second only to Ward was the contribution of Leo Garrett. The only schools which left any substantial written record of input with the Committee are Southern Seminary and Mercer University, though all of the Convention seminaries contributed to discussions regarding the document before the Committee prepared the final draft.

Chapter 7 examined evidence of significant doctrinal shifts in the document from the 1925 version. Evidence for changes in the doctrines of Scripture, Man, Salvation, and the Church served as the focus for establishing the thesis that Hobbs and the Committee produced a broad-based document and substantially altered the confessional expression of key Southern Baptist doctrines in the process. As demonstrated in chapter 7, these changes generally allowed multiple interpretations without overly stretching the text. Furthermore, the added emphasis upon individual liberty in interpretation by way of soul competency and the priesthood of the believer made such interpretative maneuvers publicly acceptable.

Whatever other doctrinal innovations he might allow, Hobbs never intended to sacrifice the Convention's conservative theological base. His expositions of Baptist doctrines in books and BP demonstrate clearly that he held to the inerrancy of the Bible and its full and complete inspiration and authority. Nevertheless, the choice of wording for Article I. The Scriptures, allowed others privately to hold views of inspiration or interpretation which undermined the nature and authority of the biblical text.

With regard to Article III. Man, the Committee moved the doctrinal standard away from a traditional Calvinistic view of the fall, original sin, and total depravity, in the direction of the New Haven Theology of Nathaniel Taylor and the popular revivalist Charles Finney. This new anthropology left Southern Baptists in a broadening evangelical doctrinal position. Again, the Committee found a way to word the article on Man in broad enough terms that persons holding any one of several possible evangelical viewpoints could find support for his or her position within the BFM.

In treating Article IV. Salvation the Committee demonstrated great skill in combining numerous articles in the 1925 version into a single article. Structurally, they separated Perseverance from Sanctification, yet they strengthened the BFM statement on both in some ways. The treatment of Sanctification, however, took a decided shift toward conditional fulfillment. Much of the article on Salvation they left open to interpretations acceptable to either Calvinists or Arminians, and this in such a way as to come across as logically incoherent at times. Here, too, the Committee produced changes which made it possible for a broad theological base to find a home.

Conclusion

Based on events at the 1963 Convention, the one truly controversial change came in Article VI. The Church. While several changes were noted in this article, the one which stood out most prominently dealt with the universal nature of the church. This represented a serious departure from the Landmarkist influences of past generations of Southern Baptists. Yet the Committee chose to emphasize, also, local church autonomy under Christ, the rights of individual members, and democratic government of the local church—themes which readily resonate with all Baptists, and the 1963 BFM passed the Convention without alteration of the Committee's work.

In the end the Committee succeeded in producing a document significantly modified from its predecessor, yet modified in such a way as to find ready acceptance among Southern Baptists. For thirty-eight years it provided information about Baptist beliefs to both Baptists and non-Baptists alike, and it served as a doctrinal guide for Southern Baptist institutions.

It is beyond the scope of this work to discuss the aftermath of the Committee's work, the uneasy peace that existed in the Convention until the mid-1970s, and the Conservative resurgence which began in earnest in 1979. Full treatments of those events can be found in the works of James Hefley (*Truth in Crisis* series and *The Conservative Resurgence in the Southern Baptist Convention*) covering the conservative resurgence, Nancy Ammerman's *Baptist Battles*, Paul Pressler's *A Hill on Which to Die: One Southern Baptist's Journey*; Walter Shurden's edited work, *The Struggle for the Soul of the SBC*; and Jerry Sutton's *The Baptist Reformation*.

Appendix One

Baptist Faith and Message

The Ward Annotated Recension

PREAMBLE

SOUTHERN BAPTISTS ARE A people with a living faith. It[1] is rooted and grounded in Jesus Christ who is "the same yesterday, today, and forever." Being a living faith it experiences a growing understanding of truth and must be continually interpreted and related to the needs of each new generation.

Through the years Baptist bodies, both large and small, have issued statements of faith which comprised a concensus [*sic*] of their beliefs, [regarding the teachings of the Bible which is the written record of God's revelation of Himself to man].[2] Such statements have never been regarded as complete, infallible statements of faith nor as binding upon the consciences of those who gave assent to them. They were not regarded as official creeds, carrying mandatory authority.

We are in historic succession of intent and purpose as this generation of Southern Baptists endeavors to state for its time those articles of the Christian faith which are most surely held among us. The sole authority for faith and practice among Baptists is the Lordship of Christ as revealed in the Holy Scriptures, especially in the New Testament.

Baptists place great emphasis on the individual soul's competency before God, freedom in religion, and the priesthood of the believer.

1. "This faith." All quoted suggestions in the footnotes come from Wayne Ward's notations or his letter. Interpretive comments have been confirmed by Wayne Ward.

2. Omit the clause which begins with "regarding" to the end of the sentence.

However, this emphasis should not be interpreted to mean that there are not certain definite doctrines that Baptists hold dear and with which they have been and are closely identified.

It is the purpose of this statement of faith to set forth [these] principles.[3]

THE BAPTIST FAITH AND MESSAGE

I. THE SCRIPTURES

[We believe that][4] the Holy Bible [was written by men divinely inspired],[5] [and][6] is a perfect treasure of [heavenly][7] instruction[; that it][8] has God for its author, salvation for its end, and truth, without any mixture of error, for its matter[; that it][9] reveals the principles by which God will judge us; and therefore is, and will remain to the end of the world, the true center of Christian union, and the supreme standard by which all human conduct, creeds, and opinions should be tried. The criterion by which the Bible is to be interpreted is the person, work and teachings of Jesus Christ.[10]

II. GOD

[There][11] is one and only one living and true God, an intelligent, spiritual, and personal Being, the Creator, Preserver, and Ruler of the universe, infinite in holiness and all other perfections, to whom we owe the highest

3. Omit "these" and adding to the end of the sentence "which we believe."

4. Omit the first three words of this sentence.

5. Omit all or part of the bracketed material (the notations are not clear at this point) and insert "is the record of God's revelation of Himself to man."

6. Break up the long sentence into numerous smaller sentences, beginning here. Drop "and" and then begin a new sentence with "It is a."

7. Replacing "heavenly" with "divine."

8. Another sentence break here, replacing the semicolon with a period, omitting "that" and beginning the new sentence with "It."

9. The same editorial changes as in seen in footnote 8 above.

10. Next to this sentence in the margin is a question mark and a notation that is difficult to read but might be the word "emotion." According to Ward, he himself had personally suggested this exact statement to Hobbs in a private conversation before the first draft of the document was prepared in response to how Christians should interpret the Mosaic law in relation to the Christian life.

11. Replace "There" with "We believe that."

love, reverence, and obedience. He is revealed to us as Father, Son, and Holy Spirit, each with distinct personal attributes, but without division of nature, essence, or being.

III. JESUS CHRIST

Jesus Christ[12] is the Eternal Son of God, [who entered history in the person of the virgin-born Jesus of Nazareth. As man, Jesus, He was completely human, and yet in His earthly life he was one with God in being.][13] In His incarnation[14] He perfectly revealed and did the will of God, taking upon Himself the demands and necessities of human nature and identifying Himself completely with mankind.[15]

In His death on the cross He made atonement for the sins of man. He [arose][16] from the dead[17] and appeared to His disciples as the person who was with them before His crucifixion. He [was then][18] exalted at the right hand of God where He is [now][19] the One Mediator partaking of the nature of God and of man, and in whose Person is effected reconciliation [between][20] God and man [and from whence][21] He will return at His second Advent to judge the world and bring His redemptive mission to a

12. Insert "We believe that."

13. Regarding this bracketed section, Ward said in a letter dated October 20, 1962, to Dick Hall Jr., "To talk about 'Jesus, as man', in distinction from his deity is to court the dangerous Nestorian heresy of separation of the two natures. Also, 'He was one with God in being' eternally; that clause should not be restricted by the words 'in His earthly life'. That restriction cuts at the doctrine of His pre-existence. Even worse, the first sentence which says that the Eternal Son 'entered history' in the person of Jesus. The Eternal Son was the agent of Creation! That was not only in history; that act was the foundation of all history. Besides, 'the rock was Christ' and the Word of God which came to the prophets was the Word Incarnate in Jesus Christ. The Eternal Son was very active in the Godhead in history from the beginning! To have him 'entering history' in Jesus of Nazareth is a few thousand years too late."

14. Insert here "as the virgin-born Jesus of Nazareth."

15. Add to the end of the sentence "yet without sin."

16. Replace "arose" with "was raised."

17. Insert "with a glorified body."

18. Omit "was then" and insert "ascended into heaven and is now."

19. Omit "now," possibly as superfluous.

20. Replace "between" with "of," and end the sentence after "God and man."

21. By ending the sentence after "man" and beginning a new sentence Ward made the phrase "and from whence" unnecessary, suggesting that the new sentence begin with "He will return."

glorious consummation. He now makes His presence known through the Holy Spirit to all believers as the Living and Ever-Present Lord.

IV. THE HOLY SPIRIT

The Holy Spirit is the third person of the Trinity. [Through inspiration He was the author of the Holy][22] Scriptures. [Through illumination He enlightens][23] man to understand truth. He convicts of sin, of righteousness and of judgment. He calls men to the Saviour, and effects regeneration. He cultivates Christian character, comforts believers,[24] bestows the spiritual gifts by which they serve God through His church.[25] He seals the believer unto the day of final redemption. His presence in the Christian is the assurance of God to bring the believer into the fullness of Christ. He enlightens and empowers [the][26] believer and [the] [C]hurch in [its][27] worship, evangelism and service.

V. MAN

Man was created by [the][28] special act of God, in His own image, and is the crown[29] of His creation. A the beginning he was innocent of sin but was endowed by His Creator with freedom and the right of choice. [By his free choice, man sinned against God and brought sin into the human race. His posterity inherit a nature corrupt and in bondage to sin, and as soon as they are capable of moral action become actual transgressors, and are under condemnation.][30] Only the grace of God can bring man

22. Replace the bracketed material with "He inspired holy men to write the." Change the period after "Scriptures" to a colon.

23. Replace this clause with "He illumines."

24. Add "and" to make the sentence flow better.

25. Change "church" to "churches" so as to be consistent with accepted Baptist ecclesiology.

26. Replace "the" with "both", and omit the second "the" in the sentence.

27. Change "Church" to "church"and omit "its" as inconsistent with the reworded sentence.

28. Change "the" to "a".

29. Change the phrase to read "crowning work."

30. Ward at first suggested numerous changes in these two sentences, but finally struck through both. In his letter to Hall, Ward states, "The article on Man contains a good reference to the 'image of God' and the race problem but is weak on the origin of sin in the race. The source of sin lies ultimately in the Tempter and not in man; otherwise,

[back][31] into His holy fellowship and enable him to fulfill the purpose of his creation. [The fact][32] that man was created in the image of God and that Christ died for him bespeaks the sacredness of human personality. [As such he][33] possesses dignity and is worthy of respect and Christian love [regardless of race or class].[34]

VI. SALVATION

Salvation involves the redemption of man in his complete being, and is made free to all by the gospel. Nothing prevents the salvation of [the greatest][35] sinner except his failure to accept Jesus Christ as Saviour and Lord. Salvation [begins in][36] regeneration, continues in sanctification, and culminates in glorification:

1. Regeneration, or the new birth, is a work of God's grace whereby we become partakers of the divine nature. It is a change of heart wrought by the Holy Spirit through conviction of sin, to which the sinner responds in repentance toward God and faith in the Lord Jesus Christ.

Repentance and faith are inseparable graces. Repentance is a deep and sincere change of thinking, feeling and willing toward sin and toward God. Faith is the acceptance of and committal to Jesus Christ as Saviour and Lord and involves the entire personality, thought, feeling and volition. Justification is God's gracious and full acquittal upon principles of His righteousness of all sinners who repent and believe in Christ.[37]

---

man would be ultimately irredeemable. Christ conquered the principalities and powers and struck the death blow at Satan—not at man. The article is completely silent on the role of the Evil One in the origin of sin in the race and thereby undercuts the doctrine of the atonement as seen in the Gospels and in Paul."

31. Omit "back."

32. Changed "The fact" but chose to leave it as it was written.

33. Change "As such he" to "Therefore every man."

34. Omit "regardless of race or class."

35. Replace "the greatest" with "a".

36. Re-write the sentence as follows: "Salvation in its broadest sense includes regeneration, sanctification, and glorification."

37. Add, "It brings us into a state of peace and favor with God."

2. Sanctification is the experience by which the regenerate person, [having been][38] set apart[39] through faith in Jesus Christ, [progressively attains to][40] moral and spiritual perfection through the presence and power of the Holy Spirit dwelling in his heart. [It] continues throughout the earthly life, [and is accomplished by the use of all the ordinary means of grace, and particularly by the Word of God.][41]

3. Glorification is the culmination of salvation and is the blessed and abiding state of the redeemed.

VII. GOD'S PURPOSE OF GRACE

Election is the gracious purpose of God, according to which he regenerates, sanctifies and [saves][42] sinners. It is consistent with the free agency of man, and comprehends all the means in connection with the end. It is a most glorious display of God's sovereign goodness, and is infinitely holy, and unchangeable. It excludes boasting and promotes humility. It encourages the use of means in the highest degree.

All real believers endure to the end. Those whom God [hath][43] accepted in the Beloved, and sanctified by His Spirit, will never [totally nor finally][44] fall away from the state of grace, but shall certainly persevere to the end; and though they may fall into sin, through neglect and temptation, whereby they grieve the Spirit, impair their graces and comforts, bring reproach on the Church, and temporal judgments on themselves, yet they shall [be renewed again unto repentance, and][45] be kept by the power of God through faith unto salvation.

38. Replace "having been" with "is" and omitting the comma after "Jesus Christ."

39. Insert "to God's purposes."

40. Change this phrase to read, "and progresses toward."

41. Re-write this sentence to read, "This growth in grace should continue throughout the earthly life."

42. Change "saves" to "glorifies."

43. Update the language with "has" instead of "hath."

44. Omit this phrase.

45. Omit this phrase.

VIII. A NEW TESTAMENT CHURCH

A New Testament Church of the Lord Jesus Christ is a [congregation][46] of baptized believers, associated by covenant in the faith and fellowship of the gospel; observing the[47] ordinances of Christ, governed by His laws, and exercising the gifts, rights, and privileges invested in them by His [w]ord,[48] and seeking to extend the gospel to the ends of the earth.

This church is an autonomous body, operating under the Lordship of Jesus Christ. In such a congregation, members are equal and equally responsible. Its Scriptural officers are pastors and deacons.

The New Testament [also][49] speaks of the church as the body of Christ which includes all of the redeemed.[50]

IX. BAPTISM AND THE LORD'S SUPPER

Christian baptism is the immersion of a believer in water in the name of the Father, the Son, and the Holy Spirit. The act is a symbol of the believer's faith in a crucified, buried and risen Saviour, of the believer's death to sin, the burial of the old life, and the resurrection to walk in newness of life in Christ Jesus. It is a pledge of his faith in the final resurrection of the dead at the second coming of Christ. It is prerequisite to the privileges of a church relation[51] and to the Lord's Supper.

The Lord's Supper is [the means of commemorating][52] the death of the Redeemer through bread and the fruit of the vine. It is a thanksgiving for all that Christ means to the believer, and is a [communion][53] with the living Lord. It is a commitment by which the believer pledges his undying loyalty and obedience to his Lord until He comes.

46. Replace "congregation" with "local body."

47. Insert "two."

48. Spell "word" as "Word."

49. Move "also" to follow "speaks."

50. Add to the sentence "of all the ages."

51. Change "relation" to "relationship."

52. Replace this phrase with "a symbol wherein members of the church commemorate."

53. Replace "communion" with "fellowship."

165

X. THE LORD'S DAY[54]

The first day of the week is the Lord's Day. It is a Christian institution for regular observance. It commemorates the resurrection of Christ from the dead and should be employed in exercises of worship and spiritual devotion, both public and private, and by refraining from worldly amusements, and resting from secular employments, work of necessity and mercy only excepted.

XI. THE KINGDOM

The Kingdom of God includes both His general sovereignty over the universe and His particular kingship over men who willfully acknowledge Him as King. Particularly the Kingdom is the realm of salvation into which men enter by trustful, childlike commitment to Jesus Christ. Christians ought to pray and labor that the Kingdom may come and God's will be done on earth. The full consummation of the Kingdom awaits the return of Jesus Christ and the end of this age.

XII. RELIGIOUS LIBERTY

God alone is Lord of the conscience, and He has left it free from the doctrines and commandments of men which are contrary to His Word or not contained in it. Church and state should be separate. The state owes to the church protection and full freedom in pursuit of its spiritual ends. In providing for such freedom no ecclesiastical group or denomination should be favored by the state,[55] more than others. Civil government being ordained of God, it is the duty of Christians to render loyal obedience thereto in all things not contrary to the revealed will of God. The church should not resort to the civil power to carry on its work. The gospel of Christ contemplates spiritual means alone for the pursuit of its ends. The state has no right to impose penalties for religious opinions of any kind. The state has no right to impose taxes for the support of any form of religion. A free church in a free state is the Christian ideal, and this implies the right of free and unhindered access to God on the part of all men, and

54. Rearrange materials at this point, making Articles X through XV cover Global Missions, Education, Stewardship, Cooperation, The Christian and the Social Order, and Religious Liberty, respectively. Ward also suggested making Article XVII Peace and War.

55. Omit the comma.

the right to form and propagate opinions in the sphere of religion without interference by the civil power.

XIII. PEACE AND WAR

It is the duty of Christians to seek peace with all men on principles of righteousness. In accordance with the spirit and teaching of Christ they should do all in their power to put an end to war.

The true remedy for the war spirit is the [pure][56] gospel of our Lord. The supreme need of the world is the acceptance of His teachings in all the affairs of men and nations, and the practical application of His law of love.

We urge Christian people throughout the world to pray for the reign of the Prince of Peace, and to oppose everything likely to provoke war.

XIV. EDUCATION

Christianity is the religion of enlightenment and intelligence. In Jesus Christ are hidden all the treasures of wisdom and knowledge. All sound learning is therefore part of our Christian heritage. The new birth opens all human faculties and creates a thirst for knowledge. An adequate system of schools is necessary to a complete spiritual program for Christ's people.

In Christian education there should be a proper balance between academic freedom and academic responsibility. Freedom in any orderly relationship of human life is always limited and never absolute. The freedom of a teacher in a Christian school, college or seminary is limited by the distinct purpose for which the school exists, by the authoritative nature of the Scriptures, and by the pre-eminence of Jesus Christ who is "the way, the truth, and the life." The cause of education in the Kingdom of Christ is co-ordinate with the causes of missions and general benevolence, and should receive along with these the liberal support of the churches.

XV. SOCIAL SERVICE

Every Christian is under obligation to seek to make the will of Christ regnant in his own life and in human society; to oppose in the spirit of Christ every form of greed, selfishness, and vice; to provide for the orphaned, the

---

56. Omit "pure."

aged, the helpless, and the sick; to seek to bring industry, government, and society as a whole under the sway of the principles of righteousness, truth and brotherly love; to promote these ends Christians should be ready to work with all men of good will in any good cause, always being careful to act in the spirit of love without compromising their loyalty to Christ and His truth. [All][57] means and methods used in social service for the amelioration of society and the establishment of righteousness among men [must finally depend on][58] the regeneration of the individual by the saving grace of God in Christ.

XVI. CO-OPERATION

Christ's people should, as occasion requires, organize such associations and conventions as may best secure co-operation for the great objects of the Kingdom of God. Such organizations have no authority over [each other][59] or over the churches. They are voluntary and advisory bodies designed to elicit, combine, and direct the energies of our people in the most effective manner. Individual members of New Testament churches should co-operate with [each other] and the churches themselves should co-operate [each other] in carrying forward the missionary, educational, and benevolent program for the extension of Christ's Kingdom. Christian unity in the New Testament sense is spiritual harmony and voluntary co-operation for common ends by various groups of Christ's people. [It][60] is permissable (*sic*) and desirable as between the various Christian denominations, when the end to be attained is itself justified, and when such co-operation involves no violation of conscience or compromise of loyalty to Christ and His Word as revealed in the New Testament.

XVII. EVANGELISM AND MISSIONS

It is the duty and privilege of every follower of Christ and every church of the Lord Jesus Christ to endeavor to make disciples of all nations. The new birth of man's spirit by God's Holy Spirit means the birth of love for others. Missionary effort on the part of all rests thus upon a spiritual

57. Omit "All" and begin the sentence with "Means."

58. Change this phrase to "can be truly and permanently helpful only when they are rooted in."

59. Each time "each other" appears replace it with "one another."

60. Replace the pronoun with "Cooperation."

necessity of the regenerate life. It is also expressly and repeatedly commanded in the teachings of Christ. It is the duty of every child of God to seek constantly to win the love to Christ by personal effort and by all other methods sanctioned by the gospel of Christ.

XVIII. STEWARDSHIP

God is the source of all blessings, temporal and spiritual; all that we have and are we owe to Him. We have a spiritual debtorship to the whole world, a holy trusteeship in the gospel, and a binding stewardship in our possessions. We are therefore under obligation to serve Him with our time, talents and material possessions; and should recognize all these as entrusted to us to use for the glory of God and helping others.[61] Christians should[62] cheerfully, regularly, systematically, proportionately, and liberally[63] [contribute of their means] advancing the Redeemer's cause on earth.

XIX. LAST THINGS

God is Sovereign in and above history. In His own time and in His own way, He will bring the world to its appropriate end. According to His promise, Jesus Christ will return[64] in glory to the earth; the dead will be raised; and Christ will judge all men in righteousness. The unrighteous will be consigned to[65] the place of everlasting punishment. The righteous in their resurrected and glorified bodies will receive their reward and will dwell forever in Heaven with God, Jesus Christ His Son, the holy angels and the saints of all the ages.

61. Insert at the end of this sentence "according to the Scriptures."

62. Insert "contribute of (or from) their means."

63. Because of the rewording in footnote 62, end the sentence with "liberally for the advancement of the Redeemer's cause on earth."

64. Insert "personally and visibly."

65. Insert "Hell."

Appendix Two

Baptist Faith and Message

The Mercer University Annotated Draft[1]

PREAMBLE

[Southern][2] Baptists are a people [with a living faith][3]. This faith is rooted and grounded in Jesus Christ who is "the same yesterday, today, and forever." [Being a living][4] faith [it experiences a growing understanding of truth and][5] must be [continually][6] interpreted and related to [the needs of][7] each new generation.

---

1. BFM file, folder 4, SBHLA. Each of the following footnotes represents suggestions for changes made by Mercer University's Christian Studies faculty. The items in quotation marks in the footnotes coorespond to the bracketed materials in the text. Footnotes are verbatim from the handwritten notes of the faculty.

2. Omit "Southern."

3. Replace with "who live by faith in Christ". Commentary: The introductory sentence of the draft statement omits the object of our faith: Jesus Christ.

4. Replace with "This."

5. Omit. Commentary related to footnotes 4–6: Omit "a growing understanding of truth": this is the notion of "progressive" revelation of 19th century liberalism and 20th century modernism, which the testimony of Scripture denies.

"to the needs of each new generation": this is a concern of humanism and not of Scripture. The gospel witnesses to individuals, and discloses to them the true nature of their needs.

6. Omit.

7. Omit.

[Through the years][8] Baptist bodies, both large and small, have issued statements of faith which [comprised a concensus [*sic*] of][9] their beliefs. Such statements have never been regarded as complete, infallible statements of faith [nor as binding upon the consciences of those who gave assent to binding upon the consciences of those who gave assent to them].[10] They were not regarded as official creeds, carrying mandatory authority.

[We are in historic succession of intent and purpose as this generation of Southern Baptists endeavors to state for its time those articles of the Christian faith which are most surely held among us.][11] The sole authority for faith and practice among Baptists is the Lordship of Christ as revealed in the Holy Scriptures, [especially in the New Testament].[12]

[Baptists place great emphasis on the individual soul's competency before God, freedom in religion, and the priesthood of the believer. However, this emphasis should not be interpreted to mean that there are not certain definite doctrines that Baptists hold dear and with which they have been and are closely identified.][13]

[It is the purpose of this statement of faith to set forth these principles.][14]

8. Replace with "Therefore" and do not make a paragraph break.

9. Replace with "confess."

10. Omit. Commentary: Omit "nor as binding upon the consciences of those who gave assent": this encourages, or at least condones, false witness. Cf. Exodus 20:16.

11. Omit and make no paragraph break. Commentary: This sentence implies that "tradition" or "historic succession" are authorities which are equal to the work of Jesus Christ.

12. Commentary: Omit "and especially in the New Testament": this denies the insistence of Scripture that its consistent testimony is to Christ. Cf. John 5:39. The phrase also implies an acceptance of the "thermometer" theory of Scriptural texts.

13. Commentary: A. This paragraph ignores that for Baptists, the object of "the individual soul's competency," "freedom in religion" and "the priesthood of the believer" is God, and not "soul" itself, "freedom" itself, the "believer" himself.

B. This draft "statement of faith" ignores in its main body the "great emphasis" of "the individual soul's competency" and "the priesthood of the believer."

C. The paragraph tends to undermine Article I, the Scriptures, by assuming that man is free to select those "certain definite doctrines" which he "holds dear."

14. Commentary: A. Repetitive.

B. Scripture's testimony is concerned with God's grace and man's rebellion, and with "principles" <u>about</u> God or man. Cf. Article III of the draft statement.

THE BAPTIST FAITH AND MESSAGE

I. THE SCRIPTURES

The Holy Bible was written by men divinely inspired and is the record of God's revelation of himself to man. It is a perfect treasure of divine instruction. It has God for its author, salvation for its end, and truth, without any mixture of error, for its matter. It reveals the [principles][15] by which God will judge us; and therefore is, and will remain to the end of the world, the true center of Christian union, and the supreme standard by which all human conduct, creeds, and opinions should be tried. [The criterion by which the Bible is to be interpreted is the person, work and teachings of Jesus Christ.][16]

II. GOD

There is [one and][17] only one living and true God, an intelligent, spiritual, and personal Being, the Creator, Preserver, and Ruler of the universe, infinite in holiness and all other perfections, to whom we owe the highest love, reverence, and obedience. He is revealed [to us][18] as Father, Son, and Holy Spirit, each with distinct personal attributes, but without division of[19] nature, essence, or being.

III. JESUS CHRIST

Jesus[20] Christ is the Eternal Son of God.[21] [In His incarnation as the virgin born Jesus of Nazareth],[22] He [perfectly][23] revealed and did the will of

---

15. Replace with "way". Commentary: Cf. 7B above (i.e., n. 14).

16. Commentary: A. The sentence in the draft statement is repetitive in the light of Article III.

B. The term "criterion", unfortunately connotes the existence of a yardstick by which man can measure or judge Scripture, rather than Scripture measuring and judging man.

Replace with "Scripture is the history of the covenant between God and man revealed in Jesus Christ, and must be read, heard, and interpreted in His light.

17. Omit.

18. Replace with "by Christ."

19. Insert "His."

20. Insert "of Nazareth, the."

21. Insert "incarnate."

22. Replace with "Conceived of the Holy Spirit, born of the virgin Mary."

23. Replace with "completely."

God, taking upon Himself [the demands of our human][24] nature [and identifying Himself completely with mankind][25] yet without sin. [In][26] His death on the cross[27] He made atonement for [the sins of man].[28] He was raised from the dead [with a glorified body][29] and appeared to His disciples [as the person who was with them before His crucifixion].[30] He ascended into heaven and is now exalted to the right hand of God where He is the One Mediator partaking of the nature of God and of man, and in whose Person is effected reconciliation between God and man.[31] He will return at His Second Advent to judge the world and bring His redemptive mission to a glorious consummation. He now makes His presence known through the Holy Spirit to all believers as the Living and Ever-Present Lord.

IV. THE HOLY SPIRIT

The Holy Spirit [is the third person of the Trinity. He inspired holy men of old to write the Scriptures. Through illumination He][32] enables man to understand truth. He convicts of sin, of righteousness, and of judgment. He calls men to the Saviour, and effects regeneration. He cultivates Christian character, comforts believers, and bestows the spiritual gifts by which they serve God through His church. He seals the believer unto the day of final redemption. His presence [in the Christian][33] is the assurance of God to bring the believer into the fulness of the stature of Christ. He enlightens and empowers both believers and church in worship, evangelism and service.

24. Replace with "our."

25. Insert a comma after "nature" and omit the bracketed material.

26. Omit.

27. Insert "both revealed the sins of men and."

28. Replace with "them."

29. Omit. Insert "bodily" after "appeared."

30. Omit.

31. Commentary: This sentence attempts too much for a single sentence, but with the time at our disposal, we are unable to suggest an alternative.

32. Omit. Commentary: The portions deleted are redundant, or are covered in Article I, the Scriptures.

33. Omit, cf. Col. 1:27; Gal. 2:20.

V. MAN

Man was created by the special act of God, in His own image, and is the crowning work of creation. At the beginning he was innocent of sin but was endowed by His Creator with freedom and the right of choice. By his free choice man sinned against God and brought sin into the human race. Through the temptation of Satan, Adam transgressed the command of God, and fell from his original holiness and righteousness; whereby his posterity inherit a nature corrupt and in bondage to sin, are under condemnation, and as soon as they are capable of moral action become actual transgressors. Only the grace of God can bring man into His holy fellowship and enable him to fulfill the purpose of his creation.[34] The fact that man was created in the image of God and that Christ died for him, bespeaks the sacredness of human personality. Therefore every man possesses dignity and is worthy of respect and Christian love.

VI. SALVATION

Salvation involves the redemption of man in his complete being, and is made free to all by the gospel. Nothing prevents the salvation of a sinner except his failure to accept Jesus Christ as Saviour and Lord.[35] Salvation, in its broadest sense includes regeneration, sanctification, and glorification:[36]

1. Regeneration, or the new birth, is a work of God's grace [whereby we become partakers of the divine nature].[37] It is a change of heart wrought by the Holy Spirit through conviction of sin, to which the sinner responds in repentance toward God and faith in the Lord Jesus Christ.

Repentance and faith are inseparable graces. Repentance is a deep and sincere change of thinking, feeling and willing toward sin and toward

34. This is an accurate state of "justification by grace alone" [and] is contradicted two sentences later by a statement which is Pelagian by the use of the phrase "nothing . . . except {man's} failure."

35. See footnote 34.

36. The attempt to organize "salvation" in terms of a three-stage scheme should be rejected. It is specifically excepted by Paul's testimony. Cf. II Corinthians 5:17ff and Galatians 2:20ff.

37. Initially Mercer suggested replacing "we" with "believers" but then decided to strike the whole phrase. Commentary: This is contradicted by Paul's testimony in Galatians 2:20ff and II Corinthians 5:17ff.

God. Faith is the acceptance of and committal to Jesus Christ as Saviour and Lord and involves the entire personality, thought, feeling and volition. Justification is God's gracious and full acquittal [upon principles][38] of His righteousness of all sinners who repent and believe in Jesus Christ. It brings [us][39] into a state of peace and favor with God.

2. Sanctification is the experience by which the regenerate person is set apart to God's purposes through faith in Jesus Christ and progresses toward moral and spiritual perfection through the presence and power of the Holy Spirit dwelling in his heart. This growth in grace should continue throughout the earthly life.[40]

3. Glorification is the culmination of salvation and is the blessed and abiding state of the redeemed.[41]

VII. GOD'S PURPOSE OF GRACE[42]

Election is the gracious purpose of God, according to which he regenerates, sanctifies, and glorifies sinners. It is consistent with the free agency of man, and comprehends all the means in connection with the end. It is a most glorious display of God's sovereign goodness, and is infinitely wise, holy, and unchangeable. It excludes boasting and promotes humility. It encourages the use of means in the highest degree.

All real believers endure to the end. Those whom God has accepted in the Beloved, and sanctified by His Spirit will never fall away from the state of grace, but shall certainly persevere to the end; and though they may fall into sin, through neglect and temptation, whereby they grieve the

38. Replace with "on the basis of." Commentary: Sentence 15 cf. Of 7B above concerning "Principles." See footnote 14.

39. Replace with "believer(s)."

40. Commentary: Article VI, lines 16–20. That the believer lives by grace, in Christ, and must hear the Apostle Paul speak the word of God in Romans 6 to the effect that the believer is the servant of righteousness is certainly the case. But spelling out the believer's obligation to live by grace in terms of an article entitles [sic] "Sanctification" is fraught with much danger (witness the "Holiness" movement). The term "progresses" sounds like the Enlightenment's "doctrine of progress," and the phrase "moral and spiritual perfection" sounds like humanism.

41. Commentary: The sentence concerning "glorification" is void of helpful content. Does it refer to the life of the redeemed before, or after, the second coming of Christ?

42. The Mercer faculty noted no further suggestions. The balance of the document is included so that the reader may see to what extent Ward's suggestions were followed in the totality of the confession.

Spirit, impair their graces and comforts, bring reproach on the Church, and temporal judgments on themselves, yet they shall be kept by the power of God through faith unto salvation.

VIII. A NEW TESTAMENT CHURCH

A New Testament church of the Lord Jesus Christ is a local body of baptized believers, associated by covenant in the faith and fellowship of the gospel; observing the two ordinances of Christ, governed by His laws, and exercising the gifts, rights, and privileges invested in them by His Word, and seeking to extend the gospel to the ends of the earth.

The church is an autonomous body, operating under the Lordship of members are equally responsible. Its Scriptural officers are pastors and deacons.

The New Testament speaks also of the church as the body of Christ which includes all the redeemed of all the ages.

IX. BAPTISM AND THE LORD'S SUPPER

Christian baptism is the immersion of a believer in water in the name of the Father, the Son, and the Holy Spirit. The act is a symbol of the believer's faith in a crucified and risen Saviour, of the believer's death to sin, the burial of the old life, and the resurrection to walk in newness of life in Christ Jesus. It is a pledge of his faith in the final resurrection of the dead at the second coming of Christ. It is a prerequisite of a church relationship and to the Lord's Supper.

The Lord's Supper is a symbol wherein members of the church commemorate the death of the Redeemer through the bread and the fruit of the vine. It is a thanksgiving for all that Christ means to the believer, and is a fellowship with the living Lord. It is a commitment by which the believer pledges his undying loyalty and obedience to his Lord until He comes.

X. EVANGELISM AND MISSIONS

It is the duty and privilege of every follower of Christ and of every church of the Lord Jesus Christ to endeavor to make disciples of all nations. The new birth of man's spirit by God's Holy Spirit means the birth of love for others. Missionary effort on the part of all rests thus upon a spiritual necessity of the regenerate life. It is also expressly and repeatedly commanded in the teachings of Christ. It is the duty of every child of God to seek constantly to win the lost to Christ by personal effort and by all other methods sanctioned by the gospel of Christ.

XI. EDUCATION

Christianity is the religion of enlightenment and intelligence. In Jesus Christ are hidden all the treasures of wisdom and knowledge. All sound learning is therefore a part of our Christian heritage. The new birth opens all the human faculties and creates a thirst for knowledge. An adequate system of schools is necessary to complete the spiritual program for Christ's people.

In Christian education there should be a proper balance between academic freedom and academic responsibility. Freedom in any orderly relationship of human life is always limited and never absolute. The free of a teacher in a Christian school, college or seminary is limited by the distinct purpose for which the school exists, by the authoritative nature of the Scriptures, and by the pre-eminence of Jesus Christ who is "the way, the truth, and the life." The cause of education in the Kingdom of Christ is co-ordinate with the causes of missions and general benevolence, and should receive along with these the liberal support of the churches.

XII. STEWARDSHIP

God is the source of all blessings, temporal and spiritual; all that we have and are we owe to Him. We have a spiritual debtorship to the whole world, a holy trusteeship in the gospel, and a binding stewardship in our possessions. We are therefore under obligation to serve Him with our time, talents, and material possessions; and should recognize all these as entrusted to us to use for the glory of God and for helping others. According to the Scriptures, Christians should contribute of their means cheerfully, regularly, systematically, proportionately, and liberally for the advancement of the Redeemer's cause on earth.

XIII. COOPERATION

Christ's people should, as occasion requires, organize such associations and conventions as may best secure co-operation for the great objects of the Kingdom of God. Such organizations have no authority over one another or over the churches. They are voluntary and advisory bodies designed to elicit, combine, and direct the energies of our people in the most effective manner. Individual members of New Testament churches should co-operate with one another in carrying forward the missionary, educational, and benevolent program for the extension of Christ's Kingdom. Christian unity in the New Testament sense is spiritual harmony and voluntary co-operation for common ends by various groups of Christ's people. Co-operation is permissable (*sic*) and desirable as between the various Christian denominations when the end to be attained is itself justified, and when such co-operation involves no violation of conscience or compromise of loyalty to Christ and His Word as revealed in the New Testament.

XIV. THE CHRISTIAN AND THE SOCIAL ORDER

Every Christian is under obligation to seek to make the will of Christ regnant in his own life and in human society; to oppose in the spirit of Christ every form of greed, selfishness, and vice; to provide for the orphaned, the aged, the helpless, and the sick; to seek to bring industry, government, and society as a whole under the sway of the principles of righteousness, truth and brotherly love; to promote these ends Christians should be ready to work with all men of good will in any good cause, always being careful to act in the spirit of love without compromising their loyalty to Christ and His truth. Means and methods used in social service for the amelioration of society and the establishment of righteousness among men can be truly and permanently helpful only when they are rooted in the regeneration of the individual by the saving grace of God in Christ Jesus.

XV. RELIGIOUS LIBERTY

God alone is Lord of the conscience, and He has left it free from the doctrines and commandments of men which are contrary to His Word or not contained in it. Church and state should be separate. The state owes to the church protection and full freedom in the pursuit of its spiritual ends. In providing for such freedom no ecclesiastical group or denomination should be favored by the state more than others. Civil government being ordained of God, it is the duty of Christians to render loyal obedience thereto in all things not contrary to the revealed will of God. The church should not resort to the civil power to carry on its work. The gospel of Christ contemplates spiritual means alone for the pursuit of its ends. The state has no right to impose penalties for religious opinions of any kind. The state has no right to impose taxes for the support of any form of religion. A free church in a free state is the Christian ideal, and this implies the right of free and unhindered access to God on the part of all men, and the right to form and propagate opinions in the sphere of religion without interference by the civil power.

XVI. THE LORD'S DAY

The first day of the week is the Lord's Day. It is a Christian institution for regular observance. It commemorates the resurrection of Christ fro the dead and should be employed in exercises of worship and spiritual devotion, both public and private, and by refraining from worldly amusements, and resting from secular employments, works of necessity and mercy only excepted.

XVII. PEACE AND WAR

It is the duty of Christians to seek peace with all men on principles of righteousness. In accordance with the spirit and teachings of Christ they should do all in their power to put an end to war.

The true remedy for the war spirit is the gospel of our Lord. The supreme need of the world is the acceptance of His teachings in all the affairs of men and nations, and the practical application of His law of love.

We urge Christian people throughout the world to pray for the reign of the Prince of Peace, and to oppose everything likely to provoke war.

XVIII. THE KINGDOM

The Kingdom of God includes both His general sovereignty over the universe and His particular kingship over men who willfully acknowledge Him as King. Particularly the Kingdom is the realm of salvation into which men enter by trustful, childlike commitment to Jesus Christ. Christians ought to pray and labor that the Kingdom may come and God's will be done on earth. The full consummation of the Kingdom awaits the return of Jesus Christ and the end of this age.

XIX. LAST THINGS

God is Sovereign in and above history. In His own time and in His own way, He will bring the world to its appropriate end. According to His promise, Jesus Christ will return personally and visibly in glory to the earth; the dead will be raised; and Christ will judge all men in righteousness. The unrighteous will be consigned to hell, the place of everlasting punishment. The righteous in their resurrected and glorified bodies will receive their reward and will dwell forever in Heaven with God, Jesus Christ His Son, the holy angels and the saints of all the ages.

Appendix Three

Comparison of Drafts as Received

by Ward and Mercer

WARD DRAFT	MERCER UNIVERSITY DRAFT
PREAMBLE	PREAMBLE
Southern Baptists are a people with a living faith. It is rooted and grounded in Jesus Christ who is "the same yesterday, today, and forever." Being a living faith it experiences a growing understanding of truth and must be continually interpreted and related to the needs of each new generation.	Southern Baptists are a people with a living faith. This faith is rooted and grounded in Jesus Christ who is "the same yesterday, today, and forever." Being a living faith it experiences a growing understanding of truth and must be continually interpreted and related to the needs of each new generation.
Through the years Baptist bodies, both large and small, have issued statements of faith which comprised a concensus (sic) of their beliefs, regarding the teachings of the Bible which is the written record of God's revelation of Himself to man. Such statements have never been regarded as complete, infallible statements of	Through the years Baptist bodies, both large and small, have issued statements of faith which comprised a concensus (sic) of their beliefs. Such statements have never been regarded as complete, infallible statements of faith nor as binding upon the consciences of those who gave assent to them. They

faith nor as binding upon the consciences of those who gave assent to them. They were not regarded as official creeds, carrying mandatory authority.

We are in historic succession of intent and purpose as this generation of Southern Baptists endeavors to state for its time these articles of the Christian faith which are most surely held among us. The sole authority for faith and practice among Baptists is the Lordship of Christ as revealed in the Holy Scriptures and especially in the New Testament.

Baptists place great emphasis on the individual's soul competency before God, freedom in religion, and the priesthood of the believer. However, this emphasis should not be interpreted to mean that there are not certain definite doctrines that Baptists hold dear and with which they have been and are closely identified.

It is the purpose of this statement to of faith to set forth principles which we believe.

were not regarded as official creeds, carrying mandatory authority.

We are in historic succession of intent and purpose as this generation of Southern Baptists endeavors to state for its time those articles of the Christian faith which are most surely held among us. The sole authority for faith and practice among Baptists is the Lordship of Christ as revealed in the Holy Scriptures, especially in the New Testament.

Baptists place great emphasis on the individual soul's competency before God, freedom in religion, and the priesthood of the believer. However, this emphasis should not be interpreted to mean that there are not certain definite doctrines that Baptists hold dear and with which they have been and are closely identified.

It is the purpose of this statement of faith to set forth these principles.

THE BAPTIST FAITH AND MESSAGE

I. The Scriptures

We believe that the Holy Bible was Written by men divinely inspired, and is a perfect treasure of heavenly instruction; that it has God

THE BAPTIST FAITH AND MESSAGE

I. The Scriptures

The Holy Bible was written by men divinely inspired and is the record of God's revelation of Himself to man. It is a perfect treasure of for its author, salvation for its end, and truth, without any mixture of error, for its matter; that it reveals the principles by which God will judge us; and therefore is, and will remain to the end of the world, the true center of Christian union, and the supreme standard by which all human conduct, creeds, and opinions should be tried. The criterion by which the Bible is to be interpreted is the person, work and teachings of Jesus Christ.

divine instruction. It has God for its author, salvation for its end, and truth, without any mixture of error, for its matter. It reveals the principles by which God will judge us; and therefore is, and will remain to the end of the world, the true center of Christian union, and the supreme standard by which all human conduct, creeds, and opinions should be tried. The criterion by which the Bible is to be interpreted is the person, work, and teachings of Jesus Christ.

II. God

There is one and only one living and true God, an intelligent, spiritual, and personal Being, the Creator, Preserver, and Ruler of the universe, infinite in holiness and all other perfections, to whom we owe the highest love, reverence, and obedience. He is revealed to us as Father, Son, and Holy Spirit, each with distinct personal attributes, but without division of nature, essence, or being.

II. God

There is only one living and true God, an intelligent, spiritual, and personal Being, the Creator, Preserver, and Ruler of the universe, infinite in holiness and all other perfections, to whom we owe the highest love, reverence, and obedience. He is revealed to us as Father, Son, and Holy Spirit, each with distinct personal attributes, but without division of nature, essence, or being.

III. Jesus Christ

Jesus Christ is the Eternal Son of God, who entered history in the person of the virgin-born Jesus of Nazareth. As man, Jesus, He was completely human, and yet in His earthly life he was one with God in being. In His incarnation He

III. Jesus Christ

Jesus Christ is the Eternal Son of God. In His incarnation as the virgin born Jesus of Nazareth, He perfectly revealed and did the will of God, taking upon Himself the demands of our human nature and identifying Himself completely perfectly revealed and did the will of God, taking upon Himself the demands and necessities of human nature and identifying Himself completely with mankind. In His death on the cross he made atonement for the sins of man. He arose from the dead and appeared to His disciples as the person who was with them before the crucifixion. He was then exalted at the right hand of God where He is now the One Mediator partaking of the nature of God and of man, and in whose Person is effected reconciliation between God and man and from whence He will return at His second Advent to judge theWorld and bring His redemptive mission to a glorious consummation. He now makes His presence known through the Holy Spirit to all believers as the Living and Ever-Present Lord.

with mankind yet without sin. In His death on the cross He made atonement for the sins of man. He was raised from the dead with a glorified body and appeared to His disciples as the person who was with them before His crucifixion. He ascended into heaven and is now exalted to the right hand of God where He is the One Mediator partaking of the nature of God and of man, and in whose Person is effected reconciliation between God and man. He will return at His Second Advent to judge the world and bring His redemptive mission to a glorious consummation. He now makes His presenceknown through the Holy Spirit to all believers as the Living and Ever-Present Lord.

IV. The Holy Spirit

The Holy Spirit is the third person of the Trinity. Through inspiration He was the author of the Holy Scriptures. Through illumination He enlightens man to understand truth. He convicts of sin, of righteousness and of judgment. He calls men to the Saviour and effects regeneration. He cultivates Christian character, comforts believers, bestows the spiritual gifts

IV. The Holy Spirit

The Holy Spirit is the third person of the Trinity. He inspired holy men of old to write the Scriptures. Through illumination He enables man to understand truth. He convicts of sin, of righteousness, and of judgment. He calls men to the Saviour, and effects regeneration. He cultivates Christian character, comforts believers, and bestows the spiritual gifts by which they by which they serve God through His church. He seals the believer unto the day of final redemption. His presence in the Christian is the assurance of God to bring the believer into the fullness of Christ. He enlightens and empowers the believer and the Church in its worship, evangelism and service.

serve God through His church. He seals the believer unto the day of final redemption. His presence in the Christian is the assurance of God to bring the believer into the fullness of the stature of Christ. He enlightens and empowers both believers and church in worship, evangelism and service.

V. Man

Man was created by the special act of God, in His own image, and is the crown of His creation. At the beginning he was innocent of sin but was endowed by His Creator with freedom and the right of choice. By his free choice, man sinned against God and brought sin into the human race. His posterity inherit a nature corrupt and in bondage to sin, and as soon as they are capable of moral action become actual transgressors, and are under condemnation. Only the grace of God can bring man back into His holy fellowship and enable him to fulfill the purpose of his creation. The fact that man was created in the image of God and that Christ died for him bespeaks the sacredness of human personality. As such he possesses dignity and is worthy of respect and Christian love regardless of race or class.

V. Man

Man was created by the special act of God, in His own image, and is the crowning work of creation. At the beginning he was innocent of sin but was endowed by His Creator with freedom and the right of choice. By his free choice man sinned against God and brought sin into the human race. Through the temptation of Satan, Adam transgressed the command of God, and fell from his original holiness and righteousness; whereby his posterity inherit a nature corrupt and in bondage to sin, are under condemnation, and as soon as they are capable of moral action become actual transgressors. Only the grace of God can bring man into His holy fellowship and enable him to fulfill the purpose of his creation. The fact that man was created in the image of God and that Christ died for him, bespeaks the sacredness of human personality. Therefore every man possesses dignity and is worthy of respect and Christian love.

VI. *Salvation*

Salvation involves the redemption of man in his complete being, and is made free to all by the gospel. Nothing prevents the salvation of the greatest sinner except his failure to accept Jesus Christ as Saviour and Lord. Salvation begins in regeneration, continues in sanctification, and culminates in glorification:

1. Regeneration, or the new birth, is a work of God's grace whereby we become partakers of the divine nature. It is a change of heart wrought by the Holy Spirit through conviction of sin, to which the sinner responds in repentance toward God and faith in the Lord Jesus Christ.

Repentance and faith are inseparable graces. Repentance is a deep and sincere change of thinking, feeling and willing toward God. Faith is the acceptance of and committal to Jesus Christ as Saviour and Lord and involves the entire personality, thought, feeling and volition. Justification is God's gracious and full acquittal upon principles of His righteousness of all sinners who repent and believe in Christ.

VI. *Salvation*

Salvation involves the redemption of man in his complete being, and is made free to all by the gospel. Nothing prevents the salvation of a sinner except his failure to accept Jesus Christ as Saviour and Lord. Salvation, in its broadest sense includes regeneration, sanctification, and glorification:

1. Regeneration, or the new birth, is a work of God's grace whereby we become partakers of the divine nature. It is a change of heart wrought by the Holy Spirit through conviction of sin, to which the sinner responds in repentance toward God and faith in the Lord Jesus Christ.

Repentance and faith are inseparable graces. Repentance is a deep and sincere change of thinking, feeling and willing toward sin and toward God. Faith is the acceptance of and committal to Jesus Christ as Saviour and Lord and involves the entire personality, thought, feeling and volition. Justification is God's gracious and full acquittal upon principles of His righteousness of all sinners who repent and believe in Jesus Christ. It brings us into a state of peace and favor with God.

2. Sanctification is the experience by which the regenerate person, having been set apart through faith in Jesus Christ, progressively attains to moral and spiritual perfection through the presence and power of the Holy Spirit dwelling in his heart. It continues throughout the earthly life, and is accomplished by the use of all the ordinary means of grace, and particularly by the Word of God.

3. Glorification is the culmination of salvation and is the blessed and abiding state of the redeemed.

VII. God's Purpose of Grace

Election is the gracious purpose of God, according to which he regenerates, sanctifies, and saves sinners. It is consistent with the free agency of man, and comprehends all the means in connection with the end. It is a most glorious display of God's sovereign goodness, and is infinitely holy, and unchangeable. It excludes boasting and promotes humility. It encourages the use of means in the highest degree.

All real believers endure to the end. Those whom God hath accepted in the Beloved, and sanctified by His Spirit, will never totally nor finally fall away from the state of grace, but shall certainly persevere to the end; and though they may fall into sin, through neglect

2. Sanctification is the experience by which the regenerate person is set apart to God's purposes through faith in Jesus Christ and progresses toward moral and spiritual perfection through the presence and power of the Holy Spirit dwelling in his heart. This growth in grace should continue throughout the earthly life.

3. Glorification is the culmination of salvation and is the blessed and abiding state of the redeemed.

VII. God's Purpose of Grace

Election is the gracious purpose of God, according to which he regenerates, sanctifies, and glorifies sinners. It is consistent with the free agency of man, and comprehends all the means in connection with the end. It is a most glorious display ofGod's sovereign goodness, and is infinitely wise, holy, and unchangeable. It excludes boasting and promotes humility. It encourages the use of means in the highest degree.

All real believers endure to the end. Those whom God has accepted in the Beloved, and sanctified by His Spirit will never fall away from the state of grace, but shall certainly persevere to the end; and though they may fall into sin, through neglect and temptation, and temptation, whereby they grieve the Spirit, impair their graces and comforts, bring reproach upon the Church, and temporal judgments on themselves, yet they shall be renewed again unto repentance, and be kept by the power of God through faith unto salvation.

VIII. A New Testament Church

A New Testament Church of the Lord Jesus Christ is a congregation of baptized believers, associated by covenant in the faith and fellowship of the gospel; observing the ordinances of Christ, Governed by His laws, and exercising the gifts, rights, and privileges invested in them by His word and seeking to extend the gospel to the ends of the earth.

This church is an autonomous body, operating under the Lordship of Jesus Christ. In such a congregation, members are equal and equally responsible. Its Scriptural officers are pastors and deacons. The New Testament also speaks of the church as the body of Christ which includes all of the redeemed.

IX. Baptism and the Lord's Supper

Christian baptism is the immersion of a believer in water in the name of the Father, the Son, and the Holy

whereby they grieve the Spirit, impair their graces and comforts, bring reproach on the Church, and temporal judgments on themselves, yet shall they be kept by the power of God through faith unto salvation.

VIII. A New Testament Church

A New Testament church of the Lord Jesus Christ is a local body of baptized believers, associated by covenant in the faith and fellowship of the gospel; observing the two ordinances of Christ, governed by His laws, and exercising the gifts, rights, and privileges invested in them by His Word, and seeking to extend the gospel to the ends of the earth.

The church is an autonomous body, operating under the Lordship of members are equally responsible. Its Scriptural officers are pastors and deacons.

The New Testament speaks also of the church as the body of Christ which includes all the redeemed of all things.

IX. Baptism and the Lord's Supper

Christian baptism is the immersion of a believer in water in the name of the Father, the Son, and the Holy Spirit. The act is a symbol

188

Spirit. The act is a symbol of the believer's faith in a crucified, buried and risen Saviour, of the believer's death to sin, the burial of the old life, and the resurrection to walk in newness of life in Christ Jesus. It is a pledge of his faith in the final resurrection of the dead at the second coming of Christ. It is prerequisite to the privileges of a church relation and to the Lord's Supper.

The Lord's Supper is the means of commemorating the death of the Redeemer through bread and the fruit of the vine. It is a thanksgiving for all that Christ means to the believer, and is a communion with the living Lord. It is a commitment by which the believer pledges his undying loyalty and obedience to his Lord until He comes.

X. The Lord's Day

The first day of the week is the Lord's Day. It is a Christian institution for regular observance. It commemorates the resurrection of Christ from the dead and should be employed in exercises of worship and spiritual devotion, both public and private, and by refraining from worldly amusements, and resting from secular employments, work of necessity and mercy only excepted.

of the believer's faith in a crucified and risen Saviour, of the believer's death to sin, the burial of the old life, and the resurrection to walk in newness of life in Christ Jesus. It is a pledge of his faith in the final resurrection of the dead at the secondcoming of Christ. It is a prerequisite of a church relationship and to the Lord's Supper.

The Lord's Supper is a symbol wherein members of the church commemorate the death of the Redeemer through the bread and the fruit of the vine. It is a thanksgiving for all that Christ means to the believer, and is a fellowship with the living Lord. It is a commitment by which the believer pledges his undying loyalty and obedience to his Lord until He comes.

X. Evangelism and Missions

It is the duty and privilege of every follower of Christ and of every church of the Lord Jesus Christ to endeavor to make disciples of all nations. The new birth of man's spirit by God's Holy Spirit means the birth of love for others. Missionary effort on the part of all rests upon a spiritual necessity of the regenerate life. It is also expressly and repeatedly commanded in the teachings ofChrist. It is the duty of every child of God to seek constantly to win the lost to Christ

XI. The Kingdom

The Kingdom of God includes both His general sovereignty over the universe and His particular kingship over men who willfully acknowledge Him as King. Particularly the Kingdom is the realm of salvation into which men enter by trustful, childlike commitment to Jesus Christ. Christians ought to pray and labor that the Kingdom may come and God's will be done on earth. The full consummation of the Kingdom awaits the return of Jesus Christ and the end of this age.

XII. Religious Liberty

God alone is Lord of the conscience, and He has left it free from the doctrines and commandments of men which are contrary to His Word or not contained in it. Church and state should be separate. The state owes to the church protection and full freedom in pursuit of its spiritual ends. In providing for such freedom no ecclesiastical group or denomination should be favored by the state, more than others. Civil government being ordained of God, it is the duty of Christians to render loyal obedience thereto in all things not contrary to the revealed will of God. The church should not resort to the civil power to carry on its work. The gospel of Christ by personal effort and by all other needs sanctioned by the gospel of Christ.

XI. Education

Christianity is the religion of enlightenment and intelligence. In Jesus Christ are hidden all the treasures of wisdom and knowledge. All sound learning is therefore a part of our Christian heritage. The new birth opens all the human faculties and creates a thirst for knowledge. An adequate system of schools is necessary to complete the spiritual program for Christ's people.

In Christian education there should be a proper balance between academic freedom and academic responsibility. Freedom in any orderly relationship of human life is always limited and never absolute. The free of a teacher in a Christian school, college or seminary is limited by thepurpose for which the school exists, by the authoritative nature of the Scriptures, and by the pre-eminence of Jesus Christ who is "the way, the truth, and the life." The cause of education in the Kingdom of Christ is co-ordinate with the causes of missions and general benevolence, and should receive along with these the liberal support of the churches.

contemplates spiritual means alone for the pursuit of its ends. The state has no right to impose penalties for religious opinions of any kind. The state has no right to impose taxes for the support of any form of religion. A free church in a free state is the Christian ideal, and this implies the right of free and unhindered access to God on the part of all men, and the right to form and propagate opinions in the sphere of religion without interference by the civil power.

XIII. Peace and War

It is the duty of Christians to seek peace with all men on principles of righteousness. In accordance with the spirit and teaching of Christ they should do all in their power to put an end to war. The true remedy for the war spirit is the pure gospel of our Lord. The supreme need of the world is the acceptance of His teachings in all the affairs of men and nations, and the practical application of His law of love.

We urge Christian people throughout the world to pray for the reign of the Prince of Peace, and to oppose everything likely to provoke war.

XIV. Education

Christianity is the religion of enlightenment and intelligence. In

XII. Stewardship

God is the source of all blessings, temporal and spiritual; all that we have and are we owe to Him. We have a spiritual debtorship to the whole world, and a binding stewardship in our possessions. We are therefore under obligation to serve Him with our time, talents, and material possessions; and should recognize all these as entrusted to us to use for the glory of God and for helping others. According to the Scriptures, Christians should contribute of their means cheerfully, regularly, systematically, proportionately, and liberally for thefor the advancement of the Redeemer's cause on earth.

XIII. Cooperation

Christ's people should, as occasion requires, organize such associations and conventions as may best secure co-operation for the great objects of the Kingdom of God. Such organizations have no authority over one another or over the churches. They are voluntary and advisory bodies designed to elicit, combine, and direct the energies of our people in the most effective manner. Individual members of New Testament churches should co-operate with one another in carrying forward the missionary, educational, and benevolent program for the exten-

Jesus Christ are hidden all the treasures of wisdom and knowledge. All sound learning is therefore part of our Christian heritage. The new birth opens all human faculties and creates a thirst for knowledge. An adequate system of schools is necessary to a complete spiritual program for Christ's people.

In Christian education there should be a proper balance between academic freedom and academic responsibility. Freedom in any orderly relationship of human life is always limited and never absolute. The freedom of a teacher in a Christian school, college or seminary is limited by the distinct purpose for which the school exists, by the authoritative nature of the Scriptures, and by the pre-eminence of Jesus Christ who is "the way, the truth, and the life." The cause of education in the Kingdom of Christ is co-ordinate with the causes of missions and general benevolence, and should receive along with these the liberal support of the churches.

XV. Social Service

Every Christian is under obligation to seek to make the will of Christ regnant in his own life and in human society; to oppose in the spirit of Christ every form of greed, selfishness, and vice; to provide for

sion of Christ's Kingdom. Christian unity in the New Testament sense is a spiritual harmony and voluntary co-operation for common ends by various groups of Christ's people. Co-operation is permissable (sic) and desirable as between the various Christian denominations whenthe end to be attained is itself justified, and when such co-operation involves no violation of conscience or compromise of loyalty to Christ and His Word as revealed in the New Testament.

XIV. The Christian and the Social Order

Every Christian is under obligation to seek to make the will of Christ regnant in his own life and in human society; to oppose in the spirit of Christ every form of greed, selfishness, and vice; to provide for the orphaned, the aged, the helpless, and the sick; to seek to bring industry, government, and society as a whole under the sway of the principles of righteousness, truth and brotherly love; to promote these ends Christians should be ready to work with all men of good will in any good cause, always being careful to act in the spirit of love without compromising their loyalty to Christ and His truth. Means and methods used in social service for the amelioration of society and the orphaned, the aged, the helpless, and the sick; to seek to bring industry, government, and society as a whole under the sway of the principles of righteousness, truth andbrotherly love; to promote these ends Christians should be ready to work with all men of good will in any good cause, always being careful to act in the spirit of love without compromising their loyalty to Christ and His truth. All means and methods used in social service for the amelioration of society and the establishment of righteousness among men must finally depend on the regeneration of the individual by the saving grace of God in Christ.

XVI. Co-Operation

Christ's people should, as occasion requires, organize such associations and conventions as may best secure co-operation for the great objects of the Kingdom of God. Such organizations have no authority over each other or over the churches. They are voluntary and advisory bodies designed to elicit, combine, and direct the energies of our people in the most effective manner. Individual members of New Testament churches should co-operate with each otherand the churches themselves should co-operate with each other in carrying

the establishment of righteousnessamong men can be truly and permanently helpful only when they are rooted in the regeneration of the individual by the saving grace of God in Christ Jesus.

XV. Religious Liberty

God alone is Lord of the conscience, and He has left it free from the doctrines and commandments of men which are contrary to His Word or not contained in it. Church and state should be separate. The state owes to the church protection and full freedom in the pursuit of its spiritual ends. In providing for such freedom no ecclesiastical group or denomination should be favored by the state more than others. Civil government being ordained of God, it is the duty of Christians to render loyal obedience thereto in all things not contrary to the revealed will of God. The church should not resort to the civil power to carry on its work. The gospel of Christ contemplates spiritual means alone for the pursuit of its ends. The state has no right to impose penalties for religiousopinions of any kind. The state has no right to impose taxes for the support of any form of religion. A free church in a free state is the Christian ideal, and this implies the right of free and unhindered access to God on the part of forward the missionary, educational, and benevolent program for the extension of Christ's Kingdom. Christian unity in the New Testament sense is spiritual harmony and voluntary co-operation for common ends by various groups of Christ's people. It is permissable (sic) and desirable as between various Christian denominations, when the end to be attained is itself justified, and when such co-operation involves no violation of conscience or compromise of loyalty to Christ and His Word as revealed in the New Testament.

XVII. Evangelism and Missions

It is the duty and privilege of every follower of Christ and every church of the Lord Jesus Christ to endeavor to make disciples of all nations. The new birth of man's spirit by God's Holy Spirit means a birth of love for others. Missionary effort on the part of all rests thus upon a spiritual necessity of the regenerate life. It is also expressly and repeatedly commanded in the teachings of Christ. It is the duty of every child of God to seek constantly to win the lost to Christ by personal effort and by all other methods sanctioned by the gospel of Christ.

all men, and the right to form and propagate opinions in the sphere of religion without interference by the civil power.

XVI. The Lord's Day

The first day of the week is the Lord's Day. It is a Christian institution for regular observance. It commemorates the resurrection of Christ from the dead and should be employed in exercises of worship and spiritual devotion, both public and private, and by refraining from worldly amusements, and resting from secular employments, works of necessity and mercy only excepted.

XVII. Peace and War

It is the duty of Christians to seek peace with all men on principles of righteousness. In accordance with the spiritand teachings of Christ they should do all in their power to put an end to war.

The true remedy for the war spirit is the gospel of our Lord. The supreme need of the world is the acceptance of His teachings in all the affairs of men and nations, and the practical application of His law of love.

We urge Christian people throughout the world to pray for the reign of the Prince of Peace,

XVIII. Stewardship

God is the source of all blessings, temporal and spiritual; all that we have and are we owe to Him. We have a spiritual debtorship to the whole world, a holy trusteeship in the gospel, and a binding stewardship in our possessions. We are therefore under obligation to serve Him with our time, talents and material possessions; and should recognize all these as entrusted to us to use for the glory of God and helping others. Christians should cheerfully, regularly, systematically, proportionately, and liberally contribute of their means advancing the Redeemer's cause on earth.

XIX. Last Things

God is Sovereign in and above history. In His own time and in His own way, He will bring the world to its appropriate end. According to His promise, Jesus Christ will return in glory to the earth; the dead will be raised; and Christ will judge all men in righteousness. The unrighteous will be consigned to the place of everlasting punishment. The righteous in their resurrected and glorified bodies will receive their reward and will dwell forever in Heaven with God, Jesus Christ His Son, the holy angels and the saints of all the ages.

and to oppose everything likely to provoke war.

XVIII. The Kingdom

The Kingdom of God includes both His general sovereignty over the universe and His particular kingship over men who willfully acknowledge Him as King. Particularly the Kingdom is the realm of salvation into which men enter by trustful, childlike commitment to Jesus Christ. Christians ought to pray and labor that the Kingdom may come and God's will be done on earth. The full consummation of the Kingdom awaits the return of Jesus Christ and the end of this age.

XIX. Last Things

God is Sovereign in and above history. In His own time and in His own way, He will bring the world to its appropriate end. According to His promise, Jesus Christ will return personally and visibly in glory to the earth; the dead will be raised; and Christ will judge all men in righteousness. The unrighteous will be consigned to hell, the place of everlasting punishment. The righteous in their resurrected and glorified bodies will receive their reward and will dwell forever in Heaven with God, Jesus Christ His Son, the holy angels and the saints of all the ages.

Appendix Four

A Declaration of Basic Beliefs

by James Leo Garrett

I. REVELATION AND THE SCRIPTURES

GOD, WHO HAS NOT left Himself without a witness through His wondrous creation, revealed Himself uniquely and savingly in history to the people called Israel and supremely, climactically, and fully in and through His Son, Jesus Christ. The authentic record of this divine self-disclosure consists of the canonical Scriptures of the Old and New Testaments, or the Bible. Written by men who were inspired by the Holy Spirit, the Bible is to be interpreted through careful exegesis under the guidance of the Holy Spirit and the criterion of the person, work, and teaching of Jesus Christ, who has fulfilled the law and the prophets and is the Way, the Truth, and the Life. Biblical truth when rightly interpreted is not in conflict with truth in any realm of knowledge. The Bible should be the standard by which all human beliefs and conduct should be tested and the basis for Christian unity.

II. GOD

God is one, the only living and true God, an intelligent, spiritual, personal and supreme being, perfect in His manifold attributes such as holiness, righteousness, and love. God is the Creator of all the universe according to His sovereign will and power and the Sustainer and Ruler of all that exists. To Him all men owe the highest love, reverence, and obedience. This one God has been revealed as the Father, the Son, and the Holy Spirit, each having personal, though not individuated, distinctions, yet the Three being One in essence or deity. God the gracious Redeemer purposes the deliverance of all His human creatures from sin.

III. MAN

Man was created by God in His own image, being the crown of His creation and having the capacity of responsible freedom before God. Occasioned by Satanic temptation man the creature freely chose to rebel against God and transgress the divine commandment and, thus falling away from fellowship with God and out of harmony with his fellow human beings, became man the sinner. All men therefore are born into a sinful world with a nature affected by sin, and, when capable of moral choice and action, become actual sinners, the consequences of which include bondage and death. All men are thus in need of deliverance or reclamation from sin and of regeneration or new life.

IV. JESUS CHRIST

Jesus, the Christ or Messiah of Israel, is the eternal and unique Son of God who entered history in the person of Jesus of Nazareth. Conceived by the Holy Spirit and born of the Marry the virgin, Jesus was completely human yet one with God as to deity and fully man yet without sin. Matchless Teacher and Worker of miracles, Jesus became the Mediator between God and men, perfectly revealing the Father's will to men and perfectly representing men before the Father. For the salvation of all men Jesus suffered at human hands shameful crucifixion, rose victoriously from the dead, appeared to his disciples as the one who was with them before his crucifixion, and ascended to the Father. Being exalted, He lives and intercedes for men. Him we confess to be our Saviour, Lord, and King.

V. BECOMING A CHRISTIAN

God purposes to save or redeem all men in Jesus Christ, whose death-resurrection is the atoning act by which God's righteousness is vindicated, God's self-giving love is supremely revealed, and God's victory over sin, death, and Satanic powers is won. By the unmerited favor of God and apart from all human works, achievements, or merits, all sinners who exercise genuine repentance toward and faith or trust in Jesus the Lord are forgiven as to sin, justified or declared righteous before God, regenerated or born anew, reconciled to the Father, and adopted into the family of God. Nothing prevents the salvation of the greatest sinner who is confronted with the Christian gospel except his own voluntary refusal to receive and confess Jesus as his Lord and Savior.

VI. THE HOLY SPIRIT AND THE CHRISTIAN LIFE

The Holy Spirit, proceeding from and yet distinct from the Father and the Son, works to fulfil the mission of the incarnate Jesus Christ. He convicts men of sin, effects their renewal or new birth, instructs, enlightens, and guides Christians, aids them in resisting temptation, produces in them the distinctively Christian qualities of character, and supplies the dynamic for effective Christian witness and service. Since God is the Source of all blessings, Christians as stewards ought faithfully to serve Him in respect to time, spiritual capacities, and material possessions. They should cheerfully, systematically, proportionately, and liberally contribute of their means to advance the mission and rule of Jesus Christ among men. The Holy Spirit is the agent of the sanctification of Christians from their initial dedication to God and through the process of Christian growth to full spiritual maturity or Christlikeness. Christians are commanded to grow in the grace and knowledge of Jesus Christ. All genuine believers endure or continue as children of God, their continuance distinguishing them from those who merely profess such faith, for Christians are kept by God's power through faith unto final salvation.

VII. THE CHURCH

Jesus Christ is calling forth from the nations of mankind His own people over whom His kingly rule is exercised, the Church, which is the temple of God, the body of Christ, and the fellowship of the Holy Spirit, the organized expression of which are particular or local congregations or churches of Christians. These congregations, when rightly constituted, consist only of genuine believers in Jesus as Lord baptized by immersion in the name of the triune God, dedicated to Jesus and to one another, and living unitedly in a disciplined fellowship of Christian love.

The immersion of believers or disciples in water is a dramatic reenactment of the death, burial, and resurrection of Jesus, an enactment of the believer's identification with Jesus in death to sin, burial with Him, and resurrection to a new life, and a symbolic portrayal of the washing of the new birth. Thereby the disciple pledges his allegiance to Jesus Christ and his participation in the community of disciples. Such baptism is prerequisite to the privilege of church membership and to participation in the Lord's Supper, that enactment by which members after solemn self-examination by the use of bread and the cup regularly commemorate together the sacrificial dying love of Jesus.

Such congregations ought regularly to engage in the public worship of God, to instruct and train their members in Christian teachings and duties, and in the name of Jesus to care to those who suffer or have particular need. While all Christians ought to minister to men in behalf of their Lord, to some are given particular gifts of ministry, especially that of the Word of God and prayer, and such pastors, deacons, and the like, called of God and chosen by the congregation are to be ordained to such ministries. Baptist churches are governed by the majority vote of their members, the ideal being one of consensus by all members through seeking the guidance of the Holy Spirit. Such churches ought to cooperate with other Baptist churches through associations, conventions, unions, and alliances, for mutual fellowship and the support of Christian missionary, educational, and benevolent enterprises and to seek, wherever possible without compromise of Christian truth, the unity of all who confess Jesus as Lord. Every congregation, as indeed every Christian, is obligated by the commission of Jesus and the nature of the gospel to seek by all available means to make disciples of all men throughout the world until the end of the age.

VIII. THE STATE AND SOCIETY

Civil government is ordained of God, and obedience thereto is the duty of Christians except in things clearly contrary to the revealed will of God. Christians ought to pay taxes to civil government and to pray for the leaders of civil government. All men have the right to religious liberty, or the freedom to choose, espouse, practice, teach, and make converts to that form of religious worship and teach which they believe to be consistent with conscience without the interference of and with the protection of civil authority. The most adequate structure for securing religious liberty and for maintaining the proper functions of government and of religion is the institutional separation of church and state. Thereby no denomination or religious body should be established or favored by the state, no religious tests for civil office imposed, and no taxes levied for the support of religion. Likewise, no religious body should seek civil power or preferment as a means of fulfilling its religious mission.

Christians ought to seek, where possible, to make the will of Jesus Christ regnant in human society. Accepting the ideal of monogamous marriage Christians ought to establish and cultivate Christian homes characterized by regular Christian devotion and nurture, Christian love, and the building of Christian character. Christians ought in the spirit of Christ to oppose every form of vice, obscenity, greed, injustice, and prejudice in human life and society. Since God is love and no respecter of persons, His children should love all men and discriminate against none. Christians ought to practice and support honesty and integrity in business, labor, and economic life. The Lord's Day, commemorating the resurrection of Jesus, ought to be observed not only by engaging in worship and devotion but also by cessation from all unnecessary employment. Christians ought to strive for provision of adequate care for the medically ill, the aged, the orphaned and neglected children, the indigent, and the helpless. Christians should pray for and actively seek peace among all nations based on international justice and adequate control of massively destructive weapons of warfare.

IX. LAST THINGS

The Kingdom of God, or God's rule or reign, includes both His general sovereignty over the universe and His particular kingship over men who wilfully acknowledge Him as King. Rooted in the election and function of Israel as the covenant people under Yahweh's kingship, the Kingdom of God was brought near to men with the advent of Jesus and actualized by the reign of God over the subjects of Christ. The Kingdom is the realm of salvation into which men enter by trustful, childlike commitment to Jesus Christ. Christians ought to pray and labor that the Kingdom may come and God's will be done on earth. Yet the full consummation of the Kingdom awaits the return of Jesus Christ and the end of this age. Christians await and expect according to His promise the coming manifestation of Jesus in power and victory; the time of which is unknown to and unpredictable by men but known by God. Christians anticipate in hope the bodily resurrection of all men, both righteous and unrighteous, and, having entered the transition of death, expect to be clothed with spiritual bodies like the resurrection body of Jesus. They likewise anticipate at the end of human history a final or last judgment by Jesus the Son of Man of all men, righteous and unrighteous, to make manifest their eternal and separate destinies and to issue rewards and punishments. The unrighteous or the unredeemed shall experience everlasting separation from God and His saints and punishment commensurate with such destiny. The righteous or the Christian believers shall live forever in the fellowship of the triune God and those who praise and serve Him in his eternal Kingdom.

Bibliography

PRIMARY SOURCES

Books

Annual of the Southern Baptist Convention Nineteen Hundred Twenty-Five. Nashville: Marshall & Bruce Co., 1925.

Annual of the Southern Baptist Convention Nineteen Hundred Twenty-Six. Nashville: Marshall & Bruce Co., 1926.

Annual of the Southern Baptist Convention, Nineteen Hundred and Forty-Six. Nashville: Executive Committee, Southern Baptist Convention, 1946.

Annual of the Southern Baptist Convention Nineteen Hundred and Sixty-Two. Nashville: Executive Committee, Southern Baptist Convention, 1962.

Annual of the Southern Baptist Convention Nineteen Hundred and Sixty-Three. Nashville: Executive Committee, Southern Baptist Convention, 1963.

Baker, Joseph S. *Queries Considered or An Investigation of Various Subjects Involved in the Exercise of Church Discipline.* Penfield, GA: The Christian Index, 1847. Reprinted in *Polity: Biblical Arguments on How to Conduct Church Life*, Mark Dever, ed. Washington, D.C.: Center for Church Reform, 2001.

Baker, Robert A. *A Baptist Sourcebook with Particular Reference to Southern Baptists.* Nashville: Broadman Press, 1966; reprint edition Eugene OR: Wipf & Stock Publishers, 2000.

The Baptist Faith and Message 1963. Nashville: The Sunday School Board of the Southern Baptist Convention, 1963.

The Baptist Faith and Message 2000. Nashville: LifeWay Christian Resources, 2000.

Blackwood, Christopher. *The Storming of Antichrist, In His Two Last and Strongest Garrisons; of Compulsion of Conscience, and Infants Baptisme.* London: n.p., 1644.

Boyce, James P. *Abstract of Systematic Theology.* Louisville: Chas T. Dearing, 1882, 1887; reprint, Christian Gospel Foundation?, 197?.

Carroll, B. H. *Baptists and Their Doctrines.* Edited by Timothy and Denise George, with a Foreword by Ken Hemphill. Nashville: Broadman & Holman Publishers, 1995, 1999.

————. *Inspiration of the Bible: A Discussion of the Origin, the Authenticity and the Sanctity of the Oracles of God.* Comp. and ed. by J. B. Cranfill. New York: Fleming H. Revell Company, 1930.

Carter, Joseph E. *Distinctive Baptist Principles.* Raleigh, NC: Edwards, Broughton, & Co., Printers and Binders, 1883.

Curtis, Thomas F. *The Progress of Baptist Principles in the Last Hundred Years.* Boston: Gould and Lincoln, 1855.

Bibliography

Dagg, John L. *Manual of Theology*. Nashville: The Southern Baptist Publication Society, 1857; reprint, Harrisonburg, VA: Gano Books, 1990.

Dargan, E. C. *The Doctrines of Our Faith*. Nashville: Sunday School Board Southern Baptist Convention, 1905.

Deweese, Charles W. *Baptist Church Covenants*. Nashville: Broadman Press, 1990.

Dobbins, Gaines S. *Baptist Churches in Action*. Nashville: Sunday School Board of the Southern Baptist Convention, 1929.

Elliott, Ralph H. *The "Genesis Controversy" and Continuity in Southern Baptist Chaos: A Eulogy for a Great Tradition*. Macon: Mercer University Press, 1992.

————. *The Message of Genesis*. Nashville: Broadman Press, 1961.

Finney, Charles G. *Finney's Systematic Theology, New Expanded Edition: Lectures on Classes of Truths, Moral Government, The Atonement, Moral and Physical Depravity, Natural, Moral, and Gracious Ability, Repentance, Faith, Justification, Sanctification, Election, Divine Sovereignty, & Perseverance of the Saints*, ed. Dennis Carroll, Bill Nicely, and L. G. Parkhurst Jr. Introduction by L. G. Parkhurst Jr. Minneapolis: Bethany House Publishers, 1994.

Fuller, Andrew. *The Complete Works of Andrew Fuller*. 3 Vol. 3d ed. London: Joseph Belcher, 1831–32; reprint, Harrisonburg, VA: Sprinkle Publications, 1988.

Gambrell, James Brut. *Baptists and Their Business*. Nashville: Sunday School Board of the Southern Baptist Convention, 1919.

George, Timothy and Denise George, eds. *Baptist Confessions, Covenants, and Catechisms*. Nashville: Broadman & Holman Publishers, 1996.

Gill, John. *A Body of Doctrinal and Practical Divinity: or A System of Evangelical Truths, Deduced from the Sacred Scriptures*. London: George Keith, 1769–1770; reprint, Paris, AK: The Baptist Standard Bearer, 1989.

Gillette, A. D. *Minutes of the Philadelphia Baptist Association, 1707 to 1807: Being the First One Hundred Years of its Existence*, Tricentennial Edition. Springfield, MO: Particular Baptist Press, 2002.

Hays, Brooks, and John E. Steely. *The Baptist Way of Life*. Englewood Cliffs, NJ: Prentice-Hall, Inc., 1963.

Howell, R. B. C. *The Terms of Communion at the Lord's Table*, 2d ed. Philadelphia: American Baptist Publication Society, 1846.

Hobbs, Herschel, H, and E. Y. Mullins. *The Axioms of Religion*, Revised Edition. Nashville: Broadman Press, 1978.

Hobbs, Herschel H. *Fundamentals of Our Faith*. Nashville: Broadman Press, 1960.

————. *My Faith and Message: An Autobiography*. Nashville: Broadman & Holman Publishers, 1993.

————. *The Baptist Faith and Message*. Nashville: Convention Press, 1971 & 1988.

Johnson, W. B. *The Gospel Developed through the Government and Order of the Churches of Jesus Christ*. Richmond: H. K. Ellyson, 1846. Reprinted in *Polity: Biblical Arguments on How to Conduct Church Life*, Mark Dever, ed. Washington, D.C.: Center for Church Reform, 2001.

Kiffin, William. *A Briefe Remonstrance of The Reasons and Grounds of those People Commonly Called Anabaptists, for their Separation, etc. Or Certaine Queries Concerning their Faith and Practice, Propounded by Mr. Robert Poole; Answered and Resolved*. London: n.p., 1645.

Knollys, Hanserd. *A Moderate Answer vnto Dr. Bastwicks Book; Called Independency not Gods Ordinance*. London: Iane Coe, 1645.

Bibliography

Machen, J. Gresham. *Christianity and Liberalism*. New York: The Macmillan Company, 1923; reprint Grand Rapids: Wm. B. Eerdmans Publishing Company, 2001.

Manly, Basil Jr. *The Bible Doctrine of Inspiration Explained and Vindicated*. Reprint edition, Harrisonburg, VA: Gano Books, 1985.

McCall, Duke, and A. Roland Tonks, *Duke McCall: An Oral History*. Brentwood, TN: Baptist History and Heritage Society, 2001.

Mullins, E. Y. *The Axioms of Religion: A New Interpretation of the Baptist Faith*. Philadelphia: The Judson Press, 1908.

———. *The Christian Religion in its Doctrinal Expression*. Philadelphia, The Judson Press, 1917, 1945.

Mullins, Isla May. *Edgar Young Mullins: An Intimate Biography*. Nashville: Sunday School Board of the Southern Baptist Convention, 1929.

Reynolds, J. L. *Church Polity or the Kingdom of Christ in its Internal and External Development* Richmond: Harrold & Murray, 1849. Reprinted in *Polity: Biblical Arguments on How to Conduct Church Life*, Mark Dever, ed. Washington, D.C.: Center for Church Reform, 2001.

Shank, Robert. *Life in the Son: A Study in the DOCTRINE of Perseverance*. Introduction by William W. Adams. Springfield, MI: Westcott Publishers, 1960.

Shurden, Walter B., ed. *Proclaiming The Baptist Vision: The Bible*. Macon: Smyth & Helwys Publishing, Inc., 1994.

Skevington, Samuel J. *The Distinctive Principle of the Baptists*. Chicago: Printed for private distribution, 1914.

Spilsbury, John. *A Treatise Concerning the Lawfull Subject of Baptism*. London, n.p., 1643.

Stokes, William. *The History of the Midland Association of Baptist Churches, From Its Rise in the Year 1655 to 1855; With a Succinct Account of Its Annual Meetings, and A Table of Chronological Events; Several Ancient Letters to the Churches, Including the Circular Letter of 1794, by the Rev. S. Pearce: With The Confession of Faith of 1689; Also an Essay on Creeds*. London: R. Theobald, 1855.

Strong, Augustus H. *Systematic Theology: A Compendium Designed for the Use of Theological Students*, Three volumes in One. Valley Forge, PA: Judson Press, 1907, 1979.

Tidwell, Josiah Blake. *Christian Teachings*. Grand Rapids: William B. Eerdmans Publishing Co., 1942.

———. *Thinking Straight About the Bible*. Nashville: Broadman Press, 1935.

Tribble, H. W., and E. Y. Mullins. *The Baptist Faith*. Nashville: The Sunday School Board of the Southern Baptist Convention, 1935.

Van Ness, I. J. *The Baptist Spirit*. Nashville: Sunday School Board of the Southern Baptist Convention, 1914, 1926.

Wallace, O. C. S. *What Baptists Believe, The New Hampshire Confession: An Exposition*. Nashville: Sunday School Board of the Southern Baptist Convention, 1913.

White, W. R. *Baptist Distinctives*. Nashville: The Sunday School Board of the Southern Baptist Convention, 1946.

Whitley, W. T. *The Witness of History to Baptist Principles*. London: Alexander & Shepheard, 1897.

Bibliography

Articles and Unpublished Papers

"A Declaration of Faith of English People Remaining at Amsterdam in Holland." In *Baptist Confessions of Faith*. Ed. by William J. McGlothlin. Philadelphia: American Baptist Publication Society, 1911, 85–93.

"A Short Confession of Faith." In *Baptist Confessions of Faith*, ed. William J. McGlothlin 56–66. Philadelphia: American Baptist Publication Society, 1911.

Armitage, Thomas. "Baptist Faith and Practice," in *Baptist Doctrines; Being an Exposition, in a Series of Essays by Representative Baptist Ministers, of the Distinctive Points of Baptist Faith and Practice*, Revised and Enlarged. St. Louis: C. R. Barns Publishing Co., 1890, 30–48.

Backus, Isaac. "An Appeal to the Public for Religious Liberty," in *Isaac Backus on Church, State and Calvinism*, ed. William G. McLoughlin. Cambridge: The Belknap Press of Harvard University Press, 1968.

Boyce, James P. "Three Changes in Theological Institutions." In *James Petigru Boyce: Selected Writings*, ed. Timothy George, 30–59. Nashville: Broadman Press, 1989.

Carroll, B. H. "Distinctive Baptist Principles," A Sermon before the Pastor's Conference at Dallas, Texas, [November 3, 1903]. BCL.

Carver, W. O. "Christianity and Liberalism, A Review," *R&E* 21 (July 1924): 346.

"Circular Letter, 1748," in *Minutes of the Philadelphia Association: 1707–1807*, Tricentennial Edition, ed. A. D. Gillette, 58. Springfield, MO: Particular Baptist Press, 2002.

C., W. C. "Fundamental Principles," *Texas Baptist*, 20 March 1879, 2.

Committee on Baptist Faith and Message. "22 Messages for 10 Million Baptists." *The Beam* November 1962, 13–21. WWC.

"Confession of Faith Put Forth by the Elders and Brethren of Many Congregations of Christians (baptized upon Profession of their Faith) in London and the Country (London: n.p., 1677, 1689)." In *Baptist Confessions of Faith*. Revised edition, ed. by W. L. Lumpkin. Valley Forge: Judson Press, 1983, 241–95.

Cornell, George W. "Church Seeks Answer to Old Question," *The Daily Oklahoman*, September 7, 1962, n.p.

"Fraternal Letter," in *A Sourcebook for Baptist Heritage*, ed. Leon McBeth, 485. Nashville: Broadman Press, 1990.

Fuller, Andrew. "Creeds and Subscription," in *The Complete Works of Andrew Fuller*. Vol. 3, 3d ed., 449–51. London: Joseph Belcher, 1831–32; reprint, Harrisonburg, VA: Sprinkle Publications, 1988.

Fuller, Ellis A. et. al., "Statement of Principles," in *Annual of the Southern Baptist Convention, 1946* (Nashville: The Executive Committee, 1946), 38.

George, Timothy. "Introduction," in *Baptist Confessions, Covenants, and Catechisms*. Nashville: Broadman & Holman Publishers, 1996, 1–18.

John F. Havlik, "Southern Baptists and the Old Testament," *BD* (30 December1961): 4.

Hobbs, Herschel H. "Southern Baptists and Confessionalism: A Comparison of the Origins and Contents of the 1925 and 1963 Confessions," *R&E* (Winter 1979): 55–68.

————. "The Baptist Faith and Message," in *The People Called Baptists and The Baptist Faith and Message: The Herschel H. & Frances J. Hobbs Lectureship in Baptist Faith and Heritage at Oklahoma Baptist University*. 28–34. Shawnee, OK: Oklahoma Baptist University Press, 1981.

————. "The Baptist Faith and Message," in *Baptist Confessions of Faith*, Revised Edition, ed. W. L. Lumpkin, 393–400. Valley Forge: Judson Press, 1969, 1983.

Bibliography

Hobbs, Herschel, et. al. "The Baptist Faith and Message of 1963," a preliminary committee draft. The Southern Baptist Historical Library and Archives, Nashville, Tennessee.

Jenkens, Charles A. "Introduction," in *Baptist Doctrines; Being an Exposition, in a Series of Essays by Representative Baptist Ministers, of the Distinctive Points of Baptist Faith and Practice*, Revised and Enlarged, ed. Charles A. Jenkens, 9–29. St. Louis: C. R. Barns Publishing Co., 1890.

Leland, John. "The Rights of Conscience," in *The Writings of John Leland*, ed. L. F. Greene, New York: G. W. Wood, 1845; reprint, Dayton, OH: Church History Research & Archives, 1986.

———. "Speech in the Massachusetts House of Representatives," in *The Writings of John Leland*, ed. L. F. Greene, New York: G. W. Wood, 1845; reprint, Dayton, OH: Church History Research & Archives, 1986.

———. "The Virginia Chronicle," in *The Writings of John* Leland, ed. L. F. Greene, New York: G. W. Wood, 1845; reprint, Dayton, OH: Church History Research & Archives, 1986.

Memminger, Thomas. "Circular Letter, 1797," in *Minutes of the Philadelphia Baptist Association, 1707 to 1807: Being the First One Hundred Years of its Existence*, Tricentennial Edition, ed. A. D. Gillette, 329. Springfield, MO: Particular Baptist Press, 2002

Minutes of Conference at Columbia, Missouri, 1923?, BCL.

Morgan, Abel. "Circular Letter, 1774," in *Minutes of the Philadelphia Baptist Association, 1707 to 1807: Being the First One Hundred Years of its Existence*, Tricentennial Edition, A. D. Gillette, 137. Springfield, MO: Particular Baptist Press, 2002.

Mullins, E. Y. Address to the Southern Baptist Convention, 1925. BCL.

———. "Introduction" to Mullins' revision of the *New Hampshire Declaration of Faith*, 6 March 1925. BCL.

———. "The Baptist Distinctive." An address before the Virginia Baptist Historical Society, 1907.

"New Hampshire Declaration of Faith," in *Baptist Confessions of Faith*, ed. J. McGlothlin, 299–307. Philadelphia: American Baptist Publication Society, 1911

Pelagius, "Letter to Demetrias," in *Theological Anthropology*, ed. J. Patout Burns, 39 Sources of Early Christian Thought. William G. Rusch, series editor. Philadelphia: Fortress Press, 1981.

Pierce, Jerry. "Elder Baptist says '63 BF&M intended to clarify Bible belief," Baptist Press, 8 January 2002.

Price, Sterling. "Liberals Versus Conservatives." *The Third Baptist Visitor*, vol 26, no 26, 28 June 1962, 1.

Rogers, Adrian, et. al. "Report of the Baptist Faith and Message Study Committee to the Southern Baptist Convention June 14, 2000." Baptist Press [online], accessed 27 May 2000, http://www.SBC_NET_files/2000_report.html; Internet.

"Second London Confession," in *Baptist Confessions of Faith*, ed. W. L. Lumpkin, 241–95. Valley Forge: Judson Press, 1959, 1983.

Taylor, Nathaniel William. "Advice to the Clergy," in *Issues in American Protestantism: A Documentary History From the Puritans to the Present*, ed. Robert L. Ferm, 138–49. Gloucester, MA: Peter Smith, 1983.

"The Kiffin Manuscript." In *A Sourcebook for Baptist Heritage*. Ed. by Leon McBeth. Nashville: Broadman Press, 1990, 26–27.

Bibliography

State Papers

Alabama Baptist (Birmingham)

"Baptist College Opens Door to Negro Graduate Students." 18 May 1961, 5.

"Baptist Unity." 30 March 1961, 9.

"In the World of Religion." 5 January 1961, 7.

"Midwestern Trustees Name Officers." 22 June 1961, 8.

"Resolution. The Trustees of Midwestern Baptist Theological Seminary." 11 January 1962, 5.

"Seminary Trustees Approve Carver Merger; Deny Moody Violated Articles of Faith." 12 April 1962, 4.

"Southern Baptist Seminary Criticizes Survey." 10 August 1961, 6.

"Southern Baptist Seminary Trustees and President Duke McCall 'Regret' King Visit." 31 August 1961, 6.

"Why An Associational Organization with Associational Meetings." 12 January 1961, 7.

"Why I Must Support Southern Seminary." 21 September 1961, 5.

Baptist Messenger. "What is Neo-Orthodoxy?" 19 April 1962, 5.

Baptist Press. "137 Found Enrolled in Other Seminaries." 25 January 1962, 16.

———. "Baylor Students Hear Perils of Communism." 11 January 1962, 4.

———. "Bible Teachers Protest Curtailment of Book." 20 September 1962, 5.

———. "C. C. Warren Names Committee to Describe Precepts of Baptists." 6 April 1961, 1.

———. "Church Schools Qualify for Educational TV Aid." 10 May 1962, 16.

———. "Counselors Talk Over Church's Divorce Stand." 20 December 1962, 4.

———. "Court Holds Taxable Some Board Property." 20 September 1962, 9.

———. "Houston Baptists Act on Integration Issue." 23 January 1961, 14.

———. "Oklahoma Pastors Attack Dale Moody." 17 August 1961, 5.

———. "Open the Book." 29 June 1961, 6.

———. "San Francisco Church Ministry Multi-Racial." 9 November 1961, 1.

———. "Seminary Trustees Approve Carver Merger; Deny Moody Violated Articles of Faith." 12 April 1962, 4.

———. "Texas Baptist Teachers State Their Convictions Relative to Higher Education." 23 November 1961, 1.

———. "Waco Baptist Association Adopts Race Resolution." 9 March 1961, 16.

Barton, L. E. "One Way American Baptists Can Unite." 20 December 1962, 5.

Bassett, Wallace. "Why I Spoke Against the Resolution." 9 August 1962, 6.

Daley, C. R. "Catholic Test in Kentucky." 8 February 1962, 7.

Eddleman, Leo. "The Doctrine of the Word of God." 11 October 1962, 6.

Edwards, W. Ross. "Southern Baptists Theological Problems." 31 May 1962, 8.

Elliott, Ralph H. "The Message of Genesis." 8 February 1962, 6–7.

Fields, W. C. "Laymen Hold Ground in Doctrinal Study." 28 September 1961, 1.

Gritz, Jack. "What Is Inspiration?" 9 August 1962, 7.

Guffin, Gilbert. "Do We Have a Paper Pope?" 1 November 1962, 6.

Harper, Shannon. "Dead Men on Furlough, or What Is Communism?" 14 September 1961, 6, 16.

Hobbs, Herschel H. "Baptist Beliefs: Ascension." 11 October 1962, 7.

———. "Baptist Beliefs: Baptism." 25 January 1962, 5.

———. "Baptist Beliefs: Election." 18 January 1962, 5.

———. "Baptist Beliefs: God." 21 September 1961, 7.

———. Baptist Beliefs: Holy Spirit." 12 October 1961, 4.

———. "Baptist Beliefs: Jesus Christ." 28 September 1961, 9.

———. "Baptist Beliefs: Man." 23 November 1961, 7.

———. "Baptist Beliefs: Salvation." 1 February 1962, 6.

———. "Baptist Beliefs: Sin." 26 October 1961, 8.

———. "Baptist Beliefs: The Bible." 14 September 1961, 7.

———. "Baptist Beliefs: The Free Will of Man." 20 December 1962, 5.

———. "What Is In a Name?" 30 August 1962, 7.

Hodges, James R. "Hodges Answers Dr. Shank." 2 March 1961, 7.

Kirkley, Harry. "Baptists and Denominational Mergers." 12 January 1961, 7.

Miley, L. Don. "Liberalism in Denominational Colleges." 3 May 1962, 5.

Macon, Leon. "About Dr. Elliott's Book." 1 February 1962, 3.

———. "A Danger Due to Court Decision." 26 July 1962, 3.

———. "Aid to Religious Colleges." 26 July 1962, 3.

———. "Analyzing the Bible." 8 November 1962, 3.

———. "Another Look at Our Seminaries." 31 May 1962, 3.

———. "An Overlooked Truth." 19 July 1962, 3.

———. "A Sense of Responsibility." 20 September 1962, 3.

———. "As a Scientist Sees the Bible." 26 April 1962, 3.

———. "As We Approach the Convention." 17 May 1962, 3.

———. "A Totalitarian Spirit." 15 March 1962, 3.

———. "At the Convention." 14 June 1962, 3.

———. "Authority and Men's Opinions." 2 February 1961, 3.

———. "Baptist DOCTRINE." 17 August 1961, 3.

———. "Baptists and Art." 28 June 1962, 3.

———. "Baptists and Creeds." 7 December 1961, 3.

———. "Beliefs of Student Ministers." 17 August 1961, 3.

———. "Broad–Mindedness." 21 September 1961, 3.

———. "Business on Sunday." 4 January 1962, 3.

———. "Christian America a Myth." 6 December 1962, 3.

———. "Christian Unity." 12 January 1961, 3.

———. "Christian Unity." 15 February 1962, 3.

———. "Church Schools Endangered." 9 February 1961, 3.

———. "Communism in America." 12 July 1962, 3.

———. "Courts and Baptist Churches." 31 May 1962, 3.

———. "Daily Prayers in Public Schools." 8 February 1962, 3.

———. "Dangers to Our Nation." 2 August 1962, 3.

———. "Decrease in Seminary Enrollment." 19 October 1961, 3.

———. "Dedication to God." 26 July 1962, 3.

———. "Delayed Action." 15 Jun 1961, 3.

———. "Evidence of Creation." 17 September 1962, 3.

———. "Experience is Acceptable Truth." 17 September 1962, 3.

———. "Four Conceptions of Creation." 5 October 1961, 3.

———. "Glossalalia." 4 October 1962, 3.

———. "Government Debts." 18 October 1962, 3.

———. "If There Were No Supernatural." 6 December 1962, 3.

———. "Intellectual Freedom." 7 December 1961, 3.

———. "Louisville Seminary Makes Statement." 10 August 1961, 3.

———. "Midwestern Comes Under Criticism." 11 January 1962, 3.

Bibliography

———. "Midwestern Continues Study of Trustees." 25 October 1962, 3.

———. "Midwestern Dismisses Elliott." 8 November 1962, 3.

———. "Minorities and Majorities." 31 May 1962, 3.

———. "Modern Biblical Interpretation." 21 June 1962, 3.

———. "Morality." 30 August 1962, 3.

———. "Movement Toward Unity." 9 February 1961, 3.

———. "Myth and the Bible." 9 November 1961, 3.

———. "Name Calling." 8 March 1962, 3.

———. "New Theology Emerging." 19 April 1962, 3.

———. "Our Doctrinal Needs." 19 July 1962, 3.

———. "Our Historical Position." 28 June 1962, 3.

———. "Overtures." 17 May 1962, 3.

———. "Pentecostals Grow in Canada." 25 October 1962, 3.

———. "Prayer in Our Public Schools." 25 October 1962, 3.

———. "Prayer in Public Schools." 5 April 1962, 3.

———. "President Kennedy and Legally Required Prayers." 12 July 1962, 3.

———. "Reflections on the Convention." 21 June 1962, 3.

———. "Religion and State Universities." 21 June 1962, 3.

———. "Religion in Our Public Schools." 12 July 1962, 3.

———. "Religion Requires an Authority." 15 February 1962, 3.

———. "Rome and U. S. Legislation." 25 January 1962, 3.

———. "School Prayer Declared Unconstitutional." 5 July 1962, 3.

———. "Scientific Interpretation." 14 September 1961, 3.

———. "Scientists and Genesis." 5 July 1962, 3.

———. "Scientists and Evangelism." 14 June 1962, 3.

———. "Science and Religion in the Space Age." 30 August 1962, 3.

———. "Scientists and Spiritual Strength." 17 May 1962, 3.

———. "Second Vatican Council." 18 October 1962, 3.

———. "Seek Unity Between Northern and Southern Baptists." 8 November 1962, 3.

———. "Senate–House Pass Bill to Provide Grants for Private Schools." 27 September 1962, 3.

———. "Solving Our Seminary Problems." 26 April 1962, 3.

———. "Sunday Laws Declared Constitutional." 15 June 1961, 3.

———. "Supporting Our Seminaries." 2 August 1962, 3.

———. "Supreme Court Rulings." 18 October 1962, 3.

———. "Taxing Religious Bodies." 5 July 1962, 3.

———. "Taxing Religious Institutions." 4 January 1962, 3.

———. "Tax Money for Religious Schools." 1 February 1962, 3.

———. "The Atonement." 17 May 1962, 3.

———. "The Bible Is True." 7 September 1961, 3.

———. "The Bodily Resurrection." 20 July 1961, 3.

———. "The Churches and Human Needs." 19 April 1962, 3.

———. "The Church and Intellectuals." 2 August 1962, 3.

———. "The Faith of Atheists." 31 May 1962, 3.

———. "The Federal Government and Education." 5 July 1962, 3.

———. "The Free Will." 17 September 1962, 3.

———. "The Historic Position." 6 December 1962, 3.

———. "The Necessity of the Virgin Birth." 8 March 1962, 3.

Bibliography

————. "The Power of God." 7 September 1961, 3.

————. "The Power to Tax." 12 July 1962, 3.

————. "The Spiritual and Material." 23 November 1961, 3.

————. "The Story of Creation." 18 January 1962, 3.

————. "The Vatican Council and Religious Liberty." 27 July 1961, 3.

————. "Theological Trends." 17 August 1961, 3.

————. "Theology and Present Day Education." 19 July 1962, 3.

————. "Theology in U. S. Schools." 26 April 1962, 3.

————. "The Story of Creation." 18 January 1962, 3.

————. "This Could Happen to Us." 29 June 1961, 3.

————. "Timely Warning." 16 November 1961, 3.

————. "Vatican Seeks U. S. Recognition." 28 September 1961, 3.

————. "Verbal Inspiration." 27 July 1961, 3.

————. "Votes Confidence in Our Seminaries." 31 August 1961, 3.

————. "Warning About Merging with American Baptist Convention." 6 July 1961, 3.

————. "What Constitutes Division." 16 November 1961, 3.

————. "Why Communists Do Not Pray." 5 October 1961, 3.

Macon, Leon, and Ralph H. Elliott. "A Letter to Dr. Elliott by the Editor and the Reply." 16 February 1962, 5–6.

McCall, Duke K. "Statement of Dr. Duke McCall Re: Oklahoma County Pastors' Conference Resolution." 24 August 1961, 6–7.

Nager, Roy. "Bible Backing for Baptist Schools." 5 January 1961, 16.

Patterson, Eugene N. "Southern Baptists and Authority." 10 May 1962, 16.

Patterson, W. Morgan. "What Is Landmarkism?" 20 December 1962, 6.

Peacock, Heber F. "Theological Education and Biblical Interpretation." 27 September 1962, 8.

Reaves, Howard M. "President's Address to the Alabama Baptist State Convention." 23 November 1961, 5.

————. "President's Address to the Alabama Baptist Convention: The Baptist Spirit." 22 November 1962, 7.

Religious News Service. "Another Texas Southern Baptist College Admits Negroes." 21 December 1961, 7.

————. "Baptist College Opens Door to Negro Graduate Students." 18 May 1961, 5.

————. "Christian Gains in Professions Slows Reds' Atheist Drive." 17 May 1962, 1.

————. "President Urged to Discuss Religious Liberty in Columbia by POAU Leaders." 25 January 1962, 4.

————. "Protestants, Catholic Leaders Join in Plea to Curb Sunday Business." 1 February 1962, 4.

————. "Protestant Groups Say Catholic Brief on Aid to Schools Invites State Control." 18 January 1962, 1.

————. "Southern Baptist Women's College Abolishes all Racial Barriers." 11 October 1962, 7.

————. "Southern Baptist President Calls for Drive Against Atheistic Communism." 21 December 1961, 4.

Roach, George. "The Bible Plan of Salvation." 5 January 1961, 4.

Wells, Keith C. "Midwestern Faculty Makes Statement." 20 September 1962, 9.

Westmoreland, N. J. "What Will Theological Liberalism Do to Southern Baptists?" 31 May 1962, 7.

White, K. Owen. "Houston Pastor Takes Stand on Liberalism Among Southern Baptists." 11 January 1962, 5.

Wright, Lloyd. "Malik Urges All–Out Battle on Communism." 28 September 1961, 8.

Arkansas Baptist (Little Rock)

"Elliott Dismissal is No. 1 Story of 1962." 20 December 1962, 2.

"Hobbs Names Those to Make Faith Study." 2 August 1962, 3.

"Hobbs Praises Ban on Governmental Prayer." 26 July 1962, 15.

"Minister's First Obligation is Feeding the Flock." 8 February 1962, 3.

"Negro Baptists Set Records." 26 July 1962, 8–9.

"President's Address: Says Baptists Must Keep to 'the Middle of Road.'" 7 June 1962, 12–14.

"Race Issue Described as Reaching all Areas." 5 April 1962, 14.

"Report to Faculty of Southern Baptist Theological Seminary." 11 January 1962, 11.

"Resolution: Board of Trustees, Midwestern Baptist Theological Seminary, Kansas City, Missouri." 11 January 1962, 11.

"Student Union: Students Take Stand on Race Issue." 15 November 1962, 19.

Adams, William W. "Southern Baptist Freedom." 31 May 1962, 4.

Alley, Reuben E. "Help the Seminaries." 8 March 1962, 12–14.

Ashcraft, Morris. "A Professor's Protest." 8 November 1962, 3.

Baptist Press. "Arkadelphia Church Adopts Policy." 15 February 1962, 15.

———. "Baptists Back Freedom from Government Prayer." 19 July 1962, 2.

———. "Baptists Discuss Higher Education." 18 October 1962, 9.

———. "Baptist Group Upholds Court Prayer Decision." 15 October 1962, 14.

———. "Catholics Pull Ahead." 23 August 1962, 14.

———. "Elliott Feels He Made a Concession." 1 November 1962, 7, 13.

———. "Good News out of K. C.: Harmony at Midwestern Seminary." 21 March 1963, 5.

———. "Midwestern Baptist Board." 11 October 1962, 14.

———. "Midwestern Trustees Dismiss Ralph Elliott." 1 November 1962, 3, 7.

———. "Most Baptist Papers Support Prayer Ruling." 6 September 1962, 14–15.

———. "Negro Baptist Speaks to National Press Club." 2 August 1962, 17.

———. "No Second Edition of Genesis Book Planned." 2 August 1962, 12.

———. "Oklahoma City Group Weighs 'Current Crisis.'" 22 March 1962, 3.

———. "Parochial Aid Battle Top Story During 1961." 11 January 1962, 14.

———. "Professor Calls Prejudice Evil as Murder, Adultery." 29 March 1962, 18.

———. "Senate Holds Hearings on Prayer Amendment to Constitution." 2 August 1962, 12.

———. "Thirteen Baptist Leaders Favor Supreme Court Ruling on Prayer." 26 July 1962, 14.

———. "World Council Speaks on Religious Liberty." 4 January 1962, 15.

Barton, V. Wayne. "Gleanings from the Greek New Testament: Not the Bible Alone." 11 January 1962, 7.

———. "Gleanings from the Greek New Testament: Prejudice and the Practice of Jesus." 22 November 1962, 9.

———. "Gleanings from the Greek New Testament: The Unofficial Priest." 28 June 1962, 7.

Bassett, Wallace. "Why I Spoke Against the Resolution." 9 August 1962. 5, 11.

Bradbury, John W. "Overdoing Self-Criticism." 15 February 1962, 4.

Carlson, Emanuel C. "Dare to be a Baptist!" 2 August 1962, 13.

Coggins, Ross. "Some Quiet Thoughts about Anti-Communism." 11 January 1962, 2.

Craft, Robert H. "Pro: Help for Pew and Pulpit." 1 February 1962, 18.

Elliott, Ralph H. "The Message of Genesis." 1 February 1962, 15–17.

Garrett, W. Barry. "The Storm in the Capital." 19 July 1962, 14–15.

Gragg, Alan W., et. al. "The Elliott Case: Midwestern Faculty Members Protest." 15 November 1962, 5.

Hart, Clyde. "New Negro Baptist Work at Pine Bluff." 8 November 1962, 20.

———. "Race Relations: Racial Intermarriage?" 7 June 1962, 26.

Hinson, Thomas. "Sunday School Lessons: God is Spirit." 18 January 1962, 22–23.

Hobbs, Herschel H. "Baptist Beliefs: Angels." 15 February 1962, 9.

———. "Baptist Beliefs: Ascension." 2 August 1962, 7.

———. "Baptist Beliefs: Authority of the Church." 22 November 1962, 9.

———. "Baptist Beliefs: Bodily Resurrection." 26 July 1962, 13.

———. "Baptist Beliefs: Confession." 17 May 1962, 7.

———. "Baptist Beliefs: Conversion." 3 May 1962, 7

———. "Baptist Beliefs: Conviction." 12 April 1962, 7.

———. "Baptist Beliefs: Deacons." 8 March 1962, 7.

———. "Baptist Beliefs: Faith." 26 April 1962, 9.

———. "Baptist Beliefs: Fatherhood of God." 14 June 1962, 7.

———. "Baptist Beliefs: Foundations of the Church." 8 November 1962, 9.

———. "Baptist Beliefs: Gehenna." 28 June 1962, 7.

———. "Baptist Beliefs: Glorification." 5 April 1962, 7.

———. "Baptist Beliefs: Hades." 21 June 1962, 16.

———. "Baptist Beliefs: Hell." 4 January 1962, 7.

———. "Baptist Beliefs: Illumination." 23 August 1962, 7.

———. "Baptist Beliefs: Inspiration." 16 August 1962, 7.

———. "Baptist Beliefs: Lordship of Christ." 7 June 1962, 7.

———. "Baptist Beliefs: Miracles." 6 September 1962, 7.

———. "Baptist Beliefs: Nature of the Church." 15 November 1962, 7.

———. "Baptist Beliefs: Pastor." 1 March 1962, 13.

———. "Baptist Beliefs: Perseverance." 24 May 1962, 20.

———. "Baptist Beliefs: Prayer," 30 August 1962, 7.

———. "Baptist Beliefs: Priesthood of Believers." 15 March 1962, 7.

———. "Baptist Beliefs: Purpose of the Church." 6 December 1962, 7.

———. "Baptist Beliefs: Regeneration." 10 May 1962, 7.

———. "Baptist Beliefs: Repentance." 19 April 1962, 7.

———. "Baptist Beliefs: Revelation." 9 August 1962, 7.

———. "Baptist Beliefs: Righteousness." 22 March 1962, 7.

———. "Baptist Beliefs: Sanctification." 29 March 1962, 9.

———. "Baptist Beliefs: Satan." 8 February 1962, 17.

———. "Baptist Beliefs: Sovereignty of God." 20 September 1962, 7.

———. "Baptist Beliefs: The Atonement." 19 July 1962, 7.

———. "Baptist Beliefs: The Free Will of Man." 27 September 1962, 7.

———. "Baptist Beliefs: The Grace of God." 18 October 1962, 8.

———. "Baptist Beliefs: The Judgment." 18 January 1962, 13.

———. "Baptist Beliefs: The Kingdom." 1 February 1962, 9.

———. "Baptist Beliefs: The Love of God." 11 October 1962, 7.

————. "Baptist Beliefs: The Mercy of God." 25 October 1962, 7.

————. "Baptist Beliefs: The Second Coming of Christ." 11 January 1962, 7.

————. "Baptist Beliefs: The Unpardonable Sin." 13 September 1962, 8.

————. "Baptist Beliefs: The Virgin March." 13 December 1962, 7.

————. "Baptist Beliefs: The Will of God." 1 November 1962, 9.

————. "Baptist Beliefs: The Wrath of God." 4 October 1962, 7.

————. "Baptist Beliefs: Trinity." 22 February 1962, 14.

————. "Baptist Beliefs: Unity of the Church." 29 November 1962, 7.

————. "Baptist Beliefs: Virgin Birth." 12 July 1962, 6.

————. "What Is in a Name?" 23 August 1962, 12–14.

Hobbs, Herschel H., et. al. "The Committee on the Baptist Faith and Message." 21 March 1963, 12–13.

Hurt, John S. Jr. "Laws Will be Enforced When Georgians Wake Up." 15 February 1962, 4.

Matthews, C. DeWitt. "No Creed but the Bible." 2 August 1962, 14–16.

————. "Understanding the Bible's Meaning." 26 July 1962, 12.

May, Lynn E. Jr. "Baptist Theological Debates are not New." 25 October 1962, 12–13.

McCray, Paul. "Danger Signals to Baptist Distinctives." 1 March 1962, 7.

McDonald, Edwin L. "More Than Orthodoxy." 22 March 1962, 4.

————. "Name Change for SBC?" 17 May 1962, 4.

————. "Our Work with Negroes." 26 July 1962, 4.

————. "Phelps of Arkansas." 21 March 1963, 3.

————. "Progress at Southern." 21 March 1963, 3–4.

————. "Re-Study of 1925 Faith Statement asked by San Francisco Convention." 14 June 1962, 2–3.

————. "San Francisco as the Editor Saw It." 21 June 1962, 10–12.

————. "The Elliott Dismissal." 8 November 1962, 4–5.

————. "The Highest Authority." 8 February 1962, 4.

————. "The Midwestern Resolution." 11 January 1962, 4.

————. "The Pastors' Conference." 4 October 1962, 4.

————. "The President's Committee." 2 August 1962, 4.

————. "The Ruling on Prayer." 12 July 1962, 4.

————. "The Seminary Controversy." 1 March 1962, 4.

————. "Who is to be Papa?" 14 June 1962, 4.

McDowell, Edward A. "Baptist Beginnings in Theological Education." 5 April 1962, 12–13.

————. "Baptist Beginnings in Theological Education." 12 April 1962, 16–17.

————. "Baptist Beginnings in Theological Education." 19 April 1962, 16–17.

————. "Last of Four in a Series: Baptist Beginnings in Theological Education." 26 April, 1962, 15, 18.

Mercer Faculty. "'Protecting' the Bible." 8 November 1962, 7.

Midwestern Baptist Theological Seminary. "Statement." 13 September 1962, 6.

Newton, Jim. "Theological Concern Receives Pastors Conference Emphasis." 21 June 1962, 13–14.

New Orleans Baptist Theological Seminary. "Says 'Witch-Hunt' is On." 1 February 1962, 2.

Phelps, Ralph A. "Academic Freedom and Academic Responsibility." 21 March 1963, 6–11.

Price, Bruce H. "New Name for Southern Convention." 17 May 1962, 3.

Reed, W. M. "Letter to the Editor: On Book Burning." 11 January 1962, 5.

Sawyer, Paul. "Letter to the Editor: 'Message of Genesis.'" 15 February 1962, 19.

Street, Mrs. J. H. "Overcoming Racial Prejudice." 19 July 1962, 6.

Swinney, S. C. "This I Believe." 29 March 1962, 7.

Torbet, Robert G. "Baptists and Biblical Authority." 24 May 1962, 14–16.

Trentham, Charles A. "Letter to the Editor: Likes Elliott's Book." 15 February 1962, 5.

Tull, Selsus E. "The Historic Baptist Position." 30 August 1962, 3.

Walker, James A. "Letter to the Editor: Highest Authority." 8 February 1962, 5.

Webb, Leland. "20 Seminary Grads Included in Baptist Statement Group." 12 July 1962, 2, 19.

———. "Oklahoma City First Refuses Negro Member." 11 January 1962, 3.

White, K. Owen. "Con: Death in the Pot." 1 February 1962, 19.

Whitlow, S. A. "Out of the Furor." 19 July 1962, 3.

Baptist Courier (Greenville)

"Baptist High Lights." 2 March 1961, 20.

"Report of Committee on Resolutions." 8 June 1961, 16, 19.

"Text of Resolution Passed by Oklahoma County Pastors' Conference." 24 August 1961, 6.

Baptist Press. "Federal College Loans Called 'Laudable' Deed." 13 July 1961, 4.

———. "Name Change Remains for Further Study." 16 March 1961, 20.

———. "Parochial School Aid Moves One Step Closer." 13 July 1961, 5.

———. "President Proclaims Prayer Day for Peace." 25 May 1961, 4.

———. "Raleigh Pastors Vote Seminaries Confidence." 7 September 1961, 7.

———. "Religious Liberty Emphasis Asked." 13 April 1961, 4.

Carroll, James P. "Christians Unashamed." 30 November 1961, 5–6.

Hobbs, Herschel H. "The Oklahoma County Resolution." 7 September 1961, 7, 19.

Jones, S. H. "Baptists and School Loans." 13 July 1961, 2.

———. "Baptist Conventions Unite?" 23 March 1961, 2.

———. "Correct Church Rolls." 16 February 1961, 2.

———. "Change of Name." 15 June 1961, 2.

———. "Change the Name?" 23 March 1961, 2.

———. "Doctrinal Arguments." 5 October 1961, 2.

———. "Seminary in the News." 24 August 1961, 2.

———. "Separation and School Support." 30 March 1961, 2.

———. "Series on Communism." 6 July 1961, 2.

———. "Sunday Law Upheld." 6 July 1961, 2.

McCall, Duke K. "Statement of Duke K. McCall Re: Oklahoma County Pastors' Conference Resolution." 24 August 1961, 6.

Moody, Dale. "Dale Moody's Reply to Resolution Adopted in Oklahoma City (Abbreviated)." 24 August 1961, 6–7, 17.

Sims, Charles F. "Christian Education on the Baptist School Level." 13 April 1961, 6–7.

Baptist Message (Alexandria)

"Baptist Record Suggests North American Pact." 12 January 1961, 1, 4.

"Cited in Campaign." 24 August 1961, 10.

"College Gets Federal Student Loan Grant." 27 July 1961, 1.

"Fallout Shelter in Churches Proposed." 21 December 1961, 1, 4.

"In New Orleans Sunday Sales Hit by Churches." 29 June 1961, 1.

"LMCF Opposes Aid to Parochial Schools." 4 May 1961, 1, 4.

"Oklahoma Judge Rules Against Parochial Buses." 2 November 1961, 1.

"Public Affairs Committee Commends Kennedy Stand: 'Firm Position' on Church-State Matters Praised." 30 March 1961, 1, 3.

"Text of Raleigh Resolution." 24 August 1961, 6.

Baptist Press. "ABC Official Calls for 3-Way Merger." 22 June 1961, 1.

———. "Alaska Baptists Oppose Federal Aid to Hospitals." 2 November 1961, 1.

———. "Alliance Names 4 Study Commissions." 13 July 1961, 12.

———. "Baptists, Other Groups Oppose Parochial Aid." 15 June 1961, 8.

———. "Baptist Urged to Decline Tax Support." 1 June 1961, 1, 10.

———. "Battle Continues over Parochial School Aid." 8 June 1961, 1, 4.

———. "Carlson Scores Cardinal's Public Education Stand: Payment of Taxes for Public School Called Privilege." 2 February 1961, 1, 4.

———. "Church College May Profit from Tax Funds: Seminaries Exempted from Aid." 7 September 1961, 1, 4.

———. "Church Groups Quite on College Aid Bill." 6 April 1961, 8.

———. "Church-State Crisis Hovers Over Nation: Says Kennedy Bewildered by Controversy." 23 March 1961, 1, 11.

———. "Church-State Problems Arise in Peace Corps." 29 June 1961, 1, 4.

———. "Church-State Relations Face National Re-Study: Protestant Era Ended, Catholic Editor Declares." 6 April 1961, 1, 4.

———. "Committee to Study Name Change for SBC." 2 March 1961, 3.

———. "Compromise Aid Bill Knocks Out Hospitals." 7 September 1961, 1.

———. "Delaying Tactic Charged: Bremond Case May Go to Federal Courts." 6 April 1961, 1, 4.

———. "Education Committees Hear Baptist Witness." 30 March 1961, 1, 3.

———. "Former SBC President Gets Post." 16 February 1961, 1.

———. "Former SBC President Visits Pope." 21 December 1961, 1, 4.

———. "Further Unity Talks." 12 January 1961, 1, 4.

———. "Glenn Archer Hits Rockefeller Plan: Calls Proposal 'Back Door' Way to Aid Churches." 23 February 1961, 1, 4.

———. "Herschel Hobbs: Former Louisiana Pastor Elected new SBC Head." 1 June 1961, 1, 6.

———. "Hobbs Calls for 'Unity of Purpose' Between ABC–SBC." 22 June 1961, 1.

———. "Hospitals Steer Clear of Government Help." 2 February 1961, 1, 4.

———. "House Group Rejects Private School Rider." 1 June 1961, 8.

———. "JFK Rejects Catholic Bid for Support." 9 February 1961, 1.

———. "Legal Report Rules Out Parochial School Loans." 6 April 1961.

———. "Malik Blasts America's Attitude Toward Reds: Says Vibrant Program Needed to Win World." 21 September 1961, 1, 4.

———. "Mob Violence Hit by SBC Messengers." 1 June 1961, 12.

———. "New Education Bill Introduced." 7 September 1961, 1, 4.

———. "Newspaper Hits Catholic Demand for Public Aid." 9 March 1961, 3.

———. "North Carolina Pastors Score Oklahoma Action." 24 August 1961, 1, 4.

———. "Official Calls for More Christianity in Politics." 23 November 1961, 5.

———. "Oklahoma Pastors Stir Theological Dispute: Dale Moody Cited in Resolution." 3 August 1961, 1, 4.

———. "On School Aid Baptist Group, JFK Express Same Views." 16 March 1961, 1, 4.

Bibliography

————. "Parochial Bus Question Goes to Supreme Court." 19 January 1961, 3.

————. "Parochial Bus Rides Upheld by Court." 9 March 1961, 1.

————. "Prayer in School Hit as Unconstitutional." 16 November 1961, 1.

————. "President Shows Concern for Religious Liberty." 9 February 1961, 3.

————. "Private Schools are Aided by Federal Lunch Program." 29 June 1961, 1.

————. "Private Schools Asked to Bombard Congress: Pictures Pasted on Post Cards to Congressmen." 15 June 1961, 1, 4.

————. "Russians Close Baptist Church." 9 November 1961, 6.

————. "SBC Name Change Urged by Northern Preachers: Say Division is Now Theological, not Regional." 16 February 1961, 1.

————. "Secretary Ribicoff Sees no Solution to Aid Impasse." 17 August 1961, 1, 4.

————. "Strategies Mapped for Aid to Church Schools." 11 May 1961, 1.

————. "Survey Shows Most Citizens Oppose Aid." 4 May 1961, 1.

————. "Tennessee's Highest Court to Rule on Tax." 2 November 1961, 1.

————. "Texas Halts Government Borrowing." 15 June 1961, 1, 4.

————. "Washington Paper Urges Church–State Separation: Cardinal's Statement on Aid Opposed." 9 February 1961, 1, 4.

————. "Wayne Morse Blasts Catholic Bishops." 24 August 1961, 1, 4.

————. "White House Conference Reveals Aid to Aging Raises Church-State Problem." 26 January 1961, 1, 4.

Barton, Wayne. "Gleanings from the Greek New Testament: Not the Bible Alone." 16 February 1961, 3.

————. "Gleanings from the Greek New Testament: Will What Will Be?" 10 August 1961, 3.

Carlson, C. Emanuel. "Carlson Says School Aid Issue not Dead." 27 July 1961, 1, 4.

Clinard, Gordon. "The Seminary Teacher and His Denomination." 21 September 1961, 8.

Cole, James F. "A Baptist Profile." 16 February 1961, 2.

————. "Added Confusion." 30 November 1961, 2.

————. "All Talk and No Give." 20 July 1961, 2.

————. "A Minority Report." 10 August 1961, 2.

————. "A New Day." 3 August 1961, 2.

————. "Baptists and Religious Liberty." 29 June 1961, 2, 3.

————. "Christianity's Cowardly Retreat." 21 September 1961, 2.

————. "Hard to Buy." 2 February 1961, 2.

————. "May Have Overplayed Their Hand." 30 November 1961, 2.

————. "The Baptist Jubilee." 26 January 1961, 2.

————. "The New President." 26 January 1961, 2.

————. "The Trojan Horse Rides Again." 13 April 1961, 2.

Daley, C. R. "A Suggestion for Seminaries." 24 August 1961, 2.

Garrett, W. Barry. "Change in Strategy on School Aid Bill is Seen as Victory." 25 May 1961, 1, 4.

————. "JFK and Catholic Bishops in Deadlock on Education: Says Kennedy Determined to Stand Ground." 9 March 1961, 1, 5.

————. "Men Recommend More Church-State Study." 21 September 1961, 1.

————. "Say President May Have Compromised on School Aid: SOS Given by Baptist Joint Committee." 18 May 1961, 1, 4.

Hobbs, Herschel H. "Are Southern Baptists Facing a Theological Revolution?" 12 October 1961, 12.

————. "Hobbs Explains Why He Voted for Resolution." 24 August 1961, 1, 6.

Lee, G. Avery. "Thus Saith the Preacher: Who's Aiding the Communists? 12 October 1961, 3.

———. "Thus Saith the Preacher: How to Tell Your Enemies from the Communists." 4 May 1961, 3.

Patterson, Thomas A. "Large Response Greets Call for Conservatism." 20 July 1961, 6.

Patterson, W. Morgan. "Baptist By Any Other Name: Survey Turns Up some Odd Suggestions as New Names for the Southern Baptist Convention." 30 March 1961, 5, 9.

Religious News Service. "Editors Oppose State Aid to Private Schools." 27 April 1961, 3.

———. "House Group Would Bar Fellowship for Clergymen, Religious Subjects." 20 July 1961, 1, 4.

———. "Methodist Bishops Urge Campaign Against Federal Aid to Church Schools." 27 April 1961, 3.

———. "Senator Pledges Fight Against Parochial Aid." 27 July 1961, 1, 4.

———. "Survey Finds Religion Influential in School." 1 June 1961, 4.

Spaid, Ora. "McCall Says Theological Revolt May Destroy SBC." 22 June 1961, 5.

Stagg, Frank. "Preaching the Gospel." 25 May 1961, 8.

Underwood, Joseph. "Religious Liberty Superior to Tolerance." 31 August 1961, 2.

Wamble, Hugh. "Battle Lines of Federal Aid." 12 January 1961, 5.

———. "Legislative Strategy on Aid-to-Education." 23 March 1961, 12.

———. "Political Factors on Aid-to-Education." 13 July 1961, 12.

———. "Why Church-State Tension?" 3 August 1961, 12.

Baptist Messenger (Oklahoma City)

"Baptist Alliance Proposed." 19 January 1961, 4.

"Board to Recommend Church-State Committee." 19 October 1961, 4.

"Constitutional Change Offered." 14 September 1961, 4.

"Convention Decisions: Praise for President." 1 June 1961, 5.

"Convention Decisions: Race Relations." 1 June 1961, 5.

"Educators Endorse Federal Loans for Colleges." 22 June 1961, 4.

"Kennedy Joins Prayer Meal." 16 February 1961, 4.

"Negro Churches Accepted." 26 October 1961, 5.

"Parochial School Issue Snarls Federal Aid Bill." 29 June 1961, 4.

"Parochial School Supporter Cripples Education Measure." 27 July 1961, 4.

"Resolutions on Schools Voted." 24 August 1961, 4.

"School Aid Fight Goes On." 8 June 1961, 4.

"The President Meets the Press." 22 June 1961, 5.

Allen, Paul C. "A Cardinal Errs." 30 March 1961, 16.

Baptist Press. "Baptist News in Brief: Desegregation." 27 April 1961, 5.

———. "Baptist News in Brief: Negroes." 11 May 1961, 5.

———. "Baptist News in Brief: Negro Ban Lifted." 13 July 1961, 4.

———. "Baptist News in Brief: "Race." 11 May 1961, 5.

———. "Baptist News in Brief: Race." 15 June 1961, 4.

———. "Baptist News in Brief: Refusal." 5 January 1961, 4.

———. "Baptists Dislike Bus Ruling." 19 October 1961. 5.

———. "Court Upholds Sunday Laws." 29 June 1961, 4–5.

———. "Cuba Doors Reported Open but Could Soon Slam Shut." 14 September 1961. 4.

Bibliography

————. "Federal Loan to Baptist Schools Ruled Out by Texas Board's Church–State Resolutions. 15 June 1961, 4.

————. "Jubilee Advance Plans Include Pulpit Exchanges." 16 March 1961, 4.

————. "Minimum School Aid Voted." 14 September 1961, 5.

————. "Private School Aid Delayed." 31 August 1961, 4.

————. "School Aid Position Stated." 16 March 1961, 4.

————. "Schools Main Board Topic." 16 March 1961, 4–5.

————. "Seminaries Draw Attention." 2 November 1961, 4–5.

————. "'Southern' Name Preferred." 8 June 1961, 4.

————. "Use of Public Funds Eyed." 23 February 1961, 5.

————. "Texans Face Race Problems." 2 March 1961, 4–5.

————. "Wichita Majority Upheld." 11 May 1961, 4–5.

Bradbury, John W. "A Growing Menace." 23 February 1961, 3.

Bryant, Cyril E. "From Washington: A Report on Catholic Growth." 19 January 1961, 3.

Carlson, C. Emanuel. "Election Reflections." 26 January 1961, 3.

Conner, W. T. "The Resurrection of Jesus." 30 March 1961, 3.

Crenshaw, Floyd. "The Good Purposes of God." 2 February 1961, 3.

Epton, T. Hollis. "My Denominational Loyalty." 24 August 1961, 8.

Gritz, Jack L. "All Baptists Are Not the Same." 12 January 1961, 2.

————. "Baptism Is by Immersion Only." 2 February 1961, 2.

————. "Baptists and Church Union." 6 July 1961, 2.

————. "Baptists Are Not Isolationists." 19 January 1961, 2.

————. "Beware of the 'Revolution.'" 13 July 1961, 2.

————. "Bishop Smith on Church Union." 26 January 1961, 2.

————. "Catholics Are Still Trying." 30 November 1961, 2.

————. "Catholic Growth Reported." 25 May 1961, 2.

————. "Catholics Keep on Trying." 9 November 1961, 2.

————. "Common Sense and Schools." 31 August 1961, 2.

————. "Each Church is Independent." 23 February 1961, 2.

————. "Every Man for Himself." 9 February 1961, 2.

————. "Federal Aid to Education Issue." 30 March 1961, 2.

————. "God Is Depending upon Us." 12 October 1961, 2.

————. "How to Study the Bible." 21 September 1961, 2.

————. "Inactive Church Members." 30 March 1961, 2.

————. "Kennedy Is not a Baptist." 22 June 1961, 2.

————. "Moving Toward the Super Church." 5 October 1961, 2.

————. "On Being Southern a Baptist." 22 June 1961, 2.

————. "Once Saved, Always Saved." 23 March 1961, 2.

————. "On Guard Against Communism." 26 January 1961, 2.

————. "Religion in the Schools." 14 September 1961, 2.

————. "Religious Liberty is for All." 16 March 1961, 2.

————. "Salvation Is by Grace." 2 March 1961, 2.

————. "Shall We Change Our Name?" 27 April 1961, 2.

————. "Southern Baptists and New Delhi." 9 November 1961, 2.

————. "Sunday Is the Lord's Day." 24 August 1961, 2.

————. "The Aid for Schools Crisis." 20 July 1961, 2.

————. "The Bible—The Word of God." 6 April 1961, 2.

————. "The DOCTRINE of Election." 11 May 1961, 2.

————. "The Drift to Union." 26 October 1961, 2.

————. "The Nature of the Church." 26 October 1961, 2.

————. "The Problem of the Seminaries." 19 October 1961, 2.

————. "The True Nature of Man." 13 April 1961, 2.

————. "Two New Testament Principles." 29 June 1961, 2.

————. "Unreasoning Prejudice." 13 April 1961, 2.

————. "What Is a Baptist?" 16 February 1961, 2.

————. "What Is Baptism?" 5 October 1961, 2.

————. "What Is Neo–Orthodoxy?" 2 November 1961, 2.

————. "What Is the Kingdom?" 15 June 1961, 2.

————. "When Negroes Visit Your Church." 23 February 1961, 2.

————. "Where Are We Advancing?" 23 March 1961, 2.

————. "Why We Cannot Unite." 4 May 1961, 2.

Harwell, Jack D. "The Invisible Killer: Fallout." 16 February 1961, 3.

Havlik, John F. "A Warning About a New Book." 24 August 1961, 3.

Hobbs, Herschel H. "Are Southern Baptists Facing a Theological Revolution?" 21 September 1961, 3, 13.

Hultgren, W. C. "Orthodoxy and the Ministry." 24 August 1961, 16.

James, E. S. "Who Opposes Public Aid?" 13 April 1961, 16.

Maston, T. B. "Criticism and Commitment." 19 October 1961, 3, 12.

Moore, L. H. "Baptist Unity." 30 March 1961. 16.

————. "Monolithic Southern Baptists." 2 November 1961, 16.

Naylor, Robert E. "Man's Ruin—The Reason and the Results." 19 January 1961, 8

————. "Plain Talk." 12 October 1961, 3.

Religious News Service. "Baptist News in Brief: Negroes Enrol." 24 August 1961, 5.

Sanderson, Leonard. "Trend in Revivals." 14 September 1961, 3.

Truett, George W. "Baptists and Religious Liberty." 10 August 1961, 2–11.

White, W. R. "Baptist Defectionists and Perfectionists." 30 November 1961, 3.

Baptist New Mexican (Albuquerque)

"California to Enter Negro Work Program." 28 September 1961, 5.

"Christianity and Communism Concern of Projected Book." 14 December 1961, 8.

"P.O.A.U. Announces Expanded Publication." 15 June 1961, 5.

"Supreme Court Upholds S. C. Sunday Movie Law." 29 June 1961, 3.

Baptist Press. "Baptist Alliance in North America Suggested." 12 January 1961, 10.

————. "Baptist 4-Way Merger Please Said 'Surprise.'" 29 June 1961, 5.

————. "Cites Federal Aid to Church Schools." 24 August 1961, 16.

————. "Committee Approves Private School Aid." 30 August 1961, 5.

————. "Dallas Negro College Slated Opening Dates." 6 April 1961, 8.

————. "Education is Prominent in Bill Before Congress." 19 January 1961, 16.

————. "Famed Negro Baptist Leader Taken by Death." 15 June 1961, 13.

————. "Freedom of Church Schools Endangered by 'Public Aid.'" 9 February 1961, 12.

————. "Historian Warns of Dim Religious Freedom Views." 6 April 1961, 8.

————. "Home Board Produces Negro Work Filmstrip." 5 January 1961, 3.

————. "Mission Policy Same After Cuba Break." 12 January 1961, 11.

————. "Mission Schools Held Among Atlanta Negroes." 9 February 1961, 12.

————. "Religious Tests Thrown Out by Supreme Court." 29 June 1961, 3.

————. "Reminds Baptists Race Issue Affects Missions." 16 March 1961, 16.

————. "SBC–ABC Merger Suggestion Draws Fire, Approval." 16 February 1961, 2.

————. "Senator Morse Clashes with Cardinal Spellman." 7 September 1961, 8.

————. "Sunday Laws Upheld by U. S. Supreme Court." 15 June 1961, 13.

————. "Texas Brotherhood Urges Sunday Closing of Stores." 19 January 1961, 5.

————. "Work With National Baptists Expands." 5 January 1961, 4.

————. "Young Baptists Request Firm Communism Stand." 21 September 1961, 13.

Brock, Delbert A. "Time for Christians to Cry Out Against Wickedness." 8 June 1961, 3.

Burns, Horace F. "A Blow to Religious Liberty." 24 August 1961, 2.

————. "A Little Toleration." 2 February 1961, 2.

————. "Business on Sunday." 5 January 1961, 2.

————. "Baptist Merger Talks Suggested." 12 January 1961, 2.

————. "Denominations." 9 February 1961, 2.

————. "Federal Aid for Church Schools." 26 January 1961, 2.

————. "Freedom in Jeopardy." 18 May 1961, 2.

————. "Have Baptists Changed?" 8 June 1961, 2.

————. "Has Religious Freedom Died in America?" 16 November 1961, 2.

————. "Important Issues to be Debated." 28 September 1961, 2.

————. "Religious Liberty for Turkey." 28 September 1961, 2.

————. "Should the Name be Changed?" 2 March 1961, 2.

————. "The Beginnings of Church Union." 2 February 1961, 2.

Garrett, W. Barry. "Parochial School Aid Fight Continues." 15 June 1961, 4.

Hancox, Jack D. "The New Look in Catholicism." 4 May 1961, 11.

Hobbs, Herschel H. "Are Southern Baptists Facing a Theological Revolution?" 28 September 1961, 4–5.

Holder, Billie. "The Security of Peace." 30 August 1961, 3.

Hurt, John J. "Who's a Bigot, Persecutor or Defender." 16 November 1961, 3.

James, E. S. "Separation of Church and State." 13 July 1961, 4–5, 12.

Long, R. A. "Convention President Asks Action on School Issue." 20 July 1961, 3.

Owen, Richard N. "Why Should Baptists Allow This?" 24 August 1961, 3.

Schroeder, George W. "Please, Not Discrimination." 20 April 1961, 5.

Sorensen, Donald J. "Faculty-Student Ties Noted at Midwestern." 14 December 1961, 3.

Underwood, Joseph B. "The Basis of Religious Liberty." 30 August 1961, 4–5.

————. "The Meaning of Separation of Church and State." 24 August 1961, 4–5.

Walker, Arthur L. "The Modern Merger Movement." 7 September 1961, 8.

White, W. R. "Baptist Defectionists and Perfectionists." 7 December 1961, 3.

Baptist Record (Jackson)

Odle, Joe T. "An American Baptist Alliance?" 5 January 1961, 4.

Religious News Service. "Kennedy Cabinet Active Churchmen." 5 January 1961, 1.

————. "St. Louis Hospital Rejects Demands." 5 January 1961, 1.

————. "The Year in Religion." 5 January 1961, 1.

Baptist & Reflector (Nashville)

"Catholics Lose Bus Dispute." 9 November 1961, 16.

"Confidence Expressed in Trustees to Deal with Race Relationship Matter." 13 April 1961, 3.

"Criswell Warns Evangelistic Conference." 26 January 1961, 5.

"Foreign Mission Work Hampered by Race Attitudes Here." 8 June 1961, 2.

"JFK and Catholic Bishops in Deadlock on Education." 16 March 1961, 5.

"Laymen State Doctrinal Views." 28 September 1961, 8–9.

"More Education Needed on Church-State Relations." 28 September 1961, 5.

"Negro Baptists Appoint First White Missionary." 20 July 1961, 10.

"Pollard Cautions Baptists Against Weakening Position." 8 June 1961, 3.

"Report of Committee on Resolutions." 8 June 1961, 10.

"Seminary President McCall Charges Poll of Preacher Students Gives False Picture." 10 August 1961, 3.

"Southern Seminary Statement May Ease Strain." 17 August 1961, 3.

Arsdale, A. B. van. "The Everlasting Gospel." 25 May 1961, 3, 18–19.

Baptist Press. "BJCPA Asks Continued Freedom for Churches." 19 October 1961, 2.

———. "Cardinal Says Opposing Protestants Expected." 14 December 1961, 2.

———. "Church-State Relations Face National Re-Study." 13 April 1961, 2.

———. "College Aid Bill Helps Public, Church Schools." 6 April 1961, 16.

———. "Declares Church-State Separation Best." 23 March 1961, 3.

———. "Education Legislation Faces Complex Forces." 16 February 1961, 3.

———. "Fall of School System Warned if Tax Aid Given." 20 April 1961, 7.

———. "Federal College Loans Called 'Laudable' Deed." 29 June 1961, 9.

———. "Former SBC President Appointed by Kennedy." 23 February 1961, 5.

———. "Freedom of Church Schools Endangered by Public Aid." 26 January 1961, 13.

———. "Funds Left by Negro to New Jersey Church." 3 August 1961, 13.

———. "Further Review Voted for American Seminary." 9 March 1961, 2.

———. "Goldwater Asks Tax Aid for Parochial Schools." 15 June 1961, 16.

———. "Groups Seek Peaceful Integration for Atlanta." 27 July 1961, 9, 12.

———. "History Says Baptists Paid Price for Liberty." 27 July 1961, 8.

———. "Houston Baptists Act on Integration Issue." 16 February 1961, 9.

———. "King's Seminary Talk Draws Alabama Critic." 4 May 1961, 5.

———. "Large Response Greets Call to Conservatism." 27 July 1961, 5.

———. "Liberty Group Fights New York State Plan." 2 March 1961, 2.

———. "Midwestern Gets Hester from William Jewell." 30 March 1961, 2.

———. "Name Change Remains for Further Study." 9 March 1961, 16.

———. "Nashville Still Tries to Tax Baptist Land." 19 January 1961, 3.

———. "New McCarthyism Said Emerging in America." 9 March 1961, 2.

———. "No Solution in Sight for Education Impasse." 24 August 1961, 5.

———. "Parochial Aid Battle Top Story During 1961." 21 December 1961, 7.

———. "Parochial Loan Bill Introduced in Senate." 13 April 1961, 2.

———. "Peace Corps Prohibits Missionary Projects." 6 July 1961, 2.

———. "President Pays Tribute to Religious Liberty." 23 February 1961, 2.

———. "President Shows Concern for Religious Liberty." 16 February 1961, 2.

———. "Religious Liberty Emphasis Asked." 6 April 1961, 13.

———. "Religious Liberty Leader Attends WCC." 23 November 1961, 2.

———. "Says Public Education Requires Support of All." 2 February 1961, 3.

———. "SBC Name Change Urged by Northern Pastors." 23 February 1961, 2.

———. "Southern Baptist Says Integration Must Come." 19 January 1961, 2.

———. "Sunday Laws Upheld by U. S. Supreme Court." 15 June 1961, 3.

———. "Waco Baptist Association Adopts Race Resolution." 23 February 1961, 5.

Bibliography

Barton, V. Wayne. "Gleanings from the Greek New Testament: Means of Grace." 12 January 1961, 16.

Bennett, Hal D. "Some Principles of People Now Called Baptists." 27 July 1961, 5.

Coggins, Ross. "Television and Christian Responsibility." 14 December 1961, 4–5, 9.

Christian Services Committee, "Progress Reports on Desegregation." 23 November 1961, 9.

Davidson, P. O., et. al. "Progress Report on Desegregation." 23 November 1961, 9.

Dyer, J. Pope. "Faith of Our Fathers." 14 December 1961, 16.

Garrett, W. Barry. "Battle Continues Over Parochial School Aid." 15 June 1961, 5, 13.

Geren, Paul. "First in a Series of Four: Cancer of Communism Requires Close Study." 22 June 1961, 2.

———. "Second in a Series of Four: Communists Thrive on Poverty, Catastrophes." 29 June 1961, 3.

———. "Third in a Series of Four: Russian Baptists Can't Plant New Congregations." 6 July 1961, 3.

———. "Fourth and Final of Series: Dream of Own Business? In Soviet Union; Nyet." 13 July 1961, 3.

Hancox, Jack D. "New Look in Catholicism." 27 April 1961, 2, 14.

Hobbs, Herschel H. "Are Southern Baptists Facing a Theological Revolution?" 21 September 1961, 3, 10.

———. "Atonement." 30 August 1961, 5.

———. "Baptist Beliefs: Baptism." 14 December 1961, 5.

———. "Baptist Beliefs: Election." 9 November 1961, 5.

———. "Baptist Beliefs: God." 5 October 1961, 5.

———. "Baptist Beliefs: Holy Spirit." 12 October 1961, 5.

———. "Baptist Beliefs: Jesus Christ." 19 October 1961, 5.

———. "Baptist Beliefs: Lord's Supper." 21 December 1961, 5.

———. "Baptist Beliefs: Man." 26 October 1961, 5.

———. "Baptist Beliefs: Sin." 2 November 1961, 5.

———. "Baptist Beliefs: The Bible." 28 September 1961, 5, 11.

———. "Baptist Beliefs: The Church." 7 December 1961, 5.

James, E. S. "Church and State." 20 July 1961, 3–6.

Kennedy, Jack R. "Government Supported Churches." 30 March 1961, 3.

Maston, T. B. "Criticism and Commitment." 19 October 1961, 5, 8.

McCarty, Doran C. "Baptists Assured About Their Future Ministers." 21 September 1961, 2.

McClellan, Albert. "How Denominations Lose Colleges." 5 October 1961, 21.

Newton, Jim. "Texas Board Interprets Church State Separation." 22 June 1961, 5.

Owen, Richard N. "Ban on Sunday Sales Upheld." 15 June 1961, 4.

———. "Battle of the Books." 7 December 1961, 4.

———. "Church Discipline." 9 February 1961, 4.

———. "Church Mergers." 16 February 1961, 4.

———. "False Gods." 19 October 1961, 4.

———. "Handing the World Over to Communism." 1 June 1961, 4.

———. "Keep Them Separate." 6 July 1961, 4.

———. "Positive Answer." 27 July 1961, 4.

———. "Principles Always Cost." 22 June 1961, 4.

———. "Restore Sunday." 27 July 1961, 4.

———. "Science and Religion." 26 January 1961, 4.

————. "Shelter from the Stormy Blast." 30 August 1961, 4.

————. "Take Care." 16 March 1961, 4.

————. "The Church." 9 February 1961, 4.

————. "The Coin Has Two Sides." 5 January 1961, 4.

————. "The Issue is Moral and Spiritual Survival." 7 December 1961, 8.

————. "Theological Controversy." 24 August 1961, 4.

————. "They Shouldn't Have Gotten by with It." 16 March 1961, 4.

————. "What Is a Church Ordinance?" 23 February 1961, 4.

————. "What Needs Changing?" 18 May 1961, 4.

————. "White Man's Religion?" 29 June 1961, 4.

Partain, G. Leon. "Training Union Department: As A Baptist, I Believe." 10 August 1961, 10.

Pitts, Charles F. "'Who Steals My Name–Steals Trash?'" 11 May 1961, 16.

Religious News Service. "Bible Society's 'Cold War Fund' Will Counter Soviet Promotion of Atheism." 30 August 1961, 22–23.

————. "Catholics Told to Revise 'Double Tax Burden' Charges." 23 February 1961, 5.

————. "J. Edgar Hoover Defends Clergy Against Charge of Red Infiltration." 22 June 1961, 10.

————. "Hearings on Loan Bill Scheduled." 13 April 1961, 2.

————. "Kennedy Says Religion Spells Difference in World Ideologies." 23 February 1961, 3.

————. "Proposes 'Great American TV Strike.'" 14 December 1961, 5.

————. "Warns Against Church Personnel in Peace Corps." 17 August 1961, 13.

Singleton, James E. "Church Unity: Good or Bad?" 5 January 1961, 5, 13.

Smothers, D. D. "Are We, As Baptists, Justified in Maintaining Our Denominational Identity?" 21 December 1961, 8–9.

Sorensen, Donald J. "Faculty-Student Ties Noted at Midwestern." 2 November 1961, 5, 11.

Southard, Samuel. "When Negroes Attend Your Church." 2 February 1961, 2, 7, 14.

Vaught, W. O. "The Enemy Within: Is Self-Criticism Going to Destroy Us?" 14 December 1961, 7.

Wamble, Hugh. "Protestant Missions Under Attack." 9 March 1961, 3, 11.

Wheatley, Melvin E. "Reflections." 19 January 1961, 3.

Baptist Standard (Dallas)

"Article by Patterson in Baptist Standard Rallies Many Conservative Supporters." 19 July 1961, 12.

"Billy Graham Urges Firm Stand in Berlin." 16 August 1961, 18.

"Bremond School Case: Board Upholds Commissioner's Ruling." 8 February 1961, 10.

"Carlson Analyzes New NDEA Parochial School Loan Bill." 12 July 1961, 12.

"Convention Adopts Federal Aid Resolution." 31 May 1961, 13.

"Cooperation between Baptist Groups Discussed at Chicago Meeting." 11 January 1961, 10.

"Dawson Lectures: Hudson to Deliver Church-State Series." 8 March 1961, 15.

"Denominational Affiliations of U. S. Senators and Representatives by States." 8 March 1961, 9.

"Federal Aid to Education Status Remains Indefinite amid Debates." 24 May 1961, 11.

"Hardin–Simmons May Admit Negroes." 22 November 1961, 13.

Bibliography

"History Reveals Baptists Paid High Price for Religious Liberty, Historians Told." 19 July 1961, 13.

"Kennedy Sees no Room for Debate on Question of Aid to Parochial Schools." 8 March 1961, 14.

"Landes Praises Kennedy for Church-State Stand." 5 April 1961, 19.

"*Look* Article Says Hierarchy's Attitude Irks Kennedy." 10 May 1961, 15.

"March Sees Kennedy's School Aid Program Collide with Catholic Bishops." 29 March 1961, 15.

"Masonic Group Publishes Church-State Treatise." 1 March 1961, 17.

"North American Baptist Alliance Proposal Gains Support." 11 January 1961, 9.

"Safeguards Against Secularization," 22 February 1961, 5.

"Senate Bill Includes Aid for Private Schools." 26 July 1961, 12.

"Sixteen Baptist Schools Receive Federal Loans." 11 October 1961, 11.

"Southern Seminary Releases Statement on Speech by King." 9 August 1961, 13.

"Statement of Conviction and Purpose of the Faculties of Texas Baptist Colleges and Universities." 1 November 1961, 1.

"Texas Institutions Answer Charges of Federal Gifts." 9 August 1961, 13.

"Two Waco Groups Pass Motion on Integration." 15 February 1961,16.

Allen, Jimmy R. "Position of Senate Candidate on Church-State Relations Given." 10 May 1961, 13.

———. "Separation or Cooperation." 8 February 1961, 6–7, 10.

Bachman, Charles. "Cautious Integration." 1 March 1961, 3.

Bailey, P. Timothy. "Baptist Theologians." 29 November 1961, 3.

Baptist Press. "Alabama Demands McCall Ouster." 3 May 1961, 14.

———. "Baptist College Administrators Vote Approval of Federal Loans." 21 June 1961, 12.

———. "Baptist Editors Call Federal Aid to Schools Most Important." 20 December 1961, 13.

———. "Baptist Representative Introduces Bill to Ban Religious Garb for Teachers." 8 February 1961, 8.

———. "Baylor Professor Named to Midwestern Seminary." 22 March 1961, 15.

———. "Bremond Case May be Switched to Federal District Court." 5 April 1961, 19.

———. "BSU Leaders Adopt Resolution Favoring Texas College Integration." 26 April 1961, 16.

———. "Catholic Congressman Cites Parochial Aid Precedents." 10 May 1961, 13.

———. "Catholic Congressman Defends Federal Aid to Church Schools." 17 May 1961, 16.

———. "Catholic Explains Vote to Kill Education-Aid Bill." 16 August 1961, 13.

———. "Catholic Leaders Argue Parochial School Future." 16 August 1961, 16.

———. "Ceylon Government Takes Over Baptist School." 25 January 1961, 13.

———. "Church-State Debate Continues in Congress." 14 June 1961, 13.

———. "Church-State Problems Arise in Peace Corps Negotiations." 28 June 1961, 15.

———. "Church-State Problems Seen in Revision of National Defense Education Act." 17 May 1961, 16.

———. "Climate Said Changing in Negro Training." 5 April 1961, 32.

———. "Congress to See New Approach to Federal Aid to Education." 1 November 1961, 11.

———. "Constitution Violation Ruled in Bremond Case." 4 January 1961, 17.

————. "Court Reaffirms Stand on Bus Rides for Students." 8 March 1961, 14.

————. "Criswell Calls Federal Aid Greatest Danger to Separation." 22 February 1961, 16.

————. "Editors Warned of New McCarthyism; Hear Layman is Forgotten 'Man' in News Coverage." 8 March 1961, 13.

————. "Federal-Aid-to-Education Proposals Face Complexity of Ideas, Carlson Says." 8 February 1961, 9.

————. "Federal Loans Approved for Baptist Institutions." 16 August 1961, 17.

————. "Federal Lunch Program Allots Almost $6 Million to Private Schools." 16 August 1961, 17.

————. "Freedom Foundation President Tells Perils of Communism." 25 October 1961, 14.

————. "Freedom of Schools Endangered by 'Public Aid,' Commission Warns." 25 January 1961, 12.

————. "Governor Gets Sunday Closing Bill." 16 August 1961, 12.

————. "Hobbs Named Midwestern's First Commencement Speaker." 10 May 1961, 13.

————. "Joint Committee Spokesman Urges End to Controversy." 29 November 1961, 15.

————. "Kennedy, Graham Pay Tribute to Liberty." 15 February 1961, 16.

————. "Kennedy Proclaims Citizenship Day, Constitution Week for September." 24 May 1961, 12.

————. "Kennedy Reaffirms 'Public' School Aid Only." 8 February 1961, 8.

————. "Merger Talk Surprises ABC; Hobbs Speaks on Unity of Purpose." 21 June 1961, 15.

————. "Negro's Will Names Jersey SBC Church." 2 August 1961, 12.

————. "New Bill Proposes Grants, Loans to Private and Public Colleges." 3 May 1961, 16.

————. "North Carolina Voices Opposition to Proposed Aid-to-Education Bill." 19 July 1961, 15.

————. "POAU Leaders Discuss Future, Review Past." 5 April 1961, 19.

————. "Presbyterian Resolution Opposes Parochial Aid." 3 May 1961, 13.

————. "President Assures Baptists of Position on Loans to Parochial Schools." 15 March 1961, 12.

————. "Prolonged Reappraisal Seen on Church–State Separation." 12 April 1961, 12.

————. "Raleigh Pastors Vote Confidence in Southern Baptist Seminaries." 16 August 1961, 18.

————. "Religious Liberty: Kennedy Assures Missionaries of Concern." 8 February 1961, 10.

————. "Resolution Lauds JFK on School-Aid Stand." 8 March 1961, 15.

————. "Ribicoff Sees no Solution to Education Aid Tangle." 16 August 1961, 12.

————. "SBC Agencies Asked to Emphasize Heritage." 5 April 1961, 19.

————. "Senators Plan Additional Aid to Parochial Schools." 10 May 1961, 14.

————. "Sunday Laws: Appellants Ask Supreme Court for Rehearing." 19 July 1961, 13.

————. "Supreme Court Refuses to Review Vermont Parochial Tuition Decision." 24 May 1961, 13.

————. "Texas House Gets Sunday Closing Bill." 2 August 1961, 12.

————. "Three South Alabama Churches Discontinue Cooperative Program Gifts to one Seminary." 2 August 1961, 30.

Bibliography

————."Union Association Pastors' Group Suggests Racial Integration of Baptist Schools." 15 February 1961, 22.

————."Wake Forest May Admit Some Negro Students." 10 May 1961, 14.

————."Wake Forest Enrolls Negro Summer Student." 21 June 1961, 14.

————."Warnings Prevalent on Segregation, Church State Relations at Convention." 31 May 1961, 7.

————."Washington Paper Defends Stand Against Federal Aid to Church Schools." 15 February 1961, 12.

Barnes, Barbara. "Origin of the Negro." 6 September 1961, 3.

Barnes, Mrs. B. "Integration." 12 April 1961, 3.

————. "Integration." 21 June 1961, 3.

Barrow, Mrs. Earnest. "Catholic Indulgences." 15 March 1961, 3.

Bradbury, J. S. "Racial Distinctions." 20 December 1961, 3.

Colton, C. E. "Our Academic Dilemma." 24 May 1961, 6.

Colyan, Larry C. "Prejudiced Publication?" 1 November 1961, 3.

Committee on Church-State Relations. "Report of Special Committee to BGCT Executive Board." 14 June 1961, 8–9.

Cooper, Owen. "The Role of the Christian College from a Layman's Point of View." 5 July 1961, 8, 10.

Cox, H. B. "Sovereignty of God." 18 October 1961, 3.

Deering, H. F. "Catholics–Politics–Freedom." 29 March 1961, 3.

Ferrer, Terry, and Abner McCall. "Judge McCall Answers Query on Aid to Education." 19 April 1961, 9.

Ford, W. Herschel. "The Gospel and the Catholic Bible." 16 August 1961, 8–9.

Garrett, James Leo. "Leo Garrett Commends Standard Position." 6 September 1961, 3.

Garrett, W. Barry. "Congress Committees Recommend Federal Aid to Parochial Schools." 28 June 1961, 14.

————. "Parochial School Issue Delays Action on Aid-to-Education Bill." 28 June 1961, 12.

Green, Joseph F. "Conservative or Fundamentalist?" 26 April 1961, 7.

Greene, Fred J. Jr. "Catholics Universal." 3 May 1961, 3.

Guffey, Mrs. J. L. "Communist Threat." 8 March 1961, 3.

Harding, F. T. "Against Integration." 21 June 1961, 3.

Harper, C. Columbus. "Negro Pastor Receives Standard." 20 September 1961, 3.

Higginbotham, F. R. "San Antonia Baptist Hospital Schools Integrated." 3 May 1961, 14.

Hobbs, Herschel H. "Are Southern Baptists Facing a Theological Revolution." 27 September 1961, 6–7.

————. "Hobbs Issues Statement to Clarify Action." 16 August 1961, 15.

————. "Oklahoma Resolution: Hobbs Issues Statement to Clarify Actions," 23 August 1961, 15.

Hopkins, Joe. "Martin Luther King." 20 September 1961, 3.

House, M. D. "National Council of Churches." 22 March 1961, 3.

Howard, Herbert R. "Crisis in Education." 26 July 1961, 5.

Hubbell, Martin Jr. "Catholics Seek Federal Aid." 20 September 1961, 3.

Hughes, Mr. and Mrs. James. "U. S. Supreme Court." 3 May 1961, 3.

Hunt, J. N. "The Baptist Conscience." 22 February 1961, 10.

Jackson, Mrs. A. T. "A Real Baptist." 25 January 1961, 3.

James, E. S. "1961 Baptist Jubilee Advance." 4 January 1961, 4.

———. "A Communist Compliment for Baptists." 9 August 1961, 4–5.

———. "A Lawyer's Convictions on Government Subsidies." 6 September 1961, 4.

———. "Alien Immersion . . . Open Communion . . . Ecumenicity . . . Apostasy . . . An Interview with Dr. Dale Moody." 30 August 1961, 6.

———. "Alternatives for Our Baptist Schools." 21 June 1961, 4.

———. "An Analysis of Government Loans to Sectarian Institutions." 21 June 1961, 5.

———. "An Incongruous Argument." 13 December 1961, 4.

———. "An Independent and Cooperative Endeavor of Baptists." 12 April 1961, 4.

———. "Are Roman Catholics a Backward People?" 29 November 1961, 4–5.

———. "Baptist Editors and the Communist Threat." 29 March 1961, 4.

———. "Baptist Theologians and Their Books." 10 January 1962, 4–5.

———. "Christians and Extravagance." 27 September 1961, 4–5.

———. "Church and State." 5 July 1961, 6–7.

———. "Church and State." 12 July 1961, 10.

———. "Compulsory Sabbath Closing." 22 November 1961, 4.

———. "Democracy." 19 July 1961, 4.

———. "Executive Board Takes Strong Position on Church and State." 14 June 1961, 4.

———. "Federal Aid for Sunday Schools." 19 April 1961, 4.

———. "Federal Funds and American Education." 25 January 1961, 4.

———. "Forty Baptist Educators Could Be Wrong." 28 June 1961, 4.

———. "Goldwater's Plea for Parochial School Aid." 30 August 1961, 4–5.

———. "Is the Virgin Birth Worth Discussing?" 8 March 1961, 4.

———. "Let Us Poll Our own Seminary Students." 9 August 1961, 4.

———. "Many Little Gods." 8 February 1961, 4.

———. "Negro Convention Sets Pattern." 26 July 1961, 5.

———. "No Other Place to Begin." 5 April 1961, 5.

———. "Operation Baptists United." 22 February 1961, 4.

———. "POAU and the Roman Catholic Church." 2 August 1961, 4.

———. "Past Masters at Evasion." 22 March 1961, 4.

———. "President-Elect Nominates Churchmen for New Cabinet." 11 January 1961, 4.

———. "President Kennedy—A Man of Courage." 12 April 1961, 5.

———. "Rockefeller Recommends Sectarian Aid." 22 February 1961, 4–5.

———. "Safeguards Against Secularization." 22 February 1961, 5.

———. "Senseless Sham." 15 November 1961, 5.

———. "Sheltering Seminary Students." 17 May 1961, 4–5.

———. "Should We Apologize for Teaching DOCTRINE?" 5 July 1961, 4–5.

———. "Some Lessons from Missouri Baptists." 18 January 1961, 4.

———. "The Bremond Captive School Case." 15 February 1961, 4.

———. "The Coming Great Church." 27 September 1961, 4.

———. "The Dale Moody Controversy." 30 August 1961, 4.

———. "The Dangers of Luxury." 5 July 1961, 5.

———. "The Peace Corps and the Churches." 12 July 1961, 4.

———. "These Uncouth, Uneducated and Bigoted Baptists." 11 January 1961, 4.

———. "Who Opposes Public Aid to Parochial School, and Why?" 5 April 1961, 4–5.

———. "Who Wants to Understand Whom?" 17 May 1961, 5.

———. "Why the Foreign Mission Board Appoints no Negro Missionaries." 6 September 1961, 4.

John, Mrs. A. "'Southern' Inappropriate?" 11 October 1961, 3.

Jones, Edward N. "The Future of Christian Education Depends Upon its Objectives." 7 June 1961, 6–7, 13.

Jones, S. H. "Doctrinal Arguments." 29 November 1961, 5.

Kasten, Frederick H. "Baptist Education for Negroes." 1 February 1961, 3.

Kitterman, Mr. and Mrs. Gene. "Wayland Baptist College Integrated." 22 March 1961, 3.

Lawrence, J. B. "The Virgin Birth." 6 September 1961, 6–7.

Leavell, Roland Q. and W. Herschel Ford, "Report from the Vice–Presidents: Principle Problems Facing Southern Baptists in the Coming Year," 12 July 1961, 11.

Lesh, March Ann. "Segregation and Foreign Missions." 19 April 1961, 3.

Lewis, Grover E. "The Attitude of the South Toward Slavery in the Pre-War Period." 2 August 1961, 8.

Lipscomb, Dixie Lea. "Baptist Alliance Proposal." 3 May 1961, 3.

Logan, W. E. "Baptists . . . Catholics . . . Politics." 1 February 1961, 3.

Maston, T. B. "Criticism and Commitment." 18 October 1961, 6–7.

———. "The Role of a Pastor in a Community Facing Desegregation." 19 July 1961, 8.

McCall, Duke K. "An Unappreciated Honor." 4 October 1961, 6.

McClellan, Albert. "How Denominations Lose Colleges." 6 September 1961, 9.

McCord, Bruce. L. "Biblical Predestination." 9 August 1961, 3.

McGregor, Don. "Executive Board Adopts Report Opposing Government Gifts, Loans." 14 June 1961, 10–11.

———. "Fund Raising, Doctrinal Emphasis, Integration Demand Attention." 15 March 1961, 10—11.

———. "Moody Answers Charges of Oklahoma Resolution." 9 August 1961, 12.

McIver, Bruce. "The Cry for Freedom." 11 January 1961, 6.

Miller, Virginia. "The Name 'Baptist.'" 15 March 1961, 3.

Moody, Dale. "Why I Reject Infant Baptism." 30 August 1961, 6–7.

Moyers, Bill. "The United States Peace Corps." 6 September 1961, 6.

Naylor, Robert E. "Plain Talk." 4 October 1961, 7.

Nelson, Richard V. "The Ecumenical Movement and the Universal Church." 16 August 1961, 6.

Newell, R. J. "Catholic Hierarchy and Kennedy." 6 September 1961, 3.

Newton, Jim. "Two Negro Churches Affiliate with Corpus Christi Association." 25 October 1961, 13.

O'Reagan, Daniel W. "Government Grants." 15 March 1961, 3.

Owen, A. Hope and Abner V. McCall. "Federal Aid to Education." 13 December 1961, 3.

Owen, Richard N. "Science and Religion." 29 March 1961, 5.

Park, Mrs. George C. "Catholic Political Activity." 3 May 1961, 3.

Patterson, T. A. "Christian Colleges." 19 April 1961, 2.

———. "Enthusiastic Promises, Disappointing Results." 12 April 1961, 2.

———. "What Is Truth?" 20 September 1961, 2.

———. "Whither Baptists?" 21 June 1961, 2.

Poe, Joe. T. "What Alternative to Communism?" 4 January 1961, 7.

Pratt, Mrs. A. C. "Integration . . . Segregation." 1 February 1961, 3.

Prescott, W. H. "Segregation." 29 March 1961, 3.

Rains, Dale O. "North American Baptist Alliance." 19 April 1961, 3.

Ransour, H. B. "Why Is Communism Godless?" 30 August 1961, 9.

Rasco, John. "The Christian Education Commission, the Convention, & Texas Baptist Schools." 1 November 1961, 5–6.

Religious News Service. "ABC Official Endorses Baptist Unity Talks." 4 January 1961, 17.

———. "Baptist Union Urged by Pastor of Nation's Oldest Baptist Church." 1 February 1961, 11.

———. "Catholic Leader Announces Plans to Seek Direct Parochial Grants." 12 April 1961, 15.

———. "Catholic Weekly Supports Kennedy on School Aid." 5 April 1961, 19.

———. "College Group Opposes State Aid to Church Schools." 11 January 1961, 9.

———. "Congressmen Find Voters Oppose Loans to Private Schools." 16 August 1961, 16.

———. "Council Lists Six Points in Opposition to Private School Aid." 12 April 1961, 12.

———. "East German Protestants defy Communists." 26 July 1961, 12.

———. "Evangelicals Oppose Federal Aid to Parochial Schools." 31 May 1961, 17.

———. "Graham Warns Against Confusion from Ideas of Leading Theologians." 29 July 1961, 11.

———. "Kennedy's Federal Aid Proposal Draws Praise and Criticism." 8 March 1961, 12.

———. "Municipal Court Releases Cleveland Preachers." 3 May 1961, 12.

———. "Negro Convention Forms Two Groups." 29 November 1961, 13.

———. "President Asks Churches to Continue Aid Abroad." 1 March 1961, 17.

———. "Priest Exerts Pressure for School Tax Exemption." 1 February 1961, 10.

———. "Sectarian Nurses Schools Receive Government Grants." 1 March 1961, 20.

———. "Spellman Praises Rockefeller's Student Aid Proposal." 22 February 1961, 14.

———. "Struggle for Money Threatens Christian Schools Prominent Educator Says." 22 February 1961, 16.

———. "Suit Seeks to Bar Aid to Segregated Schools." 22 February 1961, 15.

Rhodes, Lewis E. "Let's Have One Convention in San Francisco." 2 August 1961, 9.

Riser, George W. "Baptists and Apostolic Succession." 1 February 1961, 3.

Roach, T. A. "Public School Educator Urges Resistance to Increased College Bible Requirements." 22 February 1961, 3.

Robberson, J. S. "Racial Propagation." 29 November 1961, 3.

Rucker, Paul. "Federal Loan and Bishop College." 8 March 1961, 3.

Ryder, Gene. "School Tax Refund." 1 February 1961, 3.

Saber, Mrs. R. "Comparison of DOCTRINE." 12 April 1961, 3.

Sampey, John R. Jr. "Taboos and Freedom of the Press." 4 January 1961, 3.

Schroeder, George W. "Please, Not Discrimination." 26 April 1961, 9.

Tenery, Robert M. "Our First Line of Concern." 20 September 1961, 7.

Thomas, J. Martin. "Are We Losing our Spiritual Appetites?" 24 May 1961, 7–8.

Thompson, T. W. "The Church's Freedom." 1 February 1961, 3.

Valentine, Foy. "The Philistines be Upon Us." 28 June 1961, 8–9.

Vanderslice, Charles D. "The Cracked Wall of Morality." 20 December 1961, 8.

Walker, James A. "Upholds Negro Missionaries." 19 November 1961, 3.

Watkins, Joe James. "Education for Negroes." 1 March 1961, 3.

White, J. Eugene. "Church-State Issues, College Occupy Other State Conventions." 6 December 1961, 8.

———. "McCall Protests Claim of Fundamental Laxness." 2 August 1961, 12.

———. "Preservation of Liberties Depends on Free Conscience, Lecturer Holds." 22 March 1961, 14.

Winkle, Mrs. Owen C. "Catholic Domination." 20 December 1961, 3.

Wright, Charlotte E. "Communism in America." 25 January 1961, 3.

Bibliography

Yancey, Mrs. Kenneth W. "Negro Samaritan." 21 June 1961, 3.

Biblical Recorder (Raleigh)

"Baptists More Evenly Divided than Appears on the Surface." 10 June 1961, 19.

"Baptist Pastor Barred from Air." 21 January 1961, 5.

"Cardinal Spellman's Stand on School Aid Criticized." 4 February 1961, 13.

"Communism Major Threat to Our Liberty to Preach the Gospel." 3 June 1961, 5.

"Communists Continue to Make Big Gains in Center of Catholicism." 11 March 1961, 2.

"Denominational Loyalty Expected of Institutions." 3 June 1961, 6, 23.

"Discussion of Race Relations Most Significant Issue." 10 June 1961, 12.

"Doctrinal Differences Seldom Cause Tension in Our Churches." 16 December 1961, 2.

"Dr. Hand Lists Five Qualifications for Christian Teachers." 16 September 1961, 11.

"I Hate Negroes at Home, But Love Them in Africa." 3 June 1961, 7.

"Interracial Institutes Scheduled for October." 23 September 1961, 15.

"Letter from a Young Communist." 18 November 1961, 8.

"Mars Hill Session Probes into Most Pressing Baptist Issues." 2 September 1961, 10.

"N.C. Baptists Urged to Oppose Tax Grab." 6 May 1961, 23.

"Negro Baptists to Hold Conference on Evangelism in Raleigh, February 28–March 1." 25 February 1961, 23.

"Negro Student Drops Out of Mars Hill; Was First to be Admitted." 25 November 1961, 2.

"Protestant Minority in U. S. is Now a Reality." 11 March 1961, 3.

"Raleigh Pastors Disagree with Oklahoma Men." 19 August 1961, 7.

"Resolution on Race Relations." 3 June 1961, 18.

"Roman Catholic Church Should Pay Its Own Way, Ramsey Pollard Says." 3 June 1961, 20.

"SBC Representatives Meet with Leaders of Two Negro Conventions." 7 January 1961, 7.

"S. C. Bans Fraternities; Defeats Integration Move." 2 December 1961, 18.

"The Danger of Being Possessed by Things." 29 July 1961, 10.

"Wake Forest Board Lifts New Race Bar." 17 June 1961, 23.

"WF to Admit Negroes to Graduate School." 6 May 1961, 7.

"Wholesome Race Relations are Fostered by Cooperation." 15 July 1961, 8.

Baptist Press. "American Baptists to Attend Next Meeting with Negro Leaders." 21 January 1961, 9.

———. "Church Lets Inactive Members Drop Selves." 15 April 1961, 8.

———. "'Competition' Deplored by American and Southern Baptist Groups in Delaware." 18 March 1961, 8.

———. "Criswell Sees 'Death Struggle' Between Protestants, Catholics." 28 January 1961, 8.

———. "Dr. C. E. Autry Says Integration Must Come." 21 January 1961, 8.

———. "It's Wrong to Tax One Family to Pay for Propagation of Another Family's Faith." 9 September 1961, 7.

———. "Missionaries from ABC and SBC Take Part in Washington Program." 18 February 1961, 2.

———. "Name Change Urged by Northern Pastors." 25 February 1961, 4.

———. "New Orleans Seminary to Have Course on Relations between American, Southern Baptists." 8 April 1961, 17.

———. "Okla. Pastors Attack Dale Moody." 5 August 1961, 10.

————. "Parochial Aid Battle Top Story." 23 December 1961, 8.

————. "Pastor Should Play Key Integration Role, Dr. T. B. Maston Contends." 18 March 1961, 9.

————. "President Assures 62 Baptists Missionaries that He is Concerned for Religious Liberty." 18 February 1961, 2.

————. "Proposed SBC–ABC Talks Draw Fire, Approval." 25 February 1961, 5.

————. "Religious Issue Top SBC Story." 7 January 1961, 4.

————. "Reminds Baptists Race Issue Affects Missions." 18 March 1961, 8.

————. "Theological Education Not Job of Government, Dr. Carlson Declares." 3 June 1961, 11.

————. "Too Many Non–Resident ... Transfer of Church Membership to be Emphasized in February." 7 January 1961, 5.

————. "Washington Baptist Leader Favors Further Unity Talks; Favors Dr. Dodd's Alliance Plan." 21 January 1961, 2.

Baylor, W. H. "The Baptist Position." 11 March 1961, 3.

Bishop, George M. "Our Readers Write: Believes We Should Begin Talks with American Baptists." 4 February 1961, 16.

Bradbury, John W. "Peril of SBC Is That It Tends to be a Witness Unto Itself." 24 June 1961, 2.

Brewer, J. Street. "Prodding Colleges not Answer to Race Problem, Doctor Says." 23 December 1961, 18.

Bryan, Gainer E. Jr. "Racial Discrimination Jeopardizes Mission Work, UN Observer Declares." 14 January 1961, 9.

Cannon, W. S. "Answer to All Baptist Problems: Just Split Along Opinion Lines." 14 October 1961, 12.

Corbin, Wilford. "U. S. Baptist Convention or Baptist Convention of USA." 1 July 1961, 12.

Crabtree, Arthur B. "A British Baptist Looks at Baptists in America." 15 April 1961, 18.

Duncan, James O. "Baptist Editor in Washington Anticipates Even More Inter-Convention Cooperation." 4 February 1961, 5.

Fesperman, Mrs. Forrest. "Writing and Preaching About Racial Discrimination." 4 March 1961, 17.

Fisher, Ben C. "Lack of Impact of Gospel Message Cause for Concern." 11 February 1961, 3.

Grant, J. Marse. "Best Anti-Communist Organization is Church." 6 May 1961, 3.

————. "Catholic Priest Admires Witness of Evangelicals." 8 April 1961, 3.

————. "Editorial Causes Some Stir among the People." 11 March 1961, 3.

————. "'Get, Get, Get,' Philosophy is Damaging to Society." 6 May 1961, 3.

————. "Hierarchy Can Take Bow for Killing Federal Aid." 29 July 1961, 3.

————. "Hierarchy Flexes Muscle for All of U. S. to See." 15 April 1961, 3.

————. "Hierarchy Pushing Hard for Federal School Aid." 25 February 1961, 3.

————. "It Won't Be an Easy Year." 7 January 1961, 3.

————. "'John the Baptist' and Shades of McCarthyism." 8 April 1961, 3.

————. "Let Rep McCormick Declare Himself on Church and State." 9 December 1961, 3.

————. "Let's Hold Off on Name Changing at the Present." 20 May 1961, 3.

————. "Manipulated Gospel." 16 December 1961, 3, 18.

————. "Many Tensions Surround 20th Century Seminary." 16 September 1961, 3.

————. "Name Change Dead for Present." 3 June 1961, 3.

————. "Next Move Is Up to SBC." 21 January 1961, 3.

Bibliography

————. "Prayers, Support Needed Rather than Hasty Criticism." 16 December 1961, 3.

————. "Time for President to Speak Out on School Aid." 5 August 1961, 3.

————. "Two Points of Conflict Between Baptist Bodies." 25 March 1961, 3, 18.

————. "Why Seminary Professors Don't Write Many Books." 11 November 1961, 3.

Grigg, W. E. "Are We Merely Fighting Symptoms or Seeking a Cure?" 15 July 1961, 9, 15.

Hawkins, Leo F. "Four Reasons Given for Decline in Key Areas of Southern Baptist Life." 7 January 1961, 17.

James, E. S. "Afraid to Take Public Stand, Dr. James Says." 3 June 1961, 18.

Maston, T. B. "What if Baptists Spoke as Strongly on Race Relations as on Church and State?" 14 January 1961, 8.

Newman, Stewart A. "Is the Baptist Movement a 'Theological' Movement." 7 October 1961, 9.

Phillips, John W. "Resolution Presented by N. C. Pastor on Admittance of Negroes to Baptist Colleges." 10 June 1961, 11, 13.

Price, Sterling L. "'I'm Sorry They Apologized,' St. Louis Pastor Declares." 9 September 1961, 9.

Religious News Service. "Another Move Toward Closer Fellowship." 18 March 1961, 19.

————. "Catholic Magazine Urges Privacy for President Kennedy." 7 January 1961, 21.

————. "Catholics Predominate Group in New Congress." 14 January 1961, 9.

————. "Convention to Launch Baptist Unity Effort Urged by Dr. Trickett." 4 March 1961, 4.

————. "County Challenges Tax-Free Status of Golden Age Home Operated by Baptists in Oklahoma." 7 January 1961, 16.

————. "Georgia Paper Urges Pastors to Preach on Desegregation." 19 August 1961, 19.

————. "Opposition Expressed to Tax Deductions for Tuition Payments." 1 April 1961, 15.

————. "Pastor of Mother Church of All Baptists in America Urges One Great Fellowship." 11 February 1961, 12.

————. "POAU" Says Principle of Church-State Separation Advanced in '60." 14 January 1961, 4.

————. "Pulpit Exchanges Suggested for American and Southern Baptists." 4 March 1961, 19.

————. "Rep. McCormack Takes Issue with President on Federal School Aid." 18 March 1961, 4.

————. "SBC Hospitals Decide Against Federal Aid." 25 February 1961, 14.

————. "Seven Protestants, Two Jews, One Catholic in Kennedy Cabinet; All Active Churchmen. 7 January 1961, 5.

————. "Texas Baptist Students Pledge their Support of College Desegregation." 6 May 1961, 4.

————. "Unity Proposal by Dr. Trickett Winning Approval of Baptists." 29 April 1961, 9.

Smith, R. F. Jr. "Remember This, Joe, Baptists Believe in the Soul Competency of Individual." 2 December 1961, 8.

Stagg, Paul L. "Freedom Is the Freedom to Seek and Do the Will of God." 28 October 1961, 12—13.

Stewart, Harold B. "SBC and ABC—Why?" 25 March 1961, 12.

Tuller, Edwin H. "American Baptist Leader Says Talks are 'In Order.'" 7 January 1961, 6.

Udvarnoki, Bela. "An American Baptist Alliance?" 21 January 1961, 12, 16.

White, J. Eugene. "McCall Denies that Tomorrow's Ministers are a Liberal Lot." 19 August 1961, 8.

Bibliography

Williams, William Harrison. "In 1880, Northern and Southern Baptists Had Great Fellowship." 4 March 1961, 9.

Capital Baptist (Washington, D.C.)

"Bible Professors Protest Elliott's Dismissal; Want More Protection from Attacks." 3 January 1963, 1, 5.

"First Baptist to Use Elliott in Bible Study." 17 January 1963, 7.

"Messengers Approve New Statement of Faith." 16 May 1963, 3.

American Baptist News Service. "ABC Leaders Hold Training Session in Mexico." 24 January 1963, 1, 8.

Anderson, Paul A. "The Position of Religion in the Soviet Union." 21 February 1963, 6.

Baptist Press. "5 Negroes Seated in Alabama Church." 2 May 1963, 3.

———. "Baptist Group Stresses Freedom of Religion." 21 March 1963, 2.

———. "Bethany Press Coming Out with Elliott Book." 17 January 1963, 8.

———. "Catholic President Backs Baptist Views, Says James." 28 February 1963, 8

———. "Committee Urges Mercer Delay any Integration." 28 March 1963, 2.

———. "Fuzzy Picture Caused by Being Outdated." 24 January 1963, 1.

———. "Mercer University Drops Racial Bars." 25 April 1963, 8.

———. "Midwestern Approves Policy, Lauds Berquist." 21 March 1963, 8.

———. "Nordenhaug Welcomes Vatican Study of Religious Liberty." 31 January 1963, 3.

———. "Parochial Schools Left Out of Education Bill." 7 February 1963, 1.

———. "President Asks Huge Program of Education." 7 February 1963, 6.

———. "Race Bias Called 'Sickness of Soul.'" 14 February 1963, 8.

———. "Supreme Court Hears Bible Reading Cases." 7 March 1963, 1–2.

———. "Tax Reforms Should be Studied Carefully." 28 February 1963, 3.

Cox, James W. "The Bible Is the Word of God, Too!" 14 February 1963, 3.

Duncan, James O. "Southern Baptists to Face Several Issues at Kansas City Convention." 25 April 1963, 4.

———. "Supreme Court Has Difficult Task." 18 April 1963, 4.

Garrett, James Leo. "A Relevant Word from Dr. Schaff." 25 April 1963, 7–8.

Hobbs, Herschel H. "Blest Be the Tie that Binds . . . ." 21 February 1963, 3.

Hobbs, Herschel H., et. al. "The Baptist Faith and Message." 14 March 1963, 3–5.

Religious News Service. "American Baptists Uphold Stand on Church–State Separation." 21 February 1963, 3.

———. "Baptists Mark 300th Anniversary of Religious Freedom Charter." 28 February 1963, 6.

———. "House Passes Measure Aiding Church-Related Medical Schools." 9 May 1963, 1.

———. "Minister Sees South Solving Racial Problems before North." 17 January 1963, 2.

———. "Supreme Court to Hear Arguments on School Prayer, Bible Reading." 14 February 1963, 1–2.

Rust, Eric C. "The Miracle of the Resurrection." 28 March 1963, 3, 7.

Christian Index (Atlanta)

"Asks Life Sentence for Negro." 26 October 1961, 4.

"Baptist Appointed." 5 October 1961, 4.

"College Race Policies Hold Firm." 23 November 1961, 5.

"Continue Church–State Position; Refuse Fight on Racial Question." 1 June 1961, 3–4.

Bibliography

"Court Test Looms." 16 February 1961, 7.

"Declares for Racial Harmony." 11 May 1961, 5.

"Defends Appearance." 4 May 1961, 3.

"Defends Seminaries." 1 June 1961, 15.

"Duke K. McCall." 23 November 1961, 12.

"Election Holds Major Interest." 11 May 1961, 3.

"Integration Vote." 2 February 1961, 4.

"Meet the New SBC President." 1 June 1961, 5.

"Plan Negro Bible Institute in Douglas." 8 June 1961, 11.

"Submits Parochial Tuition Test." 6 April 1961, 3.

"Suggest North American Group." 12 January 1961, 5.

"Suggests Study of Commission." 30 November 1961, 3.

"Take Stands on Social Issues." 23 November 1961, 4.

"Texas Example on Sunday Law." 19 January 1961, 6.

Baptist Press. "Ask Integration." 16 February 1961, 7.

———. "Ask POAU Change." 9 March 1961, 7.

———. "As Racial Study." 14 December 1961, 8.

———. "Colleges Answer Aid Charges." 12 October 1961, 3.

———. "Cut Seminary Funds." 3 August 1961, 7.

———. "Education Problem Complex." 2 February 1961, 5.

———. "Endorse Integration." 27 April 1961, 23.

———. "Face Race Problem." 9 March 1961, 15.

———. "Hester Elected." 23 March 1961, 8.

———. "Kennedy Greets Baptist Group." 2 February 1961, 4.

———. "Negro in School." 22 June 1961, 7.

———. "Negro Missionaries?" 14 September 1961, 7.

———. "No Government Aid." 2 February 1961, 7.

———. "Oppose Cardinal on Federal Aid." 2 February 1961, 3.

———. "Pastors Hit SBC Theologians." 3 August 1961, 3.

———. "Study Negro School Program." 12 January 1961, 4.

———. "Test Religious Law." 4 May 1961, 3.

———. "Urges Integration." 16 March 1961, 12.

———. "Vermont School-Aid Ban Upheld." 25 May 1961, 4.

Garrett, W. Barry. "Church Lobby Loses First Test." 25 May 1961, 5.

Hanie, Ronald. "Defends Moody." 17 August 1961, 7.

Hardman, Mrs. L. G. Jr. "Busy People, Dying Religion." 4 May 1961, 2.

Hart, John J. Jr. "Atheist's Bible Disturbs Nobody." 27 July 1961, 6.

———. "Baptists Favor Cooperation, But not a Merger." 19 October 1961, 6.

———. "Baptists Show Maturity, Oneness of Purpose." 23 November 1961, 6.

———. "Cooperation but no Submerging." 9 March 1961, 6.

———. "Defeat Possible in Compromise." 6 April 1961, 6.

———. "Issue In Doubt as Separation Battle Continues in Washington." 4 May 1961, 6.

———. "Mr. Krushchev Won't Want Us." 3 August 1961, 6.

———. "New Campaign for Tax Funds." 16 February 1961, 6.

———. "Our President Needs Prayers." 26 January 1961, 6.

———. "Quit Shooting Pending Study." 10 August 1961, 6.

———. "Separation Battle Continues." 23 February 1961, 6.

———. "This Court Test is Ridiculous." 14 December 1961, 6.

————. "Watch Liquor, TV, Catholics, Churches . . . ." 12 October 1961, 6.

————. "We Thank You, Mr. President." 16 March 1961, 6.

————. "Who's a Bigot—A Persecutor or Defender?" 26 October 1961, 6.

————. "Why Our Fears without Basis?" 27 July 1961, 6.

Krainov, S. "Diary. S. Krainov, Communist Youth, Visits Moscow Baptist Church: 'Baptist Leaders Tend Toward Fanaticism without Limits . . . Blind Obedience.'" 26 January 1961, 4—5.

Mullins, E. Y. "What is the New Testament Teaching on the Relation of Baptism to the Remission of Sins and the New Birth?" 3 May 1906, 2–3, 5.

Religious News Service. "American Convention: Portrait of an Average Baptist." 2 February 1961, 5.

————. "Ban Gideon Bibles." 5 January 1961, 3.

————. "Houston: Enforce Sunday Laws." 5 January 1961, 3.

————. "Partial Integration." 11 May 1961, 5.

————. "Protestants Hit Bishop's Stand." 30 November 1961, 3.

————. "School Loan Bill." 9 March 1961, 15.

————. "Vote to Integrate." 23 February 1961, 7.

Singleton, Janice. "Five Negro Camps Planned for Summer." 13 July 1961, 13.

Wells, L. T. "Baptist Disgrace." 17 August 1961, 7.

Florida Baptist Witness (Jacksonville)

"$19 Million Budget Adopted by SBC; Herschel Hobbs is Elected President." 1 June 1961, 1, 9.

"Authority on Communism to Speak to Pastors." 23 October 1961, 2–3.

"Race Relations, Communism and Religious Liberty Evoke Strong Resolutions from SBC in St. Louis." 8 June 1961, 5, 9.

"Seminar to Alert Baptists of Dangers." 11 May 1961, 5.

Baptist Press. "Alliance in North America Suggested." 19 January 1961, 3.

————. "American, Southern Opinions Compared." 26 October 1961, 2.

————. "Another Court Holds Property Tax-Exempt." 10 August 1961, 5.

————. "'Applied Gospel' Unity Among Nation's Baptists." 20 July 1961, 2.

————. "Baptist Leader Favors Further Unity Talks." 19 January 1961, 3.

————. "Baptists Praise JFK's Church-State Position." 23 March 1961, 2.

————. "Brotherhood Urges Sunday Closing." 26 January 1961, 5.

————. "Catholic Congressman Reports School Survey." 11 May 1961, 5.

————. "Cites Federal Aid to Church Schools." 24 August 1961, 5.

————. "Colorado Commends Seminary DOCTRINE Poll." 26 October 1961, 3.

————. "Communists, Catholics Note Russian Baptists." 2 February 1961, 5.

————. "Connecticut Gets First Southern Baptist Group." 5 October 1961, 5.

————. "Court Action Upholds Vermont School Decision." 25 May 1961, 5.

————. "Criswell Blasts Catholics During Evangelism Meeting." 26 January 1961, 16.

————. "Fall of School System Seen if Tax Aid Given." 27 April 1961, 1.

————. "Freedom of Church Schools Imperiled by Acceptance of 'Public Funds.'" 2 February 1961, 2.

————. "Groups Seek Peaceful Atlanta Integration." 27 July 1961, 2.

————. "Legal Report Rules Out Parochial School Loans." 27 April 1961, 5.

————. "Legislature Passes Sunday Closing Law." 24 August 1961, 3.

———. "Mars Hill Lifts Ban on Negro Enrollment." 20 July 1961, 3.

———. "Missionary Pleads with Convention Messengers to Advance Christian Spirit in Race Relations." 8 June 1961, 1, 6.

———. "Most Baptist Schools in Ceylon are Seized." 2 February 1961, 5.

———. "Negroes Picket 3 Oklahoma Churches." 21 September 1961, 2.

———. "New Administration has Education 'Hot Potato.'" 2 February 1961, 2.

———. "Oklahoma Pastors Attack Dale Moody." 10 August 1961, 5.

———. "Parochial Bus Question Goes to Supreme Court." 26 January 1961, 5.

———. "Parochial Bus Rides Upheld by U. S. Court." 23 March 1961, 2.

———. "Parochial School Aid Issue Isn't Dead Yet." 24 August 1961, 5, 9.

———. "Parochial Tuition May Get Supreme Court Test." 27 April 1961, 5.

———. "Prayer Included in New Military Oath." 24 August 1961, 2.

———. "Proposes Federal Aid to Private Colleges." 11 May 1961, 5, 16.

———. "SBC–ABC Merger Talks Draw Fire, Approval." 16 February 1961, 5.

———. "'Sit-Ins' Said Topmost Race Story." 16 March 1961, 9.

———. "Southern Baptist Says Integration Must Come." 19 January 1961, 2.

———. "Support of Public Education Declared Privilege and Duty of Every Citizen." 2 February 1961, 3.

———. "Supreme Court to Rule on Religious Test Law. 11 May 1961, 5.

———. "Talks Studying Closer Baptist Convention Co-Operation Urged." 19 January 1961, 3.

———. "Texas Pastor Takes Stand on Desegregation." 9 March 1961, 5.

———. "Treaties Guarantee Religious Liberty." 28 September 1961, 5.

———. "Urges Caution in Peace Corps use of Churches." 1 June 1961, 9.

Bennett, Hal D. "Some Principles of the People Now Called Baptists." 24 August 1961, 3.

Coalson, C. M. "Christian Liberty Imperiled." 4 May 1961, 2.

Garrett, W. Barry. "Battle Continues Over Parochial School Aid." 15 June 1961, 5.

———. "JFK and Catholic Bishops in Deadlock on Education." 23 March 1961, 3.

Lee, Robert G. "Non-Resident or 'Lost' Members." 26 October 1961, 2.

McEniry, William Hugh. "Relationships between Church and College." 16 February 1961, 3.

Patterson, W. Morgan. "Baptists by Any Other Name." 13 April 1961, 5.

Religious News Service. "Alaska Bars Bus Service to Non-Public Schools." 31 August 1961, 3.

———. "Baptist Federation Proposal Reported Winning Approval." 4 May 1961, 1, 5.

———. "Catholics Predominate in House of Representatives." 2 February 1961, 5.

———. "Catholics Reach Record Circulation in 1960." 17 August 1961, 9.

———. "Daily Bible Reading Upheld by Florida Public Schools." 27 April 1961, 1.

———. "FBI's J. Edgar Hoover Defends Clergy Against Charge of Red Infiltration." 22 June 1961, 5.

———. "Florida Gets Its First American Baptist Church." 23 March 1961, 2.

———. "Leader Warns Against Church in Peace Corps." 31 August 1961, 3.

———. "Little Rock Ministers Elect Negro President." 29 June 1961, 9.

———. "Negro, White Baptists Map Closer Cooperation." 12 January 1961, 3.

———. "New Administration Begins with Appeal for Divine Help." 2 February 1961, 1, 7.

———. "Prayers of Four Faiths Offered at Inauguration." 2 February 1961, 3.

———. "Seminarians Forced to Withdraw Children from Integrated Schools." 5 January 1961, 6.

Schroeder, George W. "Please, Not Discrimination." 11 May 1961, 4.

Stagg, Frank. "Preaching the Gospel." 27 April 1961, 2, 7.

Stracener, W. G. "A Cautiously Constructive Convention." 8 June 1961, 4.

———. "Baptist Unity Possible without Union." 9 March 1961, 4.

———. "Baptist Unity Proposals." 23 February 1961, 4.

———. "Calling for Doctrinal Purity and Denominational Loyalty." 10 August 1961, 4.

———. "Christians Helping to Fight Communism." 4 May 1961, 4.

———. "Differing on Federal Loans to Education." 29 June 1961, 4.

———. "For Freedom *of* Religion or *from* Religion?" 27 April 1961, 5.

———. "Hierarchical Pressure Increasing." 16 March 1961, 4.

———. "Is It Time for a Name Change?" 2 March 1961, 4.

———. "More Observations on the Convention." 15 June 1961, 4.

———. "Myth and the Scriptures." 16 November 1961, 4.

———. "Praying for the President." 26 January 1961, 4.

———. "The Campaign for Church Union." 2 February 1961, 4.

———. "The Plus of Christian Education Queried." 16 February 1961, 4.

———. "Toward Better Articulating our Freedoms." 25 May 1961, 4.

Ward, Gerald M. "Canadian Baptist–Southern Baptist Relations." 18 May 1961, 16.

Hawaii Baptist (Honolulu)

Baptist Press. "Kennedy Appoints Hays." March 1961, 5.

Nash, Stanton H. "A True Denominationalism." June 1961, 2, 7.

———. "Please, Not Discrimination." May 1961, 2, 7.

———. "Southern Baptists: A New Definition." July 1961, 2.

Turner, J. Clyde. "Who Are the Baptists?" February 1961, 2.

———. "Who Are the Baptists? Continued." March 1961, 5.

Maryland Baptist (Centreville)

"A Look at Baptist Doctrines." 15 September 1961, 3–4.

"August Heat Finds Baptists Embroiled in Doctrinal Difficulties." 1 September 1961, 2–4.

"Baptist Distinctives Held Threatened." 1 March 1961, 5.

"Baptist Statements of Faith." 15 September 1961, 3.

"Church and State." 15 April 1961, 2, 11.

"Delaware Southern & American Baptists Meet." 15 March 1961, 3.

"Text of Oklahoma Resolution." 1 September 1961, 5.

Crowley, Robert D. "Enough of This!" 1 August 1961, 3.

Gainer, E. Bryan Jr. "A Time for Vigilance." 15 April 1961, 4–5.

———. "Aid for Parochial Schools." 1 March 1961, 4.

———. "Church Union in the Air." 1 January 1961, 4–5.

———. "Federal Loans to Colleges." 15 July 1961, 4.

———. "Latest Maneuver of Rome." 15 September 1961, 6.

———. "New Bishop—No Friend of 'Separation.'" 1 August 1961, 4.

———. "Oklahoma Affair Presents Difficulties." 1 September 1961, 6.

———. "Pressure for Subsidies." 15 March 1961, 4.

———. "Report from Saint Louis." 15 June 1961, 2–4.

———. "The Baptist Unity Proposal." 1 February 1961, 4.

———. "The Inauguration." 1 February 1961, 4.

———. "The Soviet Threat." 15 September 1961, 6.

————. "The Ultimate Name." 15 May 1961, 4.

Hamlet, Harvey J. "Relationships with American Baptists." 15 March 1961, 5.

Higginbotham, Leland. "School Bus Wedge Attempted in Baltimore." 15 March 1961, 5.

Religious Herald (Richmond)

"Baptist Men Divide on Ideas of Church and State." 5 October 1961, 18.

Alley, Reuben E. "A Look at the Past." 5 January 1961, 10–11.

————. "After the Convention." 8 June 1961, 10–11.

————. "Aim in Christian Education." 22 June 1961, 10.

————. "Church Union and Christian Unity." 9 March 1961, 10.

————. "Court Rulings on Sunday Closing Laws." 20 July 1961, 10.

————. "Danger in Federal Government Loans." 22 June 1961, 10–11.

————. "Evasion is Dangerous." 7 September 1961, 10.

————. "Guard Well the Seminaries." 28 September 1961, 10–11.

————. "Modern Translations of the Bible." 23 March 1961, 10–11.

————. "New Strategy for New Front." 6 April 1961, 10–11.

————. "Religious Liberty Under Test." 16 March 1961, 10–11.

————. "Statements by President McCall." 14 September 1961, 11.

————. "Sunday Work Laws." 26 October 1961, 10.

————. "The Resurrection a Revelation." 30 March 1961, 10.

————. "The Russians Join World Council." 14 December 1961, 2.

————. "The Seminary and its Students." 14 September 1961, 10.

————. "Unionism Among Baptists." 2 February 1961, 10.

Carver, W. O. "The Baptist, His Creed, and His Fellowship." 7 May 1925, 11.

Ellis, H. Cowan. "Report of the Christian Life Committee." 26 October 1961, 4.

Gambrell, J. B. "Going Forward on Two Legs." 29 January 1920, 4–5.

Jackson, E. Hilton "That Creedal Business," 16 April 1925, 3, 7.

Kersey, L. Wilbur. "Why be a Liberal Christian." 2 November 1961, 4–5, 14.

Marney, Carlyle. "Unity of the Faith." 15 June 1961, 4–5, 14.

McDowell, Edward A. "A Charge to Seminary Graduates." 13 July 1961, 12–13.

Newton, Jim. "Conventions Laud Church-State Separation." 14 December 1961, 3.

Pollard, Edward B. "An Open Letter to Dr. Love." 29 January 1920, 2.

Snow, Charles P. "Moral Un-Neutrality of Science." 26 January 1961, 4, 14.

Stancil, Ryburn T., et. al. "Report of Religious Liberty Committee." 12 October 1961, 12–13.

Stockburger, Walker N. "God of Outer Space." 14 September 1961, 4–5, 20.

Taylor, Warren F. "Taking Seriously Church Unity." 23 March 1961, 4, 14.

White, John E. "An Old and Strong Statement of the Baptist Position on Creeds," 12 April 1925, 3.

Western Recorder (Louisville)

Kruschwitz, Verlin C. "A Commendable Report." 28 March 1963, 4. Courtesy of the private collection of Wayne E. Ward, Louisville, Kentucky.

Summers, Ray. "Historic-Critical Interpretation." 23 March 1963, 3. Courtesy of the private collection of Wayne E. Ward, Louisville, Kentucky.

Word and Way (Jefferson City)

Baptist Press. "Hester Accepts Seminary Post." 6 April 1961, 4.

———. "Newspaper Hits Catholic Demand for Public Aid." 16 March 1961, 3.

———. "Parochial Bus Question Goes to Supreme Court." 26 January 1961, 5.

———. "Religious Liberty Emphasis Asked." 6 April 1961, 4.

———. "Senator Wayne Morse Hits Bishops' Stand on Education." 24 August 1961, 3.

Bryan, Gainer E. Jr. "What Hope for Peace?" 5 January 1961, 5.

Garrett, W. Barry. "Roman Catholics Concerned about Their Public Image." 12 January 1961, 2.

Hobbs, Herschel H. "Are Southern Baptists Facing a Theological Revolution?" 16 November 1961, 5, 8.

McCall, Duke K. "'In the Beginning God.'" 6 April 1961, 3.

McGinty, H. H. "A Rear View of the Convention." 15 June 1961, 2.

———. "Catholicism in the U. S. A." 12 January 1961, 4.

———. "Christianity and Communism." 18 May 1961, 2.

———. "Cooperation, Yes—Union, No." 2 February 1961, 4.

———. "Merger Under Discussion." 2 February 1961, 4.

———. "Midwestern Fulfilling Prophecy." 6 April 1961, 2.

———. "No Aid for Private Schools." 16 March 1961, 2.

———. "'Rebels and 'Revolutions.'" 17 August 1961, 2.

———. "Seminary in Spotlight Series." 24 August 1961, 2.

———. "Should We Change our Name?" 27 April 1961, 2.

———. "Some Noteworthy Unifying Forces." 9 March 1961, 2.

———. "The Breakdown of Morality." 4 May 1961, 2.

———. "The Status of Missouri Baptist Institutions." 19 January 1961, 4.

———. "The Supreme Court and Sunday." 29 June 1961, 2.

———. "Trustees of Baptist Institutions." 25 May 1961, 2.

———. "Watch This Move!" 26 January 1961, 4.

Religious News Service. "The Year in Religion." 12 January 1961, 5.

———. "U. S. Negro Priests Pass 100 Mark." 12 January 1961, 2.

Thompson, Gerald L. "The Theological and the Practical." 28 September 1961, 14.

Preliminary Drafts of the Baptist Faith and Message

Committee on Baptist Faith and Message. "The Baptist Faith and Message of 1963." A preliminary committee draft edited by the Department of Christianity, Mercer University. The Southern Baptist Historical Library and Archives, Nashville, Tennessee.

———. "The Baptist Faith and Message of 1963." First committee draft edited by Wayne E. Ward. The Southern Baptist Historical Library and Archives, Nashville, Tennessee.

———. "The Baptist Faith and Message of 1963." A committee draft for review by the Faculty of the Southern Baptist Theological Seminary. WWC.

———. "The Baptist Faith and Message, 1925 and 1963." A committee draft compared with the 1925 edition for review by the Faculty of the Southern Baptist Theological Seminary. WWC.

Bibliography

LETTERS, MEMOS, AND MISCELLANEOUS

Letters from Thomas D. Austin

To Dr. K. Owen White, Houston, Texas, 9 June 1962. The Southern Baptist Historical Library and Archives, Nashville, Tennessee.

To The Committee on the Baptist Faith and Message, 9 June 1962. The Southern Baptist Historical Library and Archives, Nashville, Tennessee.

Letters from Winn T. Barr

To Verlin C. Kruschwitz, Elizabethtown, Kentucky, 13 December 1962. The Southern Baptist Historical Library and Archives, Nashville, Tennessee.

To Verlin C. Kruschwitz, Elizabethtown, Kentucky, 28 December 1962. The Southern Baptist Historical Library and Archives, Nashville, Tennessee.

Letters from Dick Hall Jr.

To Herschel H. Hobbs, Oklahoma City, Oklahoma, 18 July 1962. The Southern Baptist Historical Library and Archives, Nashville, Tennessee.

To Herschel H. Hobbs, Oklahoma City, Oklahoma, 3 December 1962. The Southern Baptist Historical Library and Archives, Nashville, Tennessee.

To Herschel H. Hobbs, Oklahoma City, Oklahoma, 13 December 1962. The Southern Baptist Historical Library and Archives, Nashville, Tennessee.

To Members of the Committee to Study the 1925 Statement of Baptist Faith and Message, 26 October1962. The Southern Baptist Historical Library and Archives, Nashville, Tennessee.

To S. L. Stealey, Wake Forest, North Carolina, 21 November 1962. The Southern Baptist Historical Library and Archives, Nashville, Tennessee.

To Syd Stealey, Wake Forest, North Carolina, 13 December 1962. The Southern Baptist Historical Library and Archives, Nashville, Tennessee.

To Wayne Ward, Louisville, 23 November 1962. The Southern Baptist Historical Library and Archives, Nashville, Tennessee, and WWC.

Letters from Herschel H. Hobbs

To Charles H. Skutt, Memphis, Tennessee, 2 July 1962. The Southern Baptist Historical Library and Archives, Nashville, Tennessee.

To C. L. Snyder, Denton, 10 June 1963. The Southern Baptist Historical Library and Archives, Nashville, Tennessee

To C. Vinton Koons, Washington, D. C., 17 July 1962. The Southern Baptist Historical Library and Archives, Nashville, Tennessee.

To C. Z. Holland, Jonesboro, Arkansas, 24 July 1962. The Southern Baptist Historical Library and Archives, Nashville, Tennessee.

To David G. Anderson, North Charleston, North Carolina, 6 July 1962. The Southern Baptist Historical Library and Archives, Nashville, Tennessee.

To Dick H. Hall Jr., Decatur, Georgia, 10 July 1962. The Southern Baptist Historical Library and Archives, Nashville, Tennessee.

To Dick Hall Jr., Decatur, Georgia, 16 July 1962. The Southern Baptist Historical Library and Archives, Nashville, Tennessee.

To Dick Hall Jr., Decatur, Georgia, 22 October 1962. The Southern Baptist Historical Library and Archives, Nashville, Tennessee.

To D. L. Callender, Sulphur, Louisiana, 10 July 1962. The Southern Baptist Historical Library and Archives, Nashville, Tennessee.

To Dotson M. Nelson Jr., 26 July 1962. The Southern Baptist Historical Library and Archives, Nashville, Tennessee.

To Duke K. McCall, Louisville, Kentucky, 16 June 1962. The Southern Baptist Historical Library and Archives, Nashville, Tennessee.

To Duke McCall, Louisville, Kentucky, 10 December 1962. The Southern Baptist Historical Library and Archives, Nashville, Tennessee.

To Edwin D. Johnston, Macon Georgia, 8 November 1962. The Southern Baptist Historical Library and Archives, Nashville, Tennessee.

To Erwin L. McDonald, Little Rock, Arkansas, 3 July 1962. The Southern Baptist Historical Library and Archives, Nashville, Tennessee.

To Hugh Bumpass, Oklahoma City, Oklahoma, 20 June 1962. The Southern Baptist Historical Library and Archives, Nashville, Tennessee.

To James H. Hubbard, Kansas City, Missouri, 10 August 1962. The Southern Baptist Historical Library and Archives, Nashville, Tennessee.

To James H. Landes, Wichita Falls, Texas, July 16, 1962. The Southern Baptist Historical Library and Archives, Nashville, Tennessee.

To James Landes, Wichita Falls, Texas, 7 September 1962. The Southern Baptist Historical Library and Archives, Nashville, Tennessee.

To L. E. Barton, Montgomery, Alabama, 10 July 1962. The Southern Baptist Historical Library and Archives, Nashville, Tennessee.

To Majorie Dean Dockery, Colorado Springs, Colorado, 13 September 1962. The Southern Baptist Historical Library and Archives, Nashville, Tennessee.

To Members of the Seminary Subcommittees, 10 January 1963. The Southern Baptist Historical Library and Archives, Nashville, Tennessee.

To Miss Margaret Pope, Jacksonville, Florida, 10 July 1962. The Southern Baptist Historical Library and Archives, Nashville, Tennessee.

To Mr. W. E. Peeples, Gainesville, Florida, 5 July 1962. The Southern Baptist Historical Library and Archives, Nashville, Tennessee.

To Mrs. W. A. Breining, Amarillo, Texas, 9 July 1962. The Southern Baptist Historical Library and Archives, Nashville, Tennessee.

To Porter Routh, Nashville, Tennessee, 10 August 1962. The Southern Baptist Historical Library and Archives, Nashville, Tennessee.

To Robert L. Lee, Alexandria, Louisiana, 10 July 1962. The Southern Baptist Historical Library and Archives, Nashville, Tennessee.

To Roy Jennings, Memphis, Tennessee, 15 October 1962. The Southern Baptist Historical Library and Archives, Nashville, Tennessee.

To Roy Jennings, Memphis, Tennessee, 8 November 1962. The Southern Baptist Historical Library and Archives, Nashville, Tennessee.

To Ted B. Moorhead Jr., Melbourne, Florida, 10 August 1962. The Southern Baptist Historical Library and Archives, Nashville, Tennessee.

To Sydnor Stealey, Wake Forest, North Carolina, 27 November 1962. The Southern Baptist Historical Library and Archives, Nashville, Tennessee.

Bibliography

To Sydnor Stealey, Wake Forest, North Carolina, 11 December 1962. The Southern Baptist Historical Library and Archives, Nashville, Tennessee.

To V. C. Kruschwitz, Elizabethtown, Kentucky, 7 August 1962. The Southern Baptist Historical Library and Archives, Nashville, Tennessee.

To W. Boyd Hunt, Ft. Worth, Texas 3 July 1962. The Southern Baptist Historical Library and Archives, Nashville, Tennessee.

To W. E. Peeples, 5 July 1962. The Southern Baptist Historical Library and Archives, Nashville, Tennessee.

To W. Marion Lewter, Waynesboro, Tennessee, 5 October 1962. The Southern Baptist Historical Library and Archives, Nashville, Tennessee.

Letters from C. Z. Holland

To Herschel H. Hobbs, Oklahoma City, Oklahoma, 19 July 1962. The Southern Baptist Historical Library and Archives, Nashville, Tennessee.

To Millard J. Berquist, Kansas City, Kansas, [19?] July 1962. The Southern Baptist Historical Library and Archives, Nashville, Tennessee.

Letters from Verlin C. Kruschwitz

To Herschel H. Hobbs, Oklahoma City, Oklahoma, 21 December 1962. The Southern Baptist Historical Library and Archives, Nashville, Tennessee.

To Herschel H. Hobbs, Oklahoma City, Oklahoma, 8 January [1963]. The Southern Baptist Historical Library and Archives, Nashville, Tennessee.

To A. J. Smith, 22 May 2003.

Letters from Ted B. Moorhead Jr.

To Herschel H. Hobbs, Oklahoma City, Oklahoma, 25 July 1962. The Southern Baptist Historical Library and Archives, Nashville, Tennessee.

To Herschel H. Hobbs, Oklahoma City, Oklahoma, n.d. The Southern Baptist Historical Library and Archives, Nashville, Tennessee.

Letters from Robert E. Naylor

To Herschel H. Hobbs, Oklahoma City, Oklahoma, 18 June 1962. The Southern Baptist Historical Library and Archives, Nashville, Tennessee.

To Herschel H. Hobbs, Oklahoma City, Oklahoma, 28 November 1962. The Southern Baptist Historical Library and Archives, Nashville, Tennessee.

Letters from Sydnor L. Stealey

To Dick Hall, Decatur, Georgia, 14 December 1962. The Southern Baptist Historical Library and Archives, Nashville, Tennessee.

To Herschel H. Hobbs, Oklahoma City, Oklahoma, 1 December [1962]. The Southern Baptist Historical Library and Archives, Nashville, Tennessee.

Bibliography

Miscellaneous Letters

Alley, Reuben to Millard Berquist, 2 November 1961. Millard Berquist Files.

Antonson, Newman to Conrad Willard, 19 December 1961. Millard Berquist Files.

Austin, Thomas. Kansas City, to K. Owen White, Houston, 9 June 1962. The Southern Baptist Historical Library and Archives, Nashville, Tennessee.

Autrey, Allen Hill, Little Rock, to E. Y. Mullins, Louisville, 15 July 1925. BCL.

Baker, Truett, Kansas City, to Millard Berquist, Kansas City, 17 May 1962. Millard Berquist Files.

Barnett, Henley, Louisville, to Ralph Elliott, Kansas City, 6 March 1962. Millard Berquist Files.

Barr, Winn T., London, to Verlin C. Kruschwitz, Elizabethtown, 13 December 1962. The Southern Baptist Historical Library and Archives, Nashville, Tennessee.

———, to Verlin C. Kruschwitz, Elizabethtown, 28 December 1962. The Southern Baptist Historical Library and Archives, Nashville, Tennessee.

Barton, L. E., Montgomery, Alabama, to H. H. Hobbs, Oklahoma City, Oklahoma, June 29, 1962. The Southern Baptist Historical Library and Archives, Nashville, Tennessee.

Barton, Wayne to Ralph Elliott, 22 November 1961. Millard Berquist Files.

Berquist, Millard, Kansas City, to Malcolm B. Knight, 5 September 1962. Millard Berquist Files.

Box, Millard B., Houston, Texas, to H. H. Hobbs, Oklahoma City, Oklahoma, June 13, 1962. The Southern Baptist Historical Library and Archives, Nashville, Tennessee.

Breining, Mrs. A W., Amarillo, Texas, to H. H. Hobbs, Oklahoma City, Oklahoma, May 23, 1962. The Southern Baptist Historical Library and Archives, Nashville, Tennessee.

Callender, D. L., Sulphur, Louisiana, to Luther B. Hall, President of Louisiana Baptists, July 3, 1962. The Southern Baptist Historical Library and Archives, Nashville, Tennessee.

Carlson, Leslie E. Fort Worth, to Mack R. Douglas, 10 October 1961. Millard Berquist Files.

Cook, W. E. Oklahoma City, to Millard Berquist, Kansas City, 20 December 1961. Millard Berquist Files.

Copass, B. A. to E. S. James, 13 January 1962. Millard Berquist Files.

Crozier, Rufus R. to Millard Berquist, 20 Sep 1961. Millard Berquist Files.

Dockery, Majorie Dean, Colorado Springs, Colorado, to Herschel H. Hobbs, Oklahoma City, Oklahoma, n.d. The Southern Baptist Historical Library and Archives, Nashville, Tennessee.

Eddleman, H. Leo, New Orleans, Louisiana, to H. H. Hobbs, Oklahoma City, Oklahoma, 19 December 1962. The Southern Baptist Historical Library and Archives, Nashville, Tennessee.

Elliott Ralph H. to Malcolm Knight, 20 October 1962. Millard Berquist Files.

Fallis William J. to Millard Berquist, 2 November 1960. Millard Berquist Files.

Flanders, H. J. Jr., to Ralph Elliott, 11 June 1962. Millard Berquist Files.

Fly, Lovina, Middle, to Ralph Elliott, Kansas City, 21 June 1962. Millard Berquist Files.

Francisco, Clyde T., Louisville, to Ralph Elliott, Kansas City, 17 July 1961. Millard Berquist Files.

———. to Ralph Elliott, Kansas City, 5 October 1961. Millard Berquist Files.

Fuquay, C. Murray, Midwest City, to Millard Berquist, Kansas City, 20 March 1962. Millard Berquist Files.

Bibliography

Garrett, James Leo Arlington, to Nane Starnes, Asheville, 22 August 1962, courtesy of James Leo Garrett.

———, Louisville, to Nane Starnes, Asheville, 2 August 1962, courtesy of James Leo Garrett.

Garrett, J. Michael, to A. J. Smith, n.d.

Green, Joe to Millard Berquist, 27 September 1962. Millard Berquist Files.

Hockensmith, C. Hoge, Columbus, Ohio, to Herschel H. Hobbs, Oklahoma City, Oklahoma, 17 July 1962. The Southern Baptist Historical Library and Archives, Nashville, Tennessee.

Hubbard, James H., Kansas City, Missouri, to the Committee on the Baptist Faith and Message, 24 July 1962. The Southern Baptist Historical Library and Archives, Nashville, Tennessee.

Hull, William E., Ruscklikon, to Herschel H. Hobbs, Oklahoma City, n.d. The Southern Baptist Historical Library and Archives, Nashville, Tennessee.

Hunt, Boyd, Fort Worth, to Ralph Elliott, Kansas City, 17 January 1962. Millard Berquist Files.

January, James, et. al., Williamson County, Texas, to H. H. Hobbs, Oklahoma City, Oklahoma, 11 August 1962. The Southern Baptist Historical Library and Archives, Nashville, Tennessee.

Kruschwitz, Verlin C., Elizabethtown, to H. H. Hobbs, Oklahoma City, 8 January 1963. The Southern Baptist Historical Library and Archives, Nashville, Tennessee.

Kubic, Craig to A. J. Smith, 25 September 2002.

Lovelace, Marc, Wake Forest, to Ralph Elliott, Kansas City, 29 March 1962. Millard Berquist Files.

Lyon, Henry L. Jr., Montgomery, Alabama, to the Presidents of the Seminaries of the Southern Baptist Convention, 2 August 1962. The Southern Baptist Historical Library and Archives, Nashville, Tennessee.

Maquire, John to Millard Berquist, 15 January 1962. Millard Berquist Files.

———. to Millard Berquist, 23 July 1962. Millard Berquist Files.

McCall, Duke K., Louisville, to Wayne Ward, Louisville, 20 July 1962. WWC.

———, Louisville, to Verlin Kruschwitz, Elizabethtown and R. P. Downey, 1 January 1963. WWC.

McDonald, Erwin L., Little Rock, Arkansas, to Mack R. Douglas, St. Louis, Missouri, 26 June 1962. The Southern Baptist Historical Library and Archives, Nashville, Tennessee.

Moody, Dale, Louisville, to Ralph Elliott, Kansas City, 16 January 1962, courtesy Millard Berquist Files.

———, Louisville, to Duke McCall, Louisville, 7 January 1963. BCL.

Morgan, J. W., et. al., Montgomery, Alabama, to the Members of Highland Avenue Baptist Church, Montgomery, Alabama, 29 July 1962. The Southern Baptist Historical Library and Archives, Nashville, Tennessee.

Mullins, E. Y. Louisville, to L. R. Scarborough, Fort Worth, 15 June 1906. BCL.

Naylor, Robert E., Fort Worth, to H. H. Hobbs, Oklahoma City, 29 November 1962. The Southern Baptist Historical Library and Archives, Nashville, Tennessee.

Nelson, Dotson M. Jr., Birmingham, Alabama, to Herschel Hobbs, Oklahoma City, Oklahoma, May 30, 1962. The Southern Baptist Historical Library and Archives, Nashville, Tennessee.

Newman, Stewart A. Wake Forest, to Ralph Elliott, Kansas City, 28 April 1962. Millard Berquist Files.

Bibliography

Patterson, Paige, to A. J. Smith, 2 July 2002.

Peterson, Wayne H. to Ralph Elliott, 21 October 1961. Millard Berquist Files.

Pullin, Michael, to A. J. Smith. 5 July 2002.

Robbins Woodrow W. to Herschel Hobbs, 23 January 1963. The Southern Baptist Historical Library and Archives, Nashville, Tennessee.

Routh, Porter, Nashville, Tennessee, to Herschel H. Hobbs, Oklahoma City, Oklahoma, July 25, 1962. The Southern Baptist Historical Library and Archives, Nashville, Tennessee.

Rust, E. Warren, Cleveland, Tennessee, to Dr. H. H. Hobbs, Oklahoma City, Oklahoma, July 24, 1962. The Southern Baptist Historical Library and Archives, Nashville, Tennessee.

Sanders, Harold G. to Millard Berquist, 14 July 1962. Millard Berquist Files.

Scarborough, L .R. Fort Worth, to E. Y. Mullins, Louisville, 2 June 1906. BCL.

Skutt, Charles H., Memphis, Tennessee, to The Committee on the Study of Theological Interpretation, 27 June 1962. The Southern Baptist Historical Library and Archives, Nashville, Tennessee.

Southard, Samuel, Louisville, to Ralph Elliott, Kansas City,19 February 1962. Millard Berquist Files.

Starnes, Nane, Ashville, North Carolina, to H. H. Hobbs, Oklahoma City, Oklahoma, 27 June 1962. The Southern Baptist Historical Library and Archives, Nashville, Tennessee.

——, Asheville, to Wayne E. Ward, Louisville, 9 November 1962, WWC.

——, Asheville, to James Leo Garrett, Louisville, 19 July 1962, courtesy of James Leo Garrett.

Starnes, Nane, Asheville, to Herschel H. Hobbs, Oklahoma City, 27 July 1962. The Southern Baptist Historical Library and Archives, Nashville, Tennessee.

Steely, John E. Wake Forest, to Ralph Elliott, Kansas City, 9 April 1962. Millard Berquist Files.

Sullivan, James L., Nashville, to Ralph Elliott, Kansas City 24 January 1962. Millard Berquist Files.

Tate, Martin, Louisville, to Ralph Elliott, Kansas City, 9 November 1961. Millard Berquist Files.

Trentham, Charles A., Knoxville, to Millard Berquist, Kansas City, 15 January 1962. Millard Berquist Files.

Vardaman, Jerry, Louisville, to Ralph Elliott, Kansas City, 16 February 1962. Millard Berquist Files.

Ward, Wayne E., Cleveland, Tennessee, to Dick Hall Jr., Decatur, Georgia, October 20, 1962. The Southern Baptist Historical Library and Archives, Nashville, Tennessee and WWC.

Warner, Harold, Tampa, to John Maquire, 27 April 1962. Millard Berquist Files .

Watts, John D. W., Ruschlikon, to Ralph Elliott, Kansas City, 14 March 1962. Millard Berquist Files.

Westmoreland, N. J. to Millard Berquist, 26 October 1961. Millard Berquist Files.

Miscellaneous Documents

Barr, Winn T. "Universal Churchhood," The Southern Baptist Historical Library and Archives, Nashville, Tennessee. Transcribed by A. J. Smith, 11 January 2002.

Biographical Data Sheet, Millard Berquist Files.

"College of Liberal Arts, 1962–1963," *Mercer University Bulletin* 49 (March 1962), no. 2: 11–15.

Edwards, W. Ross. "Midwestern Baptist Theological Seminary," The Southern Baptist Historical Library and Archives, Nashville, Tennessee. Transcribed by A. J. Smith, 11 January 2002.

Hall, Dick Jr. Minutes of the Southern Baptist Committee to Study the 1925 Baptist Faith and Message, 19–20 November 1962. The Southern Baptist Historical Library and Archives, Nashville, Tennessee.

Hobbs, Herschel H. Press Release, n.d. The Southern Baptist Historical Library and Archives, Nashville, Tennessee.

———. Memo on the Baptist Faith and Message. The Southern Baptist Historical Library and Archives, Nashville, Tennessee.

Indian Creek Baptist Association. "Resolutions Concerning the Current Theological Problem Southern Baptists Face in These Days," Savannah, Tennessee. 14 September 1962. The Southern Baptist Historical Library and Archives, Nashville, Tennessee.

January, James, et. al. "Resolutions" of the Williamson County Missionary Baptist Association. The Southern Baptist Historical Library and Archives, Nashville, Tennessee.

Lewter, W. Marion, et. al. "Resolutions Concerning the Current Theological Problem Southern Baptists Face in These Days." Indian Creek Baptist Association, 14 September 1962. The Southern Baptist Historical Library and Archives, Nashville, Tennessee.

Moody, Dale. "A Guide to My Controversy over the Baptist Teachings on Apostasy." BCL.

Mullins, Edgar Y. Extract from Minutes of Conference at Columbia, Missouri, 1923(?). BCL.

Report of the Board of Trustees of Midwestern Baptist Theological Seminary, 25 October 1962. Millard Berquist Files.

Resolution adopted by the Highland Avenue Baptist Church of Montgomery, Alabama, 25 July 1962. The Southern Baptist Historical Library and Archives, Nashville, Tennessee

"Resolution Concerning the Dismissal of Dr. Ralph Elliott by the Midwestern Baptist Theological Seminary." Submitted by the Baptist students of North Carolina, 3 November 1962. Millard Berquist Files.

"Resolution of the 1962 Graduating Class of Midwestern Baptist Theological Seminary." The Southern Baptist Historical Library and Archives, Nashville, Tennessee.

Stagg, Bill. "Stagg Resolution," of Willow Meadows Baptist Church, Houston, Texas, August 1962. The Southern Baptist Historical Library and Archives, Nashville, Tennessee.

Tate, Martin. Interviewed by A. J. Smith, 5 August 2004.

Ward, Wayne. Interviewed by A. J. Smith, 17 April 2002.

SECONDARY SOURCES

Books

Ammerman, Nancy Tatom. *Baptist Battles: Social Change and Religious Conflict in the Southern Baptist Convention*. New Brunswick: Rutgers University Press, 1995.

Bibliography

Basden, Paul A., ed. *Has Our Theology Changed? Southern Baptist Thought Since 1845.* Nashville: Broadman & Holman Publishers, 1994.

————, and David S. Dockery, editors. *The People of God: Essays on the Believer's Church.* Nashville: Broadman Press, 1991.

Bow, J. G. *What Baptists Believe and Why They Believe It. Nashville:* Sunday School Board of the Southern Baptist Convention, n.d.

Brown, Raymond. *The English Baptists of the 18th Century.* In *A History of the English Baptists.* Gen. ed. B. R. White. London: The Baptist Historical Society, 1986.

Burrage, Champlin. *The Church Covenant Idea: Its Origin and Its Development.* Philadelphia: American Baptist Publication Society, 1904.

Bush, L. Russ and Tom J. Nettles. *Baptists and the Bible.* Revised and expanded. Nashville: Broadman & Holman Publishers, 1999.

Conner, Walter Thomas. *Christian Doctrine.* Nashville: Broadman Press, 1937.

————. *Revelation and God.* Nashville: Broadman Press, 1936.

————. *The Gospel of Redemption.* Nashville: Broadman Press, 1945.

Copeland, E. Luther. *The Southern Baptist Convention and the Judgment of History: The Taint of Original Sin.* Lanham: University Press of America, Inc., 1995.

Cothen, Grady C. *The New Fundamentalism's Impact on the Southern Baptist Convention.* Macon: Smyth & Helwys, 1995.

————. *What Happened to the Southern Baptist Convention? A Memoir of the Controversy.* Macon: Smyth & Helwys, 1993.

Deweese, Charles W., ed. *Defining Baptist Convictions: Guidelines for the Twenty–First Century.* Franklin, TN: Providence House, 1996.

Eaton, T. T. *The Faith of Baptists.* Louisville: Baptist Book Concern, 1903.

Farnsley, Arthur Emery II. *Southern Baptist Politics: Authority and Power in the Restructuring of an American Denomination.* University Park: The Pennsylvania State University Press, 1994.

Ferguson, Robert U., Jr., ed. *Amidst Babel, Speak the Truth: Reflections on the Southern Baptist Convention Struggle.* Macon: Smyth & Helwys, 1993.

Gambrell, J. B. *Baptists and Their Business.* Nashville: Sunday School Board Southern Baptist Convention, 1919.

————. *Baptist Principles Reset, Consisting of a Series of Articles on Distinctive Baptist Principles,* 3d ed. Richmond: Religious Herald, 1902.

George, Timothy, and Denise George, eds. *B. H. Carroll: Baptists and Their Doctrines,* with a Foreword by Ken Hemphill. Nashville: Broadman & Holman Publishers, 1995, 1999.

González, Justo L. *The Story of Christianity: The Reformation to the Present Day.* Vol. 2. San Francisco: HarperSanFrancisco, 1985.

Hardman, Keith J. *Seasons of Refreshing: Evangelism and Revivals in America.* Foreword by Luis Palau. Grand Rapids: Baker Books, 1994.

Haykin, Michael A. G. *Kiffin, Knollys and Keach: Rediscovering Our English Baptist Heritage.* Leeds, UK: Reformation Today Trust, 1996.

Hefley, James C. *The Conservative Resurgence in the Southern Baptist Convention.* Foreword by Lewis Drummond. Hannibal, MO: Hannibal Books, 1991.

Hudson, Winthrop S. *Baptists in Transition: Individualism and Christian Responsibility.* Foreword by Robert T. Handy. Valley Forge: Judson Press, 1979.

————. *Religion in America: An Historical Account of the Development of American Religious Life,* 3d edition. New York: Charles Scribner's Sons, 1981.

Bibliography

James, Robison B., ed. *The Unfettered Word: Confronting the Authority-Inerrancy Question.* Waco: Word Books, 1987.

Longfield, Bradley J. *The Presbyterian Controversy: Fundamentalists, Modernists, & Liberals.* New York: Oxford University Press, 1991.

Lumpkin, William L. *Baptist Confessions of Faith.* Revised edition. Valley Forge: Judson Press, 1959, 1969 and 1983.

Mauldin, Frank Louis. *The Classic Baptist Heritage of Personal Truth: The Truth as it is in Jesus*, with a Foreword by John P. Newport. Franklin, TN: Providence House Publishers, 1999.

McBeth, Leon. *The Baptist Heritage: Four Centuries of Baptist Witness.* Nashville: Broadman Press, 1987.

Mullins, Edgar Young. *Baptist Beliefs.* Philadelphia: Judson Press, 1925.

Nettles, Thomas J. *The Baptists: Key People Involved in Forming a Baptist Identity.* 3 vol. Fern, Ross-Shire, Scotland: Mentor, 2005—07.

———. *By His Grace and For His Glory: A Historical, Theological, and Practical Study of the Doctrines of Grace in Baptist Life.* Grand Rapids: Baker Book House, 1986.

———, and Russell D. Moore, editors. *Why I am a Baptist.* Nashville: Broadman & Holman Publishers, 2001.

Norman, R. Stanton. *More than a Name: Preserving our Baptist Identity.* Foreword by R. Albert Mohler Jr. Nashville: Broadman & Holman Publishers, 2001.

Olson, Roger. *The Story of Christian Theology: Twenty Centuries of Tradition and Reform.* Downers Grove: InterVarsity Press, 1999.

Parker, Gary E. *Principles Worth Protecting.* Macon: Smyth & Helwys, 1993.

Pressler, Paul. *A Hill on Which to Die: One Southern Baptist's Journey.* Nashville: Broadman & Holman Publishers, 1999.

Pool, Jeff B. *Against Returning to Egypt: Exposing and Resisting Credalism* [sic] *in the Southern Baptist Convention.* Macon: Mercer University Press, 1997.

Shurden, Walter B. *The Baptist Identity: Four Fragile Freedoms.* Macon: Smyth & Helwys, 1993.

———, ed. *The Struggle for the Soul of the S.B.C.: Moderate Responses to the Fundamentalist Movement.* Macon: Mercer University Press, 1993.

Skevington, Samuel L. *The Distinctive Principle of the Baptists.* Chicago: n.p., 1914.

Solomon, Robert C. and Kathleen M. Higgins. *A Short History of Philosophy.* New York: Oxford University Press, 1996.

Sutton, Jerry. *The Baptist Reformation: The Conservative Resurgence in the Southern Baptist Convention*, with a Foreword by James T. Draper. Nashville: Broadman & Holman Publishers, 2000.

Staton, Cecil P., Jr., ed. *Why I am a Baptists: Reflections on Being Baptist in the 21st Century.* Macon: Smyth & Helwys Publishing Incorporated, 1999.

Torbet, Robert G. *A History of the Baptists.* 3d ed. Valley Forge: Judson Press, 1980.

Truett, George W. *Baptists and Religious Liberty.* Nashville: Sunday School Board of the Southern Baptist Convention, 1920.

Tuck, William Powell. *Our Baptist Tradition.* With a Foreword by Walter B. Shurden. Macon, GA: Smyth & Helwys Publishing, 1993.

Watts, Michael R. *The Dissenters: From the Reformation to the French Revolution.* Oxford: Clarendon Press, 1978, 1999.

Wills, Greg A. *Democratic Religion: Freedom, Authority, and Church Discipline in the Baptist South, 1785–1900.* New York: Oxford University Press, 1997.

Bibliography

Theses and Dissertations

Downs, David William. "The McDaniel Statement: An Investigation of Creedalism in the Southern Baptist Convention." Th.M. thesis, The Southern Baptist Theological Seminary, 1980.

————. "The Use of the 'Baptist Faith and Message,' 1963–1983: A Response to Pluralism in the Southern Baptist Convention." Ph.D. diss., The Southern Baptist Theological Seminary, 1984.

Durden, John Allen. "A Selected Issue in Southern Baptist Ecclesiology: The Nature of the Church as Reflected in the Baptist Faith and Messages of 1925 and 1963." Th.D. diss., Mid–America Baptist Theological Seminary, 1993.

Gaines, John Steven. "An Analysis of the Correlation Between Representative Baptist Hour Sermons by Herschel H. Hobbs and Selected Articles of 'The Baptist Faith and Message', 1963." Ph.D. diss., Southwestern Baptist Theological Seminary, 1991.

Smith, L. G. "A History of the Sweetwater Baptist Association 1885–1957." M.A. thesis, Hardin–Simmons University, 1965.

Ward, Wayne E. "The Concept of Holy Scripture in Biblical Literature." Th.D. thesis, The Southern Baptist Theological Seminary, 1952.

Weber, Paul Jr. "An Investigation and Examination of Variations in Baptist Polity," Th.D. diss., Central Baptist Theological Seminary, 1943.

Articles

Avey, Albert E. "Commodious Creeds." *The Chronicle* 7 (April 1944): 59–65.

Carter, James E. "Dealing with Conflict in Associational History." *BHH* 17 (April 1982): 33–43.

————. "A Review of Confessions of Faith Adopted by Major Baptist Bodies in the United States," *BHH* 12 (January 1977): 75–91.

————. "Southern Baptists' First Confession of Faith," *BHH* 5 (January 1970): 24–28, 38.

————. "How Freely Can we Practice our Religion?" *Christian Ministry* 27(March–April 1996): 19–22.

Chesser, Larry. "'Authenticus Baptistus' Growing Extinct, Dilday Tells American Baptists." *BT* (13 July 1995):

Conner, W. T. "Theology, A Practical Discipline." *R&E* 41(October 1944): 350–60.

Coppenger, Mark. "Herschel Hobbs," in *Baptist Theologians*. Edited by Timothy George and David S. Dockery. Nashville: Broadman & Holman Press, 1990, 1999, 434–49.

————. "The Ascent of Lost Man in Southern Baptist Preaching," *FJ* 25 (Summer 1996): 5–21.

"Cothen Recommends Ideals," *F&T* 27 (June 1983): .

Cothen, Grady. "The Real Issue of Our Times," *F&T* 25 (February 1981):

Dilday, Russell. "Individuals Must Respond to God Personally," *F&T* 25 (March 1981):

Dockery, David S. "Herschel H. Hobbs," in *Theologians of the Baptist Tradition*. Edited by Timothy George and David S. Dockery. Nashville: Broadman & Holman Press, 2001, 216–31.

Dunn, James. "Church, State, and Soul Competency," *R&E* 96, No. 1 (1999): 61–73.

Estep, W. R. "Baptists and Authority: The Bible, Confessions, and Conscience in the Development of Baptist Identity." *R&E* 84 (Fall 1987): 599–615.

Bibliography

———. "The Nature and Use of Biblical Authority in Baptist Confessions of Faith, 1610–1963." *BHH* 22 (October 1987): 3–14.

Faught, Jerry. "Review of *Sacred Mandates of Conscience*," *BHH* 33 (Autumn 1998): 87–88.

Foust, Michael. "Baptist forefathers never questioned confessions," *SBT* (Arlington) 18 May 2002, 16.

Garret, James Leo. "The Concept of Biblical Authority in Historic Baptist Confessions of Faith," *R&E* 76 (Winter 1979): 43–54.

———. "Sources of Authority in Baptist Thought," *BHH* 13(July 1978): 41–49.

———. "Walter Thomas Conner," in *Baptist Theologians*, ed. Timothy George and David S. Dockery, 419–33. Nashville: Broadman & Holmann Publishers1990, 1999.

George, Timothy. "Dogma Beyond Anathema: Historical Theology in the Service of the Church." *R&E* 84 (Fall 1987): 691–713.

———. "The Priesthood of All Believers and the Quest for Theological Integrity." *Criswell Theological Review* 3 (1989): 283–94.

George, Timothy, D. A. Carson, C. Ben Mitchell, Scott Hafemann, Carl F. H. Henry, and Greg Wills. "The SBJT Forum: Overlooked Shapers of Evangelicalism," *SBJT* 3 (Spring 1999): 76–91.

Griffith, Benjamin. "The Power and Duty of an Association." *BHH* 2 (January 1967): 480–50.

Harkness, R. E. E. "Some Early Practices of Baptists in America." *The Chronicle* 7(January 1944): 13–29.

Hendricks, William L. "God, the Bible, and Authority in The Baptist Faith and Message (1963)." In *Sacred Mandates of Conscience: Interpretations of the Baptist Faith and Message*, ed. Jeffrey Pool, 102–20. Macon: Smyth & Helwys Publishers, 1997.

Hinson, E. Glenn. "Creeds and Confessions in the Christian Tradition," *R&E* 76 (Winter 1979): 5–16.

Hinson, Keith. "Baptist Faith and Message Committee members say report embraces biblical authority." Baptist Press, June 14, 2000 [online]. Accessed 15 June 2000. Available from http://www.sbcannualmeeting.org/sbc00/news.asp?ID=1927611428&page=3&num=5; Internet.

Hobbs, Herschel H. "Baptist Press Release," August 1962.

———. "Southern Baptists and Confessionalism," *R&E* 76 (Winter 1979): 55–68.

———. "The Baptist Faith and Message–Anchored but Free," *BHH* 13 (July 1978): 33–40.

Holvey, Alvah. "The Question of Creeds." *The Chronicle* 7(April 1944): 70–73 (Reprinted from *Christian Teaching and Life*, Philadelphia: American Baptist Publication Society, 1895).

Hudson, Winthrop S. "Shifting Patterns of Church Order in the Twentieth Century," in *Baptist Concepts of the Church: A Survey of the Historical and Theological Issues which Have Produced Changes in Church Order*, ed. Winthrop S. Hudson, 196–218. Chicago: The Judson Press, 1959.

Humphreys, Fisher. "E. Y. Mullins," in *Baptist Theologians*, ed. Timothy George and David S. Dockery, 330–50. Nashville: Broadman & Holman Publishers, 1990, 1999.

———. "Edgar Young Mullins," in *Theologians of the Baptist Tradition*, ed. Timothy George and David S. Dockery, 181–201. Nashville: Broadman & Holman Publishers, 2001.

Hurt, John. "Should Southern Baptists Have a Creed/Confession?—No!" *R&E* 76 (Winter 1979): 85–88.

Lawson, Linda. "Cothen Underscores Ideals," *F&T* 27 (February 1983).

Leonard, Bill J. "Types of Confessional Documents among Baptists in America," *R&E* 76 (Winter 1979): 29–42.

Littell, Franklin H. "The Problem of Discipline in American Religious Life," *Journal of Ecumenical Studies* 4 (Fall 1967): 726–29.

Lumpkin, William L. "The Bible in Early Baptist Confessions of Faith," *BHH* (July 1984): 33–41.

———. "The Nature and Authority of Baptist Confessions of Faith," *R&E* 76 (Winter 1979): 17–28.

May, Lynn E. Jr. "The Role of Associations in Baptist History." *BHH* 12 (April 1977): 69–74.

McNeal, Reggie. "The Priesthood of All Believers," in *Has Our Theology Changed? Southern Baptist Thought Since 1845*, ed. Paul A. Basden, 204–29. Nashville: Broadman & Holman Publisher, 1994.

Miller, Norm. "Southern Baptists Overwhelmingly adopt revised Baptist Faith and Message." June 14, 2000 [online]. Accessed 15 June 2000. Available from http://www.sbcannualmeeting.org/sbc00/news.asp?ID=1927611432&page=2&num=5; Internet.

Mohler, R. Albert Jr. "Baptist Theology at the Crossroads: The Legacy of E. Y. Mullins," *SBJT* v. 3, no. 4 (Winter 1999): 4–22.

Moody, Dwight A. "The Bible," in *Has Our Theology Changed? Southern Baptist Thought Since 1845*, ed. Paul A. Basden, 7–40. Nashville: Broadman & Holman Publishers, 1994.

Moore, Russell D. "For the Bible Tells Me So," *The Tie* 68, No. 4 (2000): 6–9.

Moore, Russell D., and Gregory A. Thornbury. "The Mystery of Mullins in Contemporary Southern Baptist Historiography." *SBJT* 3 (Winter 1999): 44–57.

Moyers, Bill. "On Being a Baptist." In *Best Sermons*. Vol. 7. San Francisco: Harper–Collins, 1994.

Nettles, Thomas J. *The Baptists: Key People Involved in Forming a Baptist Identity*. 3 vol. Fern, Ross-Shire, Scotland: Mentor, 2005—07.

———. "Missions and Creeds (Part 1)". *Founders Journal* 17 (Summer 1994) [CD–ROM]. Cape Coral: Founders Press, 1999.

———. "Missions and Creeds (Part 2)". *Founders Journal* 17(Fall 1994) [CD–ROM]. Cape Coral: Founders Press, 1999.

"Now I'm Scared," *F&T* 25 (June 1981).

Odle, Joe T. Should Southern Baptists Have a Creed/Confession–Yes!" *R&E* 76 (Winter 1979): 89–94.

Pollard, Edward B. "A Brief Study in Baptist Confessions of Faith." *The Chronicle* 7(April 1944): 74–85.

———. "What Shall We Think of Creeds?" *R&E* 12 (January 1915):40–54.

Pool, Jeff B. "Chief Article of Faith, The Preamble to *The Baptist Faith and Message (1963)*," in *Sacred Mandates of Conscience: Interpretations of* The Baptist Faith and Message, ed. Jeff B. Pool, 37–101. Macon, GA: Smyth & Helwys Publishing, Inc., 1997.

———. "'Sacred Mandates of Conscience': A Criteriology of Credalism for Theological Method among Baptists." *Perspectives in Religious Studies* 23 (Winter 1996): 353–86.

Richards, Jim. "FIRST–PERSON Creeds, confessions, beliefs & integrity," Baptist Press, April 16, 2002.

Bibliography

Shurden, Walter B. "Southern Baptist Responses to the 1925 and 1963 Confessions," *R&E* 76 (Winter 1979): 69–84.

Smith, Howard Wayne. "Baptists and Creeds." *The Chronicle* 7 (April 1944): 49–56.

Starnes, Todd. "New Mo. convention requires voters to sign 'agreement' form," Baptist Press, April 16, 2002.

Steely, John E. "Biblical Authority and Baptists in Historical Perspective." *BHH* 19 (July 1984): 7–15.

Stiver, Danny R. "Dale Moody," in *Baptist Theologians*, ed. Timothy George and David S. Dockery, 539–66. Nashville: Broadman & Holman Publishers, 1990, 1999.

"The Bottom Line of a Creed," *F&T* 25 (April 1981).

Tribble, Harold W. "Individual Competency and Use of Creeds." *The Chronicle* 7 (April 1944): 90–95.

Vaughn, J. Barry. "Benjamin Keach." In *Baptist Theologians*. Ed. by Timothy George and David Dockery. Nashville: Broadman & Holman Publishers, 1990, 1999), 49–76.

Webb, Leland. "20 Seminary Grads Included in Baptist 'Statement Group,'" Baptist Press, 19 July 1962.

Wills, Gregory A. "Progressive Theology and Southern Baptist Controversies of the 1950s and 1960s," *SBJT* 7 (Spring 2003): 12–31.

———. "Southern Baptists and Church Discipline," *SBJT* 4 (Winter 2000): 4–14.

Woolley, David C. "Baptist Aversion for all Creeds," *BHH* 5 (January 1970): 1–2.

Yarbrough, Slayden: "Is Credalism [*sic*] a Threat to Southern Baptists?" *BHH* 18 (April 1983): 21–33.

Unpublished Papers

Strange, Sammie P. "Backus and Leland on Liberty of Conscience and Separation of Church and State." Seminar paper, The Southern Baptist Theological Seminary, 2000.